TOWARD THE SECOND DECADE

TOWARD THE SECOND DECADE

The Impact of the Women's Movement on American Institutions

Edited by
Betty Justice and Renate Pore

CONTRIBUTIONS IN WOMEN'S STUDIES, NUMBER 25

GREENWOOD PRESS
Westport, Connecticut • London, England

Library of Congress Cataloging in Publication Data
Main entry under title:

Toward the second decade.

(Contributions in women's studies ; no. 25 ISSN 0147-104X)
Essays originating from a series of three one-day
conferences held at West Virginia University in September
1978.
Bibliography: p.
Includes index.
1. Feminism—United States—Congresses. 2. Women
in the professions—United States—Congresses. 3. Women's
rights—United States—Congresses. I. Justice, Betty,
1948- II. Pore, Renate, 1943-
III. Series.
HQ1426.T68   305.4'2'0973   80-24764
ISBN 0-313-22110-3 (lib. bdg.)

Library of Congress Catalog Card Number: 80-24764
ISBN: 0-313-22110-3
ISSN: 0147-104X

First published in 1981

Greenwood Press
A division of Congressional Information Service, Inc.
88 Post Road West, Westport, Connecticut 06881

Printed in the United States of America

10 9 8 7 6 5 4 3 2 1

Contents

Acknowledgments

Authors and editors usually acknowledge those persons who contributed to the perspective or content of a book. Almost as a dutiful afterthought, they include a reference to secretaries and/or typists who worked on the manuscript. Finally, they remember their spouses, families, and personal friends for their patient love. They follow this pattern regardless of any actual contributions by these persons.

It is no coincidence that these clerical and nurturing functions are performed primarily by women. Like most other functions socially defined as female, typing and nurturing are not taken as seriously as other socially productive activity, either in terms of pay or esteem.

Although individual departures from this familiar social pattern cannot alter it, we refuse to abide by it when it is inappropriate to do so. However, we are pleased to acknowledge that Susie Balliet Ross made significant editorial comment on this manuscript, transcribed the taped speeches, typed the manuscript, and periodically reassured us that we could accomplish this undertaking. To our friend and sister, we say thank you.

The chapters in this book originate from a series of three, one-day conferences held at West Virginia University in September 1978. Although not every speech from those conferences resulted in a chapter, and not every chapter in this book is identical to the author's presentation at those conferences, we recognize the West Virginia University Council for Women's Concerns and the dozens of persons in Morgantown, West Virginia, whose efforts produced those conferences and the seed for this undertaking. We also recognize the West Virginia Foundation for the Humanities and the West Virginia University Foundation for their financial support of the "September Festival of Women."

We are grateful to several West Virginia University faculty members who helped us formulate the context of this book, prepare the prospectus, and arrange for the book's publication. These persons are Nancy Datan, Elaine Ginsberg, Sophia Peterson, Lauralee Sherwood, Judith Stitzel, and Linda Yoder.

Noreen Aminzadeh and Judith Holley of the West Virginia University faculty secretary's office offered friendly and courteous assistance in typing portions of the the manuscript and our correspondence. We also thank Peggy Thomas and Nancy Marosy for assistance in typing and production.

TOWARD THE SECOND DECADE

————————————To Christy and her generation ———————————

Introduction

The rebirth of the women's movement in the 1960s inspired thousands of books and articles describing and analyzing a variety of forms and sources of women's oppression. It stimulated creative, new, intellectual insights and meticulous scholarship challenging traditional beliefs about women and their place in society. The dissemination of the movement's ideas through mass protest and the media has been thorough and its impact on the American consciousness profound. It would be difficult today to find a woman or man who does not have an opinion about the women's movement and the changing status of women in American society.

A materialist view of history assumes that reality creates consciousness and not vice versa. To a large extent, the growing consciousness among women of themselves as "women" has resulted from the reality that an ever increasing number of women now work for wages. Their participation in "socially productive" work has allowed and required women to experience directly the political and economic world.

The expanded consciousness of women has also grown out of the reality that the outside world has penetrated into woman's traditional domain—the family. Once perceived as a sanctuary, a "haven in a heartless world," the family today is increasingly affected by society's economic and political policies. Consequently, the women's movement has reemerged as a collective response to women's awakening recognition of their interests as wage earners and the vulnerability of their traditional position in the family.

At the beginning of this second decade of the modern women's movement, the underlying issues are well defined, and the American woman's awareness of her political and economic self-interest is high. The popular consensus is that the feminist movement has had a profound effect on American life. That effect has been understood in terms of documentable progress for women in numerous public and private areas—progress acknowledged by both proponents and opponents of women's equality. Perceptions of that effect are what the editors want to examine in this book.

After ten years of growing consciousness, dedicated activism, and visibly concrete progress, what has been the impact of the women's movement on American institutions, on society's public policies and social values? What has been the movement's impact on the law, the family, the arts, the professions, education—on the personal lives of women? How do women who are successful in their field perceive the gains of the movement? Do they relate their personal growth and professional success to that movement? To what extent have their growth and success contributed to the advancement of all women and to changing the framework of American institutions?

Not every author in this collection addresses each of these questions, nor does this book examine the impact of the women's movement on every aspect of American life. Some areas of social life, such as education and the law, are discussed in detail; others, such as religion and the organized labor movement, are not discussed at all. These limitations exist because the chapters are the result of a conference whose purpose was to discuss a variety of concerns to women. The conference featured speeches by women who are successful practitioners and scholars and who combine professional expertise and personal experience in articulating and defining particular issues. Examining the impact of the women's movement was not the principal intent of the conference, but it clearly emerged as the common underlying theme of the conference proceedings.

The focus on some areas, such as the professions, education, the law, and the arts, reflects not only the limitations of the conference but also the emphasis on certain topics in the literature on women. We suspect that the women's movement has had a greater impact on institutions that can respond to the demands of women more easily than others. Institutions that are expanding, that do not need restructuring, or that do not have to relinquish power can adapt more easily to the changing reality of women's lives. Others such as religious institutions require a fundamental change in structure and philosophy to accommodate women's demands.

Several issues are important in considering the meaning and extent of change, especially as synonymous with improvement in the status of women evident from their increasing social and professional opportunities. First, the chapters in this book offer a subjective index of change as perceived by experienced, knowledgeable observers. Without exception, the authors confirm that in literature, the theater, the law, the professions, education, and health care, some change has taken or is taking place. How enduring that change will be and whether it is structural or ephemeral, only the future will tell.

Second, the impact of progress in specific areas on the overall status of women is also problematic. In Mary Dunlap's provocative chapter, "Resistance to the Women's Movement in the United States: The ERA Controversy as Prototype," she questions whether the status of women has improved significantly. When one considers the plight of the mother on welfare and the increasing violence against all women, the notion of change as "progress" seems suspect. In the field of education, Mary Ellen Verheyden-Hilliard asserts that although some success in eradicating sexism has been achieved, "the underlying notion that if a male finds the female worthy, she need not worry about her future has not changed. It is the one belief, carefully nurtured in secondary schools, as the hidden agenda, that kills the potential of American girls."

Third, viewed historically, the importance of a high level of consciousness, either individual or collective, and even the adoption of some of women's demands as permanent changes are uncertain indicators of genuine change. The women's movement of the nineteenth century also had a high degree of consciousness and strong resolve, and it too had some impact on social institutions. For example, women gained the vote, increased their access to higher education, and achieved changes in laws relating to the rights of women to obtain a divorce and to own property.

Those were significant and concrete gains, and they made a difference in women's lives in this century. But the deeper goals and strivings of the women's movement of the nineteenth century were lost, even well before the vote was won in 1920. After the initial victories, no continued progress toward equality was evident. Wages remained unequal, women in positions of power continued to be an anomaly, and with a few token exceptions, the prestigious professions continued to exclude them. In the family, women were still junior partners, and culture and education remained male centered and male dominated. In short, women did not gain "full partnership in shaping society's course." The first phase of the women's movement suggests that the feminist consciousness of the mothers is not automatically passed on to the daughters.

As an index of change, part I contains chapters exploring the impact and experience of women in the arts and the professions. Maryat Lee and Corinne Jacker, both playwrights, argue that the theater and its contemporary offspring, television, cannot reflect the experience of women without themselves being changed. Both women have worked creatively to develop new forms of expression for women (and for others whose participation in the arts has been marginal). Elaine Ginsberg notes that the expansion of women's literary expression has given them an important forum for talking to each other but fears that the impact on literature will remain limited unless women learn to speak to men as well as to each other. Ruth Phillips and Nancy Reynolds, both health professionals, discuss the increasing opportunities for women in those professions as well as the obstacles, internal and external, they continue to face. Implicit in their chapters is the point that women's traditional role within the family as helper and healer has made their entry into the "serving" professions natural.

Part II contains chapters by three psychologists, two sociologists, and one educator. They examine the effect of the traditional male-dominant/female-submissive behavior on family interactions; on the delivery of health care, including mental health care; on the aging process; and on the education process. Marilou Burnett believes that traditional interactions in the family inhibit human potential, but a breakthrough to new behavior requires the painful renunciation of a contract made in childhood, when the child—in exchange for love and security—stifles her expressiveness and adapts herself to cultural and familial expectations.

Pauline Bart, Ellen Perlmutter, and Nancy Datan, writing on the menopausal and aging woman, see a change in the effect of those age-related processes and project a more positive experience for women as their position in society changes from subservience to equality. "The aging woman of tomorrow," Datan writes, "is the feminist of today. Thus she brings to her maturity and old age her political self-awareness, a personal self-confidence, and the professional resources and career experience that are lacking for so many of today's aging women."

Edith Breen explores the impact of the women's movement on the mental health profession, claiming that both theories of mental health and the delivery of mental health care have been challenged and changed by a growing feminist consciousness. Adelle Robertson examines the changing definition of continuing education, emphasizing its potential in fostering both personal and professional growth for women.

Part III contains chapters by three attorneys and two educators. Ruth Bader Ginsburg, Judith Lichtman, and Carol Baekey examine the development of the concept of equal rights in the law and show that discrimination against women is historically embedded in the public law. Mary Dunlap does not dismiss the significance of statutory and constitutional change but challenges the notion that progress in those areas is necessarily related to the material condition of women's lives.

Judith Stitzel, in her participation in the Modern Language Association's programs on women's literature, has been a pioneer in changing college curricula to reflect the experiences of women. She describes one example of that change and its significance to both women and men. Mary Ellen Verheyden-Hilliard identifies the pervasive sexism at the elementary and secondary levels of education and notes that although some changes have taken place, the educational system continues to socialize girls away from independence and power.

The concluding chapter, by Ann Paterson, Karen Fuchs, Carol Giesen, and Betsy Hobbs, describes the impact of all of the discussions upon the audience to whom they were first presented at a women's conference held at West Virginia University in September 1978. The authors describe how reaction to the contributors served as an index for the process of social change in general and the status of the women's movement in particular. From a survey of 1,000 audience participants, they conclude that women came to the presentation "to learn about the nature of the social changes that are in process, as well as about change processes themselves," and that the women's movement continues to attract a broad audience with diverse interests that wants to effect change.

At the beginning of this second decade of the women's movement, violence against women continues unabated, and the simple guarantee of formal constitutional equality remains elusive. Earning on the average only 59 percent of what men earn, most women continue to be economically dependent. Affirmative action is cynically subverted by those who have control over hiring and firing, and despite the legal base of Title IX, equality in education must still be won. Reproduction and motherhood are plagued with problems for many women, and the sexual division of labor, with all of its vast implications for a continuation of inequality, has barely been touched by ten years of activism. Thus the conclusion that women of diverse backgrounds and interests want to learn how to effect change seems to be the most encouraging of all of the observations made in this book. For at the beginning of the second decade, as grave national and international crises threaten to overshadow the demands for social change, much remains to be done.

PART I
Women in the Professions and the Arts: The Social and Cultural Context of These Roles

1.

Legitimate Theater Is Illegitimate

MARYAT LEE

Women in the theater have had too little to say to each other in candor and regard. It has almost become a way of life to be divided in fierce competition for too few jobs in a small field. Having only recently been allowed into this predominantly male profession, we, like many new-comers, have not wanted to appear to band together. We have too often accepted the way things are and have accommodated rather than grown, risked, and taken innovative stances. If we are to help each other, we need to forget the competitiveness and to nurture support for and thoughtful criticism of each other. We need to think in fresh terms—our own terms—about theater, our place in it, and its relation to what *we* feel about society.

It is important to know what we mean when we talk about the theater. When we refer to the male-dominated art form that stems from Greece and Europe, from Aeschylus to current American playwrights, we are referring, of course, to an import in the nineteenth century, when English and European stars were brought to the United States to tour

the provinces. This theater of European origin is what we call *the*
theater. But *theater,* in its origins, was never an import. More elastic and
catholic, incorporating all kinds of theatrical activity, theater harnesses
raw energies and sets its own standards and limits, not bound by those
of commerce or art. Although theater of this kind is virtually non-
existent in the United States, it is dormant in society and could revive
with a few nods and shoves, combined with discipline. In fact, this is the
arena in which I work. Friends jokingly tell me that I am the international
expert—in a field of one.

As a young woman, I had the naive idea that one purpose of theater
was to expose specific and universal truths hidden by appearances.
Appearances, like fashions, are specifically designed to divide us. As a
southerner, I grew up feeling that we were all hiding behind appearances
and the roles assigned to us very early. Theater offered the chance to
step out, under the protection of whatever character we played, to reveal vital, if hidden, aspects of ourselves. This sharing act of truth would
help bridge divisions and create a cleansed and loving community.
Flannery O'Connor said that the basis of art is truth, and the person who
aims after art in her work aims after truth.

When I entered drama school, I wanted to produce something concerned with values and truths. I did not want to "pretzel-ize" myself for
"the market" or the audience. I did not want to pretend what I could
not feel. But the drama school did not hold with such ideas. Acting
seemed related to someone else's truth, not one's own. My teachers did
not reckon with the curious conflicts aroused by our playing roles in
life or the distinction between these and on-stage roles. Little evidence
of any questioning of the profession could be seen—the type of questioning that a profession requires in the process of growth. I had a Kentucky
accent, and the speech instructor was trying to teach us not only good
English, but English English—broad A's and all. I was getting farther
from, not nearer to, my goal. In spite of the Declaration of Independence,
we were still dependent theatrically. Yes, I was in awe of English actors
too. Their accent was true—for them, but not for me.

To me, the idea that males were always better in male roles and females in female roles was arbitrary. I had previously attended girls'
schools where, because of my height, I had had my choice of challenging and fulfilling male roles. But at drama school, because of my height,
I had no choice of female or male roles. Later I was to discover that sex-

role switching (especially men in female roles) was not only legitimate but powerfully moving in theaters of other cultures.

Today I am occasionally sorry I left speech school after the first year. For example, I direct a theater now,[1] but I know little about stagecraft in any formal way. After many misgivings about having my ignorance exposed, and even more about a trained theater person threatening the delicate process of growth in my company, I hired a youthful stage manager. For several weeks, we tried to bring our new, condescending stage manager down to the humbling realities of indigenous theater with young mountain people. She finally set out to be a model stage manager for EcoTheater. But it is very painful and time consuming to reprogram a trained theater person to this kind of theater.

When I left the speech school, turned off as I was by unfortunate timing and choice of instructors and not committed enough to stick it out, I transferred to an eastern college, where I took a course in Greek drama in translation. Without ever seeing a performance, I recalled my original attraction to theater. I saw a few modern plays to reevaluate my decision but recognized that the theater scene had no place for me.

Subsequently, through the study of religion, I discovered examples of religion and theater before they split apart: medieval street plays— simple, unpretentious, for and about plain people, rough, crude. Such homely little plays and enactments had gone on in every public place where people carried on the daily business of life. That was where our theater started.

I recognized that Elizabethan and Greek theater were monumental because they were rooted in a broad base of people who themselves put on plays out in the bushes and back roads. I decided that the great dramatists grew up as boys (not girls), watching and participating in these naive dramas that evolved until Aeschylus and Sophocles, Marlowe and Shakespeare, stepped onto this vast male pyramid and spoke with an authority and power that has never diminished or found its equal. The audiences of Greece and medieval England were not exclusive court audiences of the wealthy and educated. These audiences were made up of the entire population, as unruly and rowdy as they were genteel, as possessive about plays and performers as a modern crowd is about its sports events.

Thus I began to see our theater as a court audience in the colonies. What we need, I thought, is an occasion for the drama and style that are

around us and crying out to be seen, to gain confidence and discipline.
If drama is all around us and in us, how deprived and cruel that, stuffed
and bursting with our own drama, we must watch others hand down
"the" theater to us, all too often with imitation accents.

One day someone dared me to prove my thesis. He said he would take
me to the back streets of New York, where people never go to the theater
but are wallowing in drama to make your hair stand on end—"like the
quill of the fretful *porpentine*" (porcupine)! This friend's voice came to
me like Hamlet's father's ghost.

List, Hamlet, oh, list! Yes, his talk froze my young blood, harrowed up
my soul, caused my knotted locks to part and each particular hair to
stand on end like the quill of the fretful porpentine. If ever I didst my
dear father (read "theater") love, I must revenge this foul and most un-
natural murder.

So began my venture into the streets empty handed, to harness the
great forces of human nature crowded together unmercifully, four thou-
sand people to a block—to channel, tame, capture, and to make a form
worthy to contain the energy, volatile power, style, and voice of the
streets.

I believed the theater had to do with truth. The crude little play in
Hamlet, for example, revealed the truth about the king's death, and the
reenactment of it brought down the court. This truth, revealed with such
dramatic consequences, was symbolic to me on many levels. The image
of revenging the murder of theater itself—a broad-based, primitive
theater built on bedrock in the unpolished voices of real people—obsessed
me, on the one hand. On the other hand, what I felt and believed to be
a spiritual murder in the bosom of my own family, was one that was not
known except by me, for I was the only witness to it. Since it was the
murder of a spirit—the breaking of a spirit, if you will—no law pertained
to it. There was no one to talk with, and no way to accuse. So only a reenactment could expose the truth for all to see who could see, a reenactment that could make right a wrong, a reenactment of a true story by
simple players that could bring down a court—a kingdom. Finally, there
was, of course, the simple, primitive troupe of actors themselves, perhaps
like the little troupes that preceded Shakespeare, providing the bedrock
on which he built, and indeed how ready they were to do his (Hamlet's)
bidding.

I did a play on drugs.[2] A somewhat smug junkie sees his loved sister initiated into the rite of drug taking. (Drugs, incidentally, were not the family problem I referred to above.) The process of reenacting a true story is somehow transformed and seldom as transparent as Hamlet's play—unless one's sole purpose is to use it as a tool. Yet didn't I start with the idea of using it as a tool?

I began to get interested not so much in the drugs but in the addiction itself. In Roman law, *addiction* was a word used for the judicial act of giving someone to a master by sentence of a court. Later it meant becoming attached by one's own act. I soon found myself affected in unexpected ways. Although I started wanting to use theater for revenge, proof, truth, or whatever, I began to see that to use a play for my own schemes would be as calculating as to use a person for my intentions, however good they might be. In short, I was not comfortable with that idea. I was not actually comfortable until the play was its own master, not my slave. It was quite a wrestling match. Since then, this master-slave duel has become my primary struggle in writing a play—the play (characters, action) fighting against me, struggling for its own autonomy. It often ends in a draw (or in a drawer).

I researched the play on East 100th Street, later discovered to have the heaviest drug traffic in New York. I wrote it, cast it from the neighborhood, directed it, designed it, and learned another unforgettable lesson. Because of the difficulty of the central role, I was afraid of casting the addict from the block. So I advertised that one role in various drama schools and held auditions for it. A young actor from the Piscator workshop got the role. I made clear to him that he was not to impose his ways but was to fit in with the street actors. Yet he tested this. He wanted quiet during rehearsals. I did not give in on this point. I knew that in the streets it would not be quiet, and I was training the actors to use the sounds, play against them, repeat words, and so on. He wanted them to stand still during his long speech. This was an artifice.

After a while, I noticed that the other actors were becoming withdrawn and unhappy, and I could not pinpoint the source of the problem. Eventually they skipped rehearsals. Then it came to me that I had given in here and there, tempted by the actor's knowledge and seduced from my original position. The actors knew my compromise before I did. So I confessed to them that I had let them down and made them feel stupid and inferior. I asked them to give me another chance. They came back, and when they saw me take a tough position with hapless Neil McKenzie,

a strong and dedicated actor, they began to float and soar, and vitality
was restored. This is the sort of thing that in the nineteenth century
stopped the development of provincial theater in this country. When the
great English actors toured, they undoubtedly made the locals feel foolish.

This play did not bring down the kingdom or the court of my family.
It didn't even stir a hair. But it did momentarily bring down a kingdom
of another order that, however, quickly restored itself. It generated a few
weeks of sensational notoriety about drugs: banner headlines, network
television exposure, *Life* photos, accounts in the *New Yorker,* and cele-
brity visits. Then the experience was buried. No one in the 1950s was
concerned with the streets. I could find no way and no one to help continue with other productions, in spite of the publicity. Not until fifteen
years later did I again work in the streets—when the streets of the 1960s
were themselves a theater.

It is not fashionable to dissect plays or books to discover things about
the author's private life. This is a good thing, because it protects the
writers from nosiness and from becoming more self-conscious than they
already are. I can bring this up because that first play is so far in my past
that I have no uneasiness about it now. However, although it appears to
be removed from me, theater is not something happening elsewhere. It
is here and now. It is what is happening with you and me. One can have
the direct experience of theater, and one's personal word in it, while
writing out of a specific community that may be, in outward appearances, very remote from one's personal life.

I was white and southern and had been to boarding schools. Yet
underneath these surface differences between me and the blacks and
Puerto Ricans with whom I worked was another world in which we
shared a few important attitudes and circumstances in different degrees.
Not only were we kept in our places, for instance, and thought to be
inferior, we also shared an understanding about addiction. No one recognized my own personal story that found its way through the play, not
even I, until ten or so years later, when it came to me what the story
really was. Most people thought it was a documentary street play. But
as much as the play came out of the streets, threads of myself sewed it
together.

It is true that limitations in theater are found outside "the" theater.
Limitations are also found in a two-part fugue.

Louis is talking to two younger boys. He must repeat words, but not as if to morons. He cannot be too subtle perhaps, but he can lace into an image with an edge. One of the younger boys says, "I heard it takes ten years off your life."

LOUIE: So. Who wants to live a hundred years around here in this—this cage? (The word turns him on.)[3]

The other boy says, "That stuff must do a lot for you." Turned on by a word, Louis repeats it and other key words, building a cage of words.

> A cage! Yeah. Ssh, don't interrupt. I'm seeing this whole jungle, all of it, man, inside a cage. And look at them—all these faces, thousands of faces in that cage. Flattened out and dead, man—and one or two soft alive faces—their bodies stuffed in there, too—their heads hanging out, trying to sneak through—or breathe. Yeah—Porse and them are in there too. They're all in there. We're all inside! See—[4]

From the initial success in the streets, I retired indoors for a long time, buried inside, working in and around the theater until the street 1960s revived performances of *Dope!* uptown and downtown, and street theater companies were forming everywhere. I too started a new company in 1968, Soul and Latin Theater, and we did five plays over a two-year period about the scandalous classroom, homosexuality, drugs, and a liberated street woman—subjects taken directly from the company's experiences and meshed with my own.[5]

By this time, my own street theater experiment was tried twice, seventeen years apart, in the same neighborhood. At the end of the 1960s, however, it was time for a lot of us to go back to the South to deal with various personal and social problems we had run away from. I moved to a farm in West Virginia in 1970. While waiting for general understanding and trust to develop with and from the community in which I settled before attempting a rural theater, I wrote a play, *Fuse*. A virtuoso piece for two actresses, *Fuse* is about a middle-class woman in her forties who is split within—appearances versus reality—trying to come together with herself.

Although the play is of interest to the conventional theater especially because of its protagonist, who is from their world, and in spite of its technical difficulties, I include it here to illustrate the variety outside the theater. Trained actresses have difficulty reading the play with any comprehensibility initially, but many nonactresses get to the heart of it. So intent are the actresses on reading it properly, they miss or resist letting the play, the action, happen to them. They impose themselves (their training, that is) on the play.

MONA (looking at the mirror): Funny. I can see out through slits in the armor. I can see through it, always did. But nobody sees me through it anymore, and sometimes lately I can't see myself either.

Can a person—can a person—change?

I don't mean changing a job, an address, a shrink, a husband, even a "life style." That's easy. I mean can you change? Inside? When I think about that, a big silence, a big sadness comes around like a cloud and everything quivers slightly as if in the deepest sleep. Oh, eternal night, uncradle us gently, open our eyes to the movements of the deep!

Here we go. Whimper time, folks, Self-pityville. (Business with table.)

Do you know one person who's changed? I've heard. I've read about it. But do I know anyone? Do you?

Listen, self-pity—self-pity stinks, because it's *so small.* Furtive. Now—take BIG pity. The Greeks had BIG pity. So did Jesus. (Pours a drink in glass.) BIG pity! Not squnching it down! Letting it well up, letting it flow over, letting it roll and thunder and spill and gather and include the lame, halt, blind—which, when you come right down to it, is any, every one of us, right?

That's how they got rid of that little teaspoon that gets sour if you keep it pinched into a whine. That's how they did it! BIG pity. Includes self-pity. Starts with self-pity. Mine, yours, really it's a beginning, self-pity, of something that could flower, but that—in our supposed wisdom—we try to root out. Oh, me. It emboldens me like mud. (Takes glass and sniffs.) Hmm. And if you can't root it out (*and you can't*), then *drown* it, right? Drug it! (Pause. Hesitates. Then pours drink back in bottle.)

Okay. Let's have it. (Blank.) I'm waiting. I'm listening. And I'm thinking—about—the office. My promotion shafted, third time in a row. Boo hoo. So an outsider comes in with his "fresh blood" (sleazy Ivy League bum) and I'm up again for the "next" time. Okay. Bitter blow. (To mirror). So? Don't stop there. Move on further. Further. More BIG pity. That's the game we're after, not this whining stuff. . . .

I can't see, can't really hear any more. (Lith smiles.) I hear a little bell ring—way off. (Fingers glass thoughtfully.)

Oh, boy. I'm stuck. Yes, I can't see. If I look at someone, it's one manikin to another. Excuse me. Womanikin. I can't even ask a real question or listen to a real answer. I don't know. Don't know. Half-way through life's journey, and I know less, feel less. Halfway through life's journey, and I am a *wo-manikin*! A *woe* manikin. Yet not too far away, inside there, is a little something, way inside this manikin. Sometimes I can smell a smoky little fire. Sometimes it's a little package and I can hear it tick. I think almost anything could set it off—only it never does. That's the point, isn't it. Do you know, do you understand where I am? (To audience). Do you know, really where? That's right. BIG pity. Oh, I would, if I could, uncradle you gently, myself, and open all our eyes and ears to the movement of the dark.

But how can I. Nobody can do it for me. Nobody has done it for me. In fact—can anybody do it at all? Isn't it your own—personal—private—(Notices Lith.) Oh—(Continues absently.) Struggle in this—life? (Pause.)

I can't see. (Squints.) Can you speak? Is she there?[6]

On this particular day, Mona starts the painful step of recognition, realization, integration—a most difficult play, perhaps impossible, to perform. It seemed to involve, the performers, in some mysterious way, in the same process of realization, although this was not my intention.

EcoTheater, a rural counterpart of Soul and Latin Theater (SALT), was born in 1975 in the Appalachian spring. As I did in New York, I chose a group of young mountain people hired by the state during the summer, ordinarily to work at menial jobs that required them to put in thirty-two hours a week. We set about with a colleague, Fran Belin, to train them from scratch for performances that were booked four weeks later throughout August at flea markets, the state fair, and other arenas of community life.

The plays were written by me out of oral history sessions with the company, local people, and neighbors. One play is about John Henry, the local legendary figure, and one is about an old mountain woman of great individuality, integrity, and imagination. The criterion for casting is based on who is best in the role regardless of gender. John Henry has been played by a woman each summer and Miz Dacey by a man. The audiences accept this without question. The company is black and white, sometimes with senior citizen actors. Among other things, both plays explore the race polarity—John Henry by no overt reference to race at all, and Miz Dacey with the visit of two black girls wanting to use her phone. She has never had a black person on her porch and says as much as she sits down to enjoy their company.

The truth—theater as reenactment of the truth underneath appearances, under veils of fears and suspicions, and theater setting forth explicitly the limits defined and imposed like a mask on our normal lives and then breaking through this mask, leaving the verities intact but the lies broken in tiny pieces—this is how Miz Dacey acts. Her world is small and her learning is limited. Yet when confronted by the appearance of what she thought was inferior—two ordinary black girls—she discerns the ridiculousness of all of the fears and breaks through in her own way to a new stage—an acceptance of what life has thrown her way. She also announces that she will marry the twenty-year-old TV repairman who is wooing her.

The play would hardly be controversial elsewhere in 1978. But it was heavy for Summers County, West Virginia. Miz Dacey says to her nosy neighbor who comes to check on things:

MIZ DACEY: Well, Tatter Lee, I'll tell you one thing. I used to think like
        you, the Lord wanted us all separate and pure. But to tell the truth,
        it's the ones tryin' so hard to keep pure that's bringing on the end
        of the world, this bunch thinkin' they can't mix or share with
        some other bunch. That kinda talk has got us a world tearin' itself
        to pieces. Now, look—isn't this fine we can set on the porch and
        talk, all of us, young and old, and all different colors. If the Maker
        didn't want us to mix, why, he woulda fixed it so we couldn't—
        like the horses and cows![7]

Tatter Lee shrieks as she falls out. But Miz Dacey goes into the house to
get her fiddle, saying in passing, "Come on, Tatter, wake up. I haven't
tole you the real news—me and Orfin is getting married."[8]

Miz Dacey also deals with the bureaucrat who visits her and tells her
how to eat and with a real estate man who is trying to buy her farm at a
low price. She is unwavering with each visitor. She tries to help the nutrition lady whose pill bottle has one of those devilish lids that torment the
elderly—a lid that "it would take a blacksmith and a little boy to open."
Her surefire way of getting the pills is to put the bottle on the floor and
stamp on it. She tells the real estate man to come back when he can't
stay so long. She asks the nutrition lady if she's from the agency that
had them plant those rose bushes long ago that have taken over so not
even a place is left for a cow to drop a pie. The play takes pokes at the
favorite butts of country humor: the doctors, agriculture people, real
estate people, nosy neighbors. Treating the blacks as equal is the only
departure from the norm, and bedded between the usual familiar objects of derision, it works.

I have tried to show through examples of my own work, the variety
that is possible in theater outside the theater. But far more astounding
theatrical activity is taking place elsewhere in the world. In a book published by the Harvard Press a decade ago, James Brandon said Southeast
Asia has so many troupes that no one has ever tried to count them.[9]
The United States had 50 troupes outside New York in 1967,[10] but
Brandon estimates that Southeast Asia has 1,168 known professional
troupes and double or triple that number of amateur troupes operating
today. Three out of four people living in Southeast Asia see these troupes
perform every year. In a comparable population in the United States,
two out of one hundred people, by recent count, annually attend "the"
theater. The variety in Southeast Asia is equally staggering—theater at
every level, for all ages, all degrees of education, as well as all dialects
and languages.

I love to go to good theater in London or New York, especially
London. But I am suggesting today that we begin to think and consider
that the theater we know and love is only part, and a small part, of a
total theater picture, just as classical music is only part of the music picture. Those of us who are discontent with the limitations of conventional
or commercial theater should start now to develop our own diverse
theater language, to explore the bottom or neglected part of society,
and to capture some of its voices.

The word *professional* is confusing and misleading. It does not describe anything distinctive any more, except possibly that payment is
involved. As for skill and quality, professional performances are too often
marred by sloppiness, ineptitude, indulgence, ineffectuality—all of the
things commonly attributed only to amateurs.

At times amateurs produce what is considered state of the art. Free
from pressures of profit and unions, they can devote extra time and care
to achieve high quality. One thinks of one of the most sublime of theaters
today in terms of discipline and perfection: the Noh theater.[11] Traditionally, Noh performers have been dedicated amateurs, and males play
both genders.

Occasionally I am asked, how do you start your own theater from the
bottom up? To clear the mind of stereotypes, you can think and read
about theater of other cultures. You can also pick an audience that
never attends the theater and for whom you feel affection. Like families,
an audience unmistakably influences and shapes you. It is not something
to be ashamed of. You affect and change each other as you grow. As in
sex, shame comes only if you try to please those you do not respect.
Young anthropologists pick their people to study with great care, hoping
to like them.

Any community will do: a rural white community, a prison, women's
groups, church, children, adolescents, senior citizens, ethnic communities.
Any of these communities will be more rewarding than the well-educated
theatergoing group that is sated and tired out from the heavily subsidized
programs designed for them, which they are obliged to attend. You can't
learn much from them. They don't yell "louder" when the sound is bad;
they don't whistle; they don't walk out if they are bored. They are in
fact so nice that theater companies don't know what to do when they
get a rowdy audience. As a performer or playwright, one is positively
driven to beating this kind of audience over the head, insulting it, abusing—or placating it. Rarely does one feel affection. Great stars seldom
break through it. Estelle Parsons told me she regards the audience as the
enemy and prepares each night as if for combat.

Once you choose your people, simply go to them; be with them;
listen to them; let them happen to you; record them; be sensitive to their
voices, cadences, and concerns and to the stories and messages between
the lines. Improvise with them, cast your play with them—these experts
who have experienced the action. Rehearse, set up performance dates,
announce the opening, invite friends, and—do it.

At some point, you find a sense of identity, a freedom, a pride, that you have done theater from scratch without looking over your shoulder or having someone breathing down your back. Theater people have a way of saying at least once a year that the theater is dying. It is not dying. It has not yet been born.

NOTES

1. EcoTheater, which began in 1975, has to do with the mutual give and take of the people with the environment, including that of the local culture. We try not to impose external standards but to isolate and develop an inherent style and to find the voice of the community, its concerns, language, color, and will and let this be heard in these mountains and beyond. The troupe has consisted of fifteen to twenty young people (ages, fifteen to twenty-one years) from Summers County, West Virginia, who are eligible for low-income Governor's Summer Youth Programs. Instead of cutting brush along the highways, the young people learn a variety of skills, gathering oral history, acting, building, and so on, in a farm setting at the Women's Farm, home of Maryat Lee.
2. Maryat Lee, *Dope!* (New York: Samuel French, 1956). Also published in ed. Margaret Mayorga, *Best Short Plays of 1952-1953,* (New York: Dodd, Mead, and Company, 1953): and ed. Rachel France, *A Century of Plays by American Women,* (New York: Richards Rosen Press, 1979.).
3. Maryat Lee, *Dope!,* p. 9.
4. Ibid., p. 10.
5. Soul and Latin Theater (SALT). A. D. Coleman, in the *Village Voice* (August 29, 1968), wrote:

There was something in the work of the SALT troupe, and in the audience's response to it, which represented to me the very essence of theater.

If I seem to impose a double standard on the work of ghetto street-theater groups, remember that contemporary theater imposes a double standard on me. Maryat Lee's plays may be irrelevant and useless to the audience for avant-garde theater; but avant-garde theater is irrelevant and useless to the audience for Maryat Lee's plays.

At a time when the avant-garde theater is deeply concerned with total theater and "participatory theater," the SALT troupe's biggest problem is keeping members of the audience from leaping onto the stage.

What all that adds up to I truly don't know; but if it's patronization, I'll eat every word of it.

I was never able to find another review of theater work after this date by A. D. Coleman. He apparently wrote photography criticism.

6. Maryat Lee, *Fuse* (unpublished play, 1970-1979).

7. Maryat Lee, "Miz Dacey."

8. Ibid.

9. James R. Brandon, *Theatre in Southeast Asia* (Cambridge, Mass.: Harvard University Press, 1967).

10. William J. Baumol and William G. Bowen, *Performing Arts: The Economic Dilemma* (New York: Twentieth Century Fund, 1966).

11. The Noh theater is the classic theater of Japan. It is subtle to the point of invisibility to Western eyes until one has seen several performances. One then experiences a shift of perception, an opening of a door to another world, that has little to do with plot, character, and action in our terms. It is difficult, exasperating, and completely worth the pains.

2.

Better Than a Shriveled Husk: New Forms for the Theater

CORINNE JACKER

The theater has always been a sort of exclusive club. Nowadays we refer to anyone who is not in the business as a "civilian." For most of its history, the theater club has been for men only.

Drama began as a part of a religious ceremony in a place consecrated to Dionysius, a male god. The playwrights and performers were all male. Ancient Athens itself was a world where all citizens were male and in which the slaves and women belonged together.

But women's exclusion from the club was not a phenomenon only of the ancient period. Virginia Woolf wrote a fable about William Shakespeare's imaginary sister Judith, a writer with a talent equal to his. Judith, however, did not end up at the Globe as playwright in residence. She hung around the stage door, trying to get work as an actress or a writer, until she was noticed by the company manager, who befriended her, got her pregnant, and left her. While brother Will went on to write great plays, sister Judith killed herself and lies in some anonymous grave.

Judith was right to try to get acting work. That is where women made their breakthrough. In England, actresses appeared around 1600, charming the audiences and soon becoming the only reason that many people went to see plays. However, they did not manage the companies or write or direct the plays. With few exceptions, that was the reality of the theater until only a hundred years ago.

One exception was Hrotsvitha of Gandersheim, a Benedictine nun who lived and wrote in the latter half of the tenth century, and who began her work when there were no theaters, few active original dramatists, and no secular drama. "Unknown to all around me," she wrote,

I have toiled in secret, often destroying what seems to me ill written and rewriting it. . . . Up to the present I have not submitted the work to any experts, much as I needed their advice, for fear that the roughness of the style would make them discourage me to such an extent that I might give up writing altogether.[1]

But plays cannot exist without an audience. Fortunately, she found one. Her plays—moral tales of seduced virgins, dreadful torture, and the triumph of virtue—were performed by her sister nuns for visiting royalty.

As playwrights have to be, she was fascinated by the ways of the world, by the "dreadful frenzy of those possessed by unlawful love and the insidious sweetness of passion." In one of her plays, Abraham finds his long-lost niece Mary, who has become a prostitute in a brothel. He poses as a client and the madam teases Mary about the advanced age of her client.

MARY: It is all one to me. It is my business to love those who love me.

ABRAHAM: Come nearer, Mary, and give me a kiss.

MARY: I will give you more than a kiss. I will take your head in my
        arms and stroke your neck.

ABRAHAM: Yes, like that!

MARY: What does this mean? What is this lovely fragrance, so clean, so
        sweet? It reminds me of the time when I was good.[2]

Perhaps the second oldest profession is a reasonable concern for the mother of all women dramatists. But worldly as her plays were, they were confined to the convent. After limited performances, they vanished into obscurity for hundreds of years and were not revived and translated until the nineteenth century.

Hrotsvitha had no women successors until the middle of the 1600s. Soon after actresses appeared on the English state, Aphra Behn, who made her living as a writer, became a cause célèbre as a dramatist. Many members of her audiences considered her plays indecent, but not indecent enough to be avoided. Consequently, many of her plays had substantial runs on the professional London stage.

However, Behn did not receive the recognition she thought she deserved. Some of her work was not successful, and many of the dramas were reviled by the audiences and the critics. To her, only one thing explained her mixed success: the plays had been written by a woman, not a man. She wrote:

> This one thing I will venture to say, though against my nature, because it has a vanity in it: that had the plays I have writ come forth under any man's name, and never known to have been mine, . . . all unbiased judges of sense [would have] said that [I] had made as many good comedies as any one man that has writ in our age; but a devil on't. The woman damns the poet. All I ask, is the privilege for my masculine part, the poet in me. . . . If I must not, because of my sex, have this freedom, I lay down my quill and you shall hear no more of me.[3]

What did she mean by her "masculine part"? Was it that men were welcomed as playwrights and women were not, or did she feel an androgynous quality in her work, a kind of masculine energy or voice that was responsible for the poetry, the drama? Certainly we know that even the worldly Behn, making a living with the best of them, considered herself an interloper in a man's world.

Hrotsvitha of Gandersheim and Aphra Behn are two landmarks, one more a curiosity than a playwright, the other competent at her craft. This is the bleak landscape that existed for another two hundred years. A thin trickle of plays appeared during the nineteenth century but were, mostly, merely interesting. Only a few of them are still performed—most notably Anna Cora Mowatt's *Fashion.*

Not until the early 1920s, when writers such as Susan Glaspell, Zoe Atkins, Sophie Treadwell, and Edna St. Vincent Millay achieved productions both on and off Broadway, were women recognized as serious writers of drama. Treadwell's *Machinal,* which dealt with the terrible robotization of the office worker, was perhaps the first play to look sympathetically at the plight of the female white-collar worker. With Lillian Hellman, however, the theater at last found a truly distinguished woman writer, with abiding creations such as *The Little Foxes, The Children's Hour, Another Part of the Forest, Toys in the Attic,* and *The Autumn Garden.*

Since World War II, more women have been writing plays, and more women's plays are being produced. When I went to the Eugene O'Neill playwrights conference in its eighth year, only two women had ever previously attended. In 1977 seven women and seven men were there. Now one sees collections of plays by women playwrights, courses for women on dramaturgy, women's theaters, and women's theater collectives all over the United States. Megan Terry, who was a well-known playwright of the beginning of the off-off-Broadway theater, left New York to work exclusively with a women's theater collective in Omaha. We can now name a long list of women playwrights whose names are recognized, including Lorraine Hansberry, Alice Childress, Eve Merriam, Anne Burr, Megan Terry, Rochelle Owens, Ntozake Shange, Elizabeth Swados, Wendy Wasserstein, and Susan Miller. At last we do not have to search through obscure reference books for a few token writers; the list of talented women goes on and on.

Somehow that isn't enough. Why do we still have a nagging feeling of incompletion? What more do we want? In part, we want to be taken seriously. Women dramatists know that, despite their successes, they are not yet viewed with the seriousness accorded other playwrights.

Many of the new women playwrights of the 1960s and 1970s came out of the women's movement. Their work has been regarded as theatrical, but as something other than drama. Some women's collectives presented evenings that were political and sociological statements first and drama second. Others used theater as a kind of psychological exploration of the female predicament. Their works were sincerely conceived, and many of them were remarkably effective. But the audience for such productions was limited. If men came to the theater at all, they felt uncomfortable and unwanted, as though they were the enemy at whom the play was directed. Many of the women who came were already aware of or sympathetic with the viewpoints expressed. Somehow the plays never seemed to attract the audience that the writers thought should be seeing the plays.

These women writers were seeking ways to liberated consciousness and new forms of expression but were not able to move into the commercial theater. Producers did not believe plays that were dealing with women's topics or were trying to make an agit-prop statement about women were money-making properties. Beyond that, the women's theater movement had no pool of talent to draw upon. Women directors were, and still are, scarce. Women designers are just beginning to find work. Women stage managers are still something of an oddity. Like the dilemma facing women who make films, two choices were available: to use men who had the skills and reputations the plays needed to "make it," or to be true to the philosophy behind the drama and employ only women, regardless of the current state of their skills.

It is interesting that Eve Merriam's *The Club* was produced by women but directed by a man. Its production signified the beginning of women working with men to create a kind of theater that was for an audience of both women and men. The most popular off-off-Broadway institutional theater, the Manhattan Theater Club, is run by a woman, Lynne Meadow, who also directs (usually plays by men). Although their opportunities are still limited, many other women directors have entered the mainstream of theater, television, and film. Like the blacks who brought about the change in the black theater in recent years, many women playwrights are reaching out for a larger, more conservative audience while still retaining their political philosophies.

Nevertheless, playwriting continues to be a man's occupation. Recently, the *New York Times* listed the twenty-five American writers of this generation who were going to form the backbone of our theater. Of the twenty-five, only two were women. Yet this imbalance was not simply that the men were better qualified.

Why aren't women being taken seriously? Relatively few women are writing plays, and they can look back to only a small body of women's work; the playwright's life seems to conflict with what is often thought to be a woman's sensibilities and behavior; the relationship with actors, directors, even actresses, is often difficult; and women have sometimes found difficulty in writing central male characters. Perhaps most importantly, when women forget about writing well-made plays, or imitations of other forms, the drama that results is often surprising—shocking rhythmically, told in subtly different ways, aiming at different reactions from the audience, and affecting them in a new way. Critics and viewers are sometimes confused about what they think and feel or about what they think they are supposed to feel.

The first two reasons are interrelated. Until the last hundred years or so, women who chose to write did not choose playwriting. Where were the women dramatists when Sappho was writing her poetry, when Jane Austen and George Eliot were writing their novels? They were at home, and playwrights cannot stay at home.

Women who were working in the truly literary arts—novel, short story, poetry, biography, or essay—had a specific predicament, however difficult, that had a solution. The "angel in the house" might come to Virginia Woolf and talk to her about her womanly domestic duties. There were children, household responsibilities, and the fact that "nice" women did not try to do something as mannish as writing. But literary writing is done, or can be done, in solitude, in a room of one's own. Short of that, one has secrecy. Jane Austen put a squeak in one of the floorboards in the room where she wrote, so when someone intruded on her privacy, she would have time to hide her papers. The Brontës hid behind male names.

The theater has no hiding place, no privacy, and a play cannot be created by one person working alone in a room. The theater works by fixed hours and a scheduled opening date. Rehearsals do not wait for nursing mothers. The script that goes into rehearsal is usually only a shadow of the finished work. The writer has to be available, go out of town, and work long hours after rehearsal, often with the director or the actors, so the rewrite can be put in the next day. In short, the writer has to lead the life of a gypsy from the moment her play is optioned until it opens. The writer is there, not on the stage, but fully there, intimately exposed.

What happens in rehearsal? The director is usually a man, and it is easy to fall into familiar patterns, to allow the man to be authoritative, to be father and instructor, to lecture the woman playwright on what is wrong with her work, and to protect and take care of her. Assertiveness training is an important part of consciousness raising. The woman who is in the theater in any occupation other than actress needs to understand assertiveness.

When I was eighteen, I got my first job as a professional director. A community theater near my college was going to do *Time Out for Ginger,* a comedy about a young girl who wants to play football but discovers she is a girl. The play has a little love scene between Ginger's mother and father. They were being played by a real-life husband and wife. He was a professional actor of twenty years' standing; her credentials were about the same.

I did not like the way they were playing the love scene. He did not know how to kiss her, how to behave seductively, and so on. So I had to tell a man, a professional actor old enough to be my father, that he did not know how to kiss his own wife. I blushed, I stuttered, I took the most delicate approach. It didn't matter. I *told* him how to kiss her. He went right on kissing her his way, in rehearsals and in performance, and what was I supposed to do about it?

I felt that same embarrassment, that same fear and timidity, when I tried to write a male character. If a man is in the play, he has to behave a certain way. That means he has thoughts, emotions, actions, conflicts, a whole life that as a character he must bring to the drama. If I had trouble telling an actor how to kiss his wife, a minor issue in a play already written, think what I went through making a character live out his life.

At first I ignored the problem. I avoided subjects that were primarily male (if I wrote a war play, I wrote about women's camps with no men in them). I never wrote a play about the presidents of the United States, or molecular biologists, or generals, or almost anything that springs from exterior action in the real world. If I did have to write a man, I kept him one dimensional, a shadow. They might say he was not fully drawn, but I would not be shown up as a fool who did not know how a man's mind works. I avoided any depth of conflict between men and men or men and women. My plays became superstructures of avoidance.

Of course, I had to face the dialogue. Men had to speak. I had the answer to that too. I wrote men who were peculiar—who came from outer space, or who were mentally ill, or who came from extremely odd backgrounds, so their language would not be like a man's usually is. But what do men talk about? I solved that too. I never had men alone on stage; a woman always had to be present. Better yet, I always told the story from the woman's point of view, from her head. Then the men had to be hidden, or what they said was always tempered by the fact that it was filtered through her mind. Best of all, I made the play somehow fantastic, or expressionistic, or highly stylized. Then I didn't have to deal with conflict, with the reality of human behavior.

I had solved my problems, but I was left with plays that were either bland or of deep intellectual eccentricity, inaccessible to the audience. What was missing from my work was honesty, confrontation, true human behavior—all of the stuff that drama is made of. In despair, I left the theater. I wrote fiction and books about science, sociology, history— anything that freed me from the awful confrontation with the man. I could not break through the taboos in my mind. I could not allow my- self to write the forbidden. Writing male characters was one taboo; writing as a woman was another.

That second taboo looms large right now as women are moving into life and leaving traditional occupations behind. A woman truck driver, lawyer, doctor, senator—these are reasonable, or somewhat reasonable, occupations now. Women are working communally with other women, and that means they have to deal with that great taboo in their conscious- ness—womanhood. Stronger than the taboos, though, was the fact that I was a playwright. I was devoted to the theater. It was the kind of writing I needed to do. I had to find some way to break through this block.

The way appeared, and as happens with most self-discovery, I was well on the road before I realized it. The way was television. Through a series of coincidences, I was hired to write for TV. No one at the networks was interested in my agony about the male psyche. My tasks were a series of commissions in which the scripts were about men—the Benjamin Franklin series of CBS, the "Adams Chronicles," and so on.

I was paid to write, and I had to write. Luckily for me, I was writing about real people and actual events in their lives. Because I was dealing with real men and events that really happened, I found the secret. Men are human. That means that it is possible to figure them out. I found out that it was not an act of hubris to write a male character. Now I have the opposite kind of problem. A television producer will frequently say to me, "Yes, but have you written anything about women?"

Two years ago, a play of mine called *My Life* was being produced. It happened entirely in the mind of the protagonist. One of the actors came to the auditions only because he knew a woman could not have written the play. The men were too real. At first I was proud. Then I was angry. Why couldn't a woman write male characters? They always seem to take it for granted that they can write about us.

Another writer commented that I do write real men—but men seen through a woman's eyes. That is the crux of the problem and the joy of it. I am a woman. I see the world through my eyes. How do I learn to write with my own individual, unique, woman's voice?

For instance, in writing for the television miniseries, "Best of Families," I wrote a short scene, the culminating romantic moment between James Lathrop and the woman he loved, Sarah Baldwin. The director, a man, said, "It won't play." The producer, a man, said, "Rewrite it, the audience will never get it." The actor who played James was troubled by it. But, luckily, the executive producer was a woman. "Shoot it," she said, "it'll play. It's the best scene in the show." It did work, but what was it about the scene that made the men so hesitant? Why were they so sure it would not play or be understood? The sensibility was not what they were used to. The whole rhythmic and emotional arc of the scene was not predictable, but it was written the way that seemed true to its requirements and to me.

When I write of women's sensibilities, I mean that we approach drama in a way that inevitably results in the making of another form. First, many women playwrights seem concerned with the inner drama of life much more than with exterior events. Perhaps it is because women have not been out in the world all that much—have not had a chance to lead armies and run countries. Historically, drama has been concerned with the large event—wars, kingship, power. This interest, the different rhythmical quality, the difference in world view, even a different approach to character and conflict, makes for a new kind of theater, one that has never had a chance to grow and flower before.

This is not a *women's* theater. It is a theater made by a woman's vision, but it is for the world to see. It is a new exploration of the human condition. What we women who write plays are now insisting on is that we have to make these explorations our way. I cannot go on imitating what I have seen, trying to make my plays neat and predictable because that is the way it has always been done. This generation is saying for the first time, "I don't have to write like a man any more."

We are here. We are being produced. For the first time in 2,500 years, the audience is being given a new vision of dramatic action. We will not simply take an old form and shape it to our female bodies. The clothes don't fit. We join the anonymous Victorian feminist who first asked, "Isn't it better to find a new form, than cling with perverse tenacity to the dried-up and shriveled husk?"

NOTES

1. Trans. Christopher St. John, *The Plays of Hrotvuitha,* (London: Chatto & Windus, 1923) p. xxii.

2. Ibid., p. 83.

3. From Behn's introduction to her play, "The Lucky Chance," contained in *The Works of Apara Behn with a Memoir,* 6 vols., ed. Rev. Montague Summers (Blom Publications, 1915).

3.

Playwrights, Poets, and Novelists: Sisters under the Skin

ELAINE GINSBERG

The literary arts—fiction, drama, poetry, even biography and autobiography—are as diverse as the artists who practice them. Women writers likewise differ: one can hardly imagine two persons—let alone two women—as different as Virginia Woolf and Tillie Olsen. But my purpose here is to explore the similarities, to explore what women writers of all times have had, and still have, in common and what effect the women's movement has had on women writers.

One thing women writers, or perhaps I should say "would-be writers," have had in common, as both Tillie Olsen and Virginia Woolf so eloquently told us, is "silences." Woolf in 1929 speculated about those women of genius who because of societal restrictions were never able to express their gift:

When . . . one reads of a woman possessed by devils, of a wise woman selling herbs, or even of a very remarkable man who had a mother, then I think we are on the track of a lost novelist, a suppressed poet, of some

mute and inglorious Jane Austen, some Emily Brontë who dashed her
brains out on the moor . . . crazed with the torture that her gift had put
her to.[1]

They shared a lack of education, lack of opportunity, lack of freedom.
Had there been a female Shakespeare, Woolf told us, she

. . . would certainly have gone crazed, shot herself, or ended her days in
some lonely cottage outside the village, half witch, half wizard, feared
and mocked at. For it needs little skill in psychology to be sure that a
highly gifted girl who had tried to use her gift for poetry would have
been so thwarted and hindered by other people, so tortured and pulled
asunder by her own contrary instincts, that she must have lost her health
and sanity to a certainty.[2]

Those women who did manage, with a bit of freedom and a great deal
of courage, to produce works of literature have shared other problems.
One significant problem has always been a difficulty in dealing with men
and power. Adrienne Rich, in an essay written in 1972, pointed out that
in the work of two twentieth-century poets, Sylvia Plath and Dianne
Wakoski,

Man appears as, if not a dream, a fascination and a terror; and that the
source of the fascination and the terror is, simply, man's power—to dom-
inate, tyrannize, choose, or reject the woman. . . . And, in the work of
both of these poets, it is finally the woman's sense of *herself*—embattled,
possessed—that gives the poetry its dynamic charge, its rhythms of
struggle, need, will, and female energy.[3]

Rich added the important point that "until recently this female anger
and this furious awareness of man's power over her were not available
materials to the female poet."[4]
This is not to imply that earlier women writers never expressed their
resentment toward the power that men held over their lives. Virginia
Woolf in *A Room of One's Own* is almost apologetic as she appeals for
women's freedom to write, to have the time and the place to create,
but the anger is obvious beneath the surface. Much earlier, the American
Puritan poet, Ann Bradstreet, in a prologue to her volume of poetry published in 1650, wrote the following lines as she anticipated male judgment of her creation:

I am obnoxious to each carping tongue
Who says my hand a needle better fits,
A poet's pen all scorn I should thus wrong,
For such despite they cast on female wits:
If what I do prove well, it won't advance,
They'll say it's stol'n, or else it was by chance.

But sure the antique Greeks were far more mild,
Else of our sex, why feigned they those nine
And poesy made Galliope's own child;
So 'mongst the rest they placed the arts divine:
But this weak knot they will full soon untie,
The Greeks did nought, but play the fools and lie.
Let Greeks be Greeks, and women what they are,
Men have precedency and still excel,

It is but vain unjustly to wage war;
Men can do best, and women know it well.
Preeminence in all and each is yours;
Yet grant some small acknowledgment of ours.

And oh ye high flown quills that sour the skies,
And ever with your prey still catch your praise,
If e'er you deign these lowly lines your eyes,
Give thyme or parsley wreath, I ask no bays;
This mean and unrefined ore of mine
Will make your glist'ring gold but more to shine.[5]

Bradstreet's contemporary, Margaret Cavendish, Duchess of Newcastle, expressed similar sentiments in several of her poems, and in her preface to *The World's Olio,* she affirmed that

Men from their first creation usurped a supremacy to themselves, although we [women] were made equal by nature, which tyrannical government they have kept ever since, so that we could never come to be free, but rather more and more enslaved, using us either like children, fools, or subjects. . . .[6]

But the tone of these seventeenth-century lines is not quite so angry as twentieth-century poet Sylvia Plath's tone when she wrote about the two men—her father ("Daddy") and her husband—who had power over her life; the anger here is open and shrill:

I made a model of you,
A man in black with a Meinkampf look

And a love of the rack and the screw.
And I said I do, I do.
So daddy, I'm finally through.
The black telephone's off at the root,
The voices just can't worm through.

If I've killed one man, I've killed two—
The vampire who said he was you
And drank my blood for a year,
Seven years, if you want to know,
Daddy, you can lie back now.

There's a stake in your fat black heart
And the villagers never liked you.
They are dancing and stamping on you.
They always knew it was you.
Daddy, daddy, you bastard, I'm through.[7]

Women writers have had to free themselves not only from the power men exert over their bodies and their psyches—free themselves from the subtle exertion of power—but also from the tentativeness, lack of confidence, and sense of inadequacy from which women suffer in their relationships with male agents, editors, publishers, directors, actors, and critics. A consequence of the women's movement, the freedom to express anger and to be assertive, will change considerably not only women's writing but also their lives as writers.

Another "problem" related to men, which all women in the literary arts have shared until recently, is a lack of female models to imitate. Throughout the nineteenth and early twentieth centuries, approximately one published book in five was written by a woman. Until the advent of the women's studies movement and the pressure of groups like the women's caucus of the Modern Language Association, works by women writers represented less than 10 percent of the works included in literature courses, textbooks, and anthologies.

Thus women who would be poets, playwrights, and novelists have grown up reading poems, plays, and novels by men, all identified in school as "great art." Tillie Olsen affirmed that "in a writer's young years, sus-

ceptibility to the vision and style of the great is extreme."[8] Prospective
writers would find their styles, as Adrienne Rich did, being influenced
by male writers and, more damaging, would find themselves adopting
the images, myths, and symbols of male writers.

Add the aspiration-denying implication, consciously felt or not, that (as
Woolf noted years ago) women writers, women's experience, and literature written by women, are by definition minor. . . . No wonder that
[Elaine] Showalter observes: "Women [students] are estranged from
their own experience and are unable to perceive its shape and authenti-
city, in part because they do not see it mirrored and given resonance
in literature. . . . They have no faith in the validity of their own perceptions and experiences, rarely seeing them confirmed in literature, or
accepted in criticism."[9]

Thus women writers or would-be writers had no models to imitate, no
affirmation or confirmation of their own experiences, no way to model
themselves as writers after great writers who were also women.

    A third problem common to all women in the literary arts is the fear
and timidity women have experienced when trying to create male characters. Avoidance is a possibility, although a writer can hardly ignore
one-half of the human race. But is it not presumptuous of a woman to
try to understand how men think and why they act the way they do?
Well, men have never thought it presumptuous to write about women,
although, admittedly, American men have had less success than men of
other nationalities, as Leslie Fiedler so well demonstrated in *Love and
Death in the American Novel.*

    But now most women writers seem to be writing about women. In
fact, they seem to be writing mostly about themselves, a kind of con-
fessional literature. In fiction we have books about women by women,
written with women's sensibilities. We think of Marge Piercy, *Small
Changes;* Sarah Davidson, *Loose Change;* Judith Rossner, *Looking for
Mr. Goodbar;* Marilyn French, *The Women's Room;* and Lisa Alther,
Kinflicks. These books come immediately to mind, all of them best-
selling novels of the late 1970s. In drama and in poetry too, we have
seen a great outpouring from women writers, poets, and playwrights.

    In one sense, this is exhilarating—women are sharing their experiences,
their visions, their sensibilities and sensitivities, and, yes, their anger too,
confirming and affirming their womanness and their humanness. They

are creating new forms, and creating those new forms is far better than "clinging with perverse tenacity" to the old. But in this, one senses a danger. Not only are women writing about women, they seem to be writing only *to* women. Thus we may become so engrossed in our own joy at talking to each other, of communicating with kindred souls, that we fall into the trap of creating a literature for women alone (as women's theater has had an audience of only women and thus has never been a commercial success), further dividing the human race and creating the possibility that literature by and about women will continue to be classified "inferior."

As readers, we can hardly dictate to creative artists what their subjects should be, but if twentieth-century literature by and about women finds only a female audience, it will suffer the same fate as the work of those popular nineteenth-century American women who, in their own day, outsold both Hawthorne and Melville but who are remembered today only by Hawthorne's epithet "damned scribbling women." For the sake of the women of the twenty-first century, we cannot let literary history repeat itself.

NOTES

1. Virginia Woolf, *A Room of One's Own* (New York: Harcourt, Brace, and World, 1929), pp. 50-51.

2. Ibid.

3. Adrienne Rich, "When We Dead Awaken: Writing as Revision," *College English* 34, no. 1 (October 1972): 19.

4. Ibid.

5. Ann Bradstreet, "Prologue," in ed. Jane Eberwein, *Early American Poetry*, (Madison, Wis.:, University of Wisconsin Press, 1978), p. 15.

6. Margaret Cavendish, Preface to "The World's Olio," in ed. Joan Goulianos, *By A Woman Writt*, (Baltimore: Penguin Books Inc., 1974), p. 55.

7. Sylvia Plath, "Daddy," in *Ariel* (New York: Harper and Row, 1966).

8. Tillie Olsen, "One Out of Twelve: Writers Who Are Women in Our Century," in *Silences* (New York: Dell Publishing Company, 1978), p. 29.

9. Ibid.

4.

Women in the
Dental Profession

NANCY REYNOLDS

> . . . the profession of dentistry, involving as it does,
> the vital interest of humanity, in the relief of human
> suffering, and the perpetuation of the comforts and
> enjoyments of life in civilized and refined society, has
> nothing in its pursuits foreign to the instincts of women,
> and, on the other hand, presents in almost every appli-
> cant for operations, a subject requiring a kind and
> benevolent consideration of the most refined and
> womanly nature.
>
> Resolution passed
> by the Iowa State
> Dental Society in 1865.[1]

Twenty years later, on the other side of the Atlantic, the *British Journal of Dental Science* also supported and recommended dentistry as a suit-able profession for women, because "the tact, the good temper, the quiet

sympathetic ways of a woman adapt her admirably for such a post."[2]
Nevertheless, the journal speculated that in England, "lady dentists will
prove a development only of the far distant future, if at all."[3] While
England was waiting for its first "lady dentist," the profession was already being practiced by women in France and the United States.

In his *Bygone Women Dentists,* Dr. J. Menzies Campbell chronicled
the career of the exotic Madame Desclaux, who "claimed to have
attended to the dental requirements of the Nobility" and who attributed
her outstanding success to the fact that she possessed the lightest touch
of any dental operator in the city.[4] Madame Desclaux apparently made
house calls in pursuit of her profession and did not limit herself to ailments of the mouth but "sold a solution which cured inflamed eyes:
and even dispelled black specks resulting from a hangover!"[5]

In the United States, women entered the profession by serving appren-
ticeships under practicing dentists, often their husbands. In 1854
Emeline Roberts, age seventeen, married Dr. Daniel Albion Jones, a
practicing dentist, and began to observe his techniques and to practice
them. In 1859 she became his partner, and when he died five years later,
she continued his practice. Their son studied dentistry under her for
three years and then entered Harvard's dental school. In 1893 she was
publicly acknowledged to be *the* pioneer woman dentist.[6]

The best known of the pioneer women dentists was Lucy Hobbs, who
became the first woman doctor of dental surgery. Initially she had hoped
for a career in medicine, but opted for an apprenticeship under Dr.
Samuel Wardle, a dentist, when she discovered that medical schools were
closed to her. Not satisfied to practice without a degree, Lucy Hobbs
persisted and was finally granted one from the Ohio College of Dentistry.
Later she married a painter of trains, and he immediately became her
apprentice in dentistry. They practiced together for many years.[7]

Despite such pioneering efforts, dentistry in the United States has
remained until recently an almost exclusively male profession. In 1967
less than 1 percent of practicing dentists were women. However, 25 percent of the dentists in Sweden and France were female, and more than
80 percent in Finland and Russia were women.[8] Obviously, the profession is not inherently male; yet people continue to be surprised to find
a woman dentist. However, change is occurring; today, 13 percent of all
dental students and 15 percent of students in their first year of dental
school are women.

The desirable characteristics for people entering the helping professions, including dentistry, medicine, and law, are not unique to one sex. First, any profession requires a good scholar, one who can absorb undigested data and put it to use. The straight-A student who is a memorizer is not as suitable as someone who can compare, discriminate, and make choices. These functions do not require a male brain. A female brain can do them just as well.

Second, the professions require self-actualizers. It is good in a society to have both leaders and followers, but the person making decisions about lives needs to be a self-starter, able to change courses when necessary to achieve goals.

Third, the professions demand that their practitioners have a high frustration tolerance. One does not go through life finding the wind always at one's back and the road smooth and straight. One does not go through life without some failures. Coping means that one can struggle with a problem with some degree of success. It means that one may experience difficulty in doing something, yet learn to do it or at least find a way to get it done. A doctor has to be able to cope with his or her world or else will have no success helping others cope with theirs. Women have always been copers. It is the nature of nurturing a family, and this has been the traditional female role.

Fourth, the professions involve an element of trust. To assume responsibility for another's welfare implies a trusting situation. The client has to relinquish some degree of control to the professional. This makes the client extremely vulnerable and dependent on the professional not to take advantage of that vulnerability. The doctor must be worthy of that trust. Nothing in this quality is uniquely male.

Fifth, a good professional is an effective communicator. Dentists are in the people business, and a people person has to learn not to talk but to communicate. Many people believe that talking to someone is communicating. Who would argue that men have a corner on the market in communication skills?

Finally, and most importantly, the professions expect that their members will be "servers." I recently heard a speaker talk about women in the health professions, commenting that they suit the role so well because their traditional role has been that of server. To *serve,* as defined in the dictionary, is "to exert oneself continuously for the benefit of others," and that says it all. Dentistry's reason for being a profession is to serve humanity. The essential ingredients are caring and recognizing the needs of others.

By this time, any rumors that the perfect doctor has to be male should have been dispelled; yet barriers remain in the minds of many people. Females in the United States are expected to be warm, dependent, passive, and gentle. Males are expected to be competitive, independent, objective, and assertive. Assuming a choice exists between a male or a female who typifies these qualities, wouldn't you prefer the warm and gentle person to the competitive, totally objective, and assertive one? However, the characteristics traditionally considered "male" are those deemed essential for success. Certainly objectivity in making decisions and assertiveness in executing them are critical for a doctor; yet aren't social consciousness and concern for people essential too?

It seems, then, that to be a good doctor, a female must possess some traditionally male qualities. But wouldn't a male doctor with some critical female qualities be a better doctor also?

The existence of deviants in any profession has long been recognized. Deviants are those who reject the subculture, who cannot or will not accept the customs, the symbols, and the acceptable behavior of the group to which they are attached. They can be destructive, or they can be the catalysts for progress, depending upon the way in which they resist or try to effect change within the profession. Women who enter a characteristically male profession are often categorized as deviant.

In one survey male dental students saw female dental students as assertive, unfriendly, and task oriented.[9] A subsequent study by Howard Rosenberg and Norman Thompson explored whether male dental students and faculty viewed the role of the female dental student as deviating from the sex role of woman and the potential role as dentist. The male dental students saw the female dental students as neither wives nor dentists. They saw as congruent the following roles: wife and adult woman, dentist and adult man, and dental student and adult man. The faculty also saw the female student as close to neither wife nor dentist. Although both male students and faculty gave the female dental students high evaluative scores, the females were nonetheless viewed as deviant in terms of role identity.[10]

Women entering a "male" profession must be prepared in four dimensions. These dimensions are the emotional, mental, psychological, and physical.

The emotional dimension may be one of the most powerful aspects of preparation. It is a psychic and physical reaction subjectively experienced as strong feeling. Try as one may, when strong feelings flood an individual, mental control of thoughts and behavior becomes extremely difficult. The key, of course, is to learn to understand the reasons for the feelings, to accept the feelings as neither good nor bad but for what they are, and not to permit *them* to gain control. The woman dentist has a plus in her emotional, caring approach to health care and can use it to greater advantage for her own fulfillment and for service to humanity.

Mental preparation has two aspects. One aspect is the intellectual, academic preparation. A woman dentist must have the ability to learn and to solve problems. She also must be able to make decisions based on careful evaluation of the objective conditions tempered by the influences of the emotional world. Another aspect is the psychological preparation. It embodies both the mental and the emotional dimensions but as the interaction of the two, with the resulting behavior forming the substratum for the life patterns of the individual.

Critical to a woman's preparation for a professional career is her recognition that her identity as a woman may be questioned. She may be perceived as different, and not in a flattering way. She may be made to feel conflict in the multiple roles she wants to assume. If she knows herself conflict in the multiple roles she wants to assume. If she knows herself and is confident and if she sets her goals realistically and can handle the tilting of the environment toward the male—not necessarily accepting it but coping—she will emerge whole and strong.

Physical preparation is also important. Some people believe that women do not have the endurance of men, that they need time off once a month, that they take time out for their pregnancies, that their work attendance records are not good. However, the statistics indicate that when women ask for acceptance as mature persons, they *do* accept the responsibility that goes with it. Their attendance record in professional schools is good, and their dropout rate is no higher than that for males. The years of interrupted practice average four years, with interruptions for pregnancy, family demands, or husbands changing jobs. However, what women take out in the middle, they can give back at the end, because most women outlive men.

A profile of the professional dental student reveals some differences and similarities between male and female students in recruitment, influences associated with career choice, deterrents to the choice, and finally personality traits.

Recruitment for the profession does not exist with any significance. In a study by Jeanne Coombs, the three major positive influences for both male and female dental students on their career choice were their father, mother, and family dentist. Counselors and teachers were listed as having a negative influence in most cases. In addition, women dental students also listed male friends, female friends, and spouses as influencing their decision.[11]

The influence of parents on women was conflicting. Thirty-eight percent of the women listed parents as both positive and negative influences. One woman reported that her mother liked the status and educational opportunity afforded by dentistry but did not like the idea of looking in mouths all day. Men were more frequently influenced by their family dentist than by anyone else.[12]

Women were also attracted to dentistry by the intellectual stimulation it provides and the opportunity to improve the system. Men more often cited prestige and the opportunity to work with their hands. In this study, the five most frequently mentioned positive influences were the opportunity to be independent, flexible hours, income, public service, and working with people. For all students, male and female, independence was by far the most important factor. The next most important for men—but not for women—was salary.[13]

Previous experience in the field was an important positive indicator for women. Sixty percent of the women had had a health-related job, compared with 26 percent of the men. Twenty-five percent of the women had had experience in the dental profession, compared with 3 percent of the men.[14]

Coombs concluded that sustained commitment to a profession is enhanced by an accurate idea of what the work entails. One can conclude, then, that women will make a continuing contribution in providing health care to the public.

Stereotyped role images and the absence of role models are probably the most significant deterrents to career choices in the male-dominated professions. Sex discrimination is seen as a dominant influence on women even after they enter dental school. Interestingly, in a study by Deborah Zeitler, Elizabeth Ramsey, and James Fuller, 46 percent of the female dental students thought that school was no harder or easier because of their sex and that the male faculty was never guilty of sexism. Seventy percent saw no difference in the attitude of patients, but 82 percent perceived their male classmates as biased. All of the males (faculty and students) reported no perceived bias toward the female students, indicating perhaps that men do not recognize their own sexism and that sexist behavior in these instances is more subtle than overt.[15]

Do male and female dental students differ in personality types, and do they differ from their norms in the general population? J. A. Gershen and J. M. McCreary administered the Comrey Personality Scales to two first-year dental classes at the University of California in an effort to assess the personalities of males and females. The test sought to measure whether women dental students possess traits traditionally attributed to females, such as empathy, or whether women dental students were different from the characteristic female. The study also sought to determine if female dental students are more similar to male dental students than they are to other females.

The study measured trust (belief in basic honesty) versus defensiveness; orderliness (carefulness and organization) versus lack of compulsion; social conformity (acceptance of society and respect for law) versus rebelliousness; activity (energy, endurance, and a desire to excel) versus lack of energy; emotional stability (stable, confident person) versus neuroticism; extroversion versus introversion; masculinity (toughminded person who does not cry easily) versus femininity; and empathy versus egocentrism.

The males tested were similar to their norms in every characteristic except three. Dental students reported high scores in neatness and orderliness, conformity, and emotional stability. Interestingly, these three traits reflect more similarity with women in general as well as with the female dental students.[16]

The female dental students were more similar to female norms than male dental students were to male norms. In one notable exception, female dental students scored higher on masculinity versus femininity than their normative group. Apparently it takes a great deal of assertiveness and competitiveness to enter this male-dominated profession.[17]

The number of women in the professions is growing because of the women's movement and the resulting government pressures. However, a profession is also enhanced by the qualities women bring to it. Hopefully the professions will become more socially minded, more humanistic. Where dentistry will go from here depends on those in it. Its members, both male and female, have some critical fields to plow to leave a legacy that will favorably influence the future.

NOTES

1. Miriam S. Kinsler, "The American Woman Dentist: A Brief Historical Review from 1855 through 1968," *Bulletin of the History of Dentistry* 17, no. 2 (December 1969): 25.

2. "Female Dentists," *British Journal of Dental Science* 28 (1885): 453.

3. Ibid.

4. Kinsler, "The American Woman Dentist," p. 26.

5. Ibid.

6. Ibid., p. 27.

7. Ibid., p. 28.

8. Howard M. Rosenberg and Norman L. Thompson, "Attitudes toward Women Dental Students among Male Dental Students and Male Dental Faculty Members," *Journal of Dental Education* 40, no. 10 (1976): 696.

9. Ibid., p. 679.

10. Ibid.

11. Jeanne A. Coombs, "Factors Associated with Career Choice among Women Dental Students," *Journal of Dental Education* 40, no. 11 (1976): 724-31.

12. Ibid.

13. Ibid.

14. Ibid.

15. Deborah L. Zeitler, Elizabeth F. Ramsey, and James L. Fuller, "The Dental Education Environment as Perceived by the Female Student," *Journal of Dental Education* 41, no. 5 (1977): 271-72.

16. "Comparing Personality Traits of Male and Female Dental Students: A Study of Two Freshman Classes," *Journal of Dental Education* 41, no. 10 (1977): pp. 618-22.

17. Ibid.

5.

Women in Medicine

_____RUTH M. PHILLIPS

INTRODUCTION

Currently, over 30,000 physicians in the United States are women,
representing more than 8 percent of all physicians,[1] and this number
will no doubt increase with time. Although the number of young people
applying for medical schools across the country has decreased, particularly in 1980, more women are seeking futures in the "traditional"
careers of engineering, law, and medicine. Twelve years ago, about 6
percent of the women in the twelfth grade expressed an interest in entering these professions. This percentage had increased to 17 percent by
1975. (Conversely, the interest of men in following the same career goals
fell from 50 percent in 1966 to 39 percent in 1975.)[2]

  However, in spite of the increased visibility of women as physicians,
in the 1960s, the United States had the lowest percentage of women
doctors of all countries except Spain, Madagascar, and South Vietnam.[3]

HISTORICAL BACKGROUND

Young women entering medicine at the beginning of the twentieth century already had a notable heritage. The Female Medical College founded in 1850, now called the Medical College of Pennsylvania, was already established.[4] Also, a few special hospitals for women had been established, usually through the combined efforts of medical, nonmedical, and public-spirited men and women. These hospitals were directed by women physicians *for* women physicians, many of whom, because of sex bias, were unable to admit their patients to established hospitals. The first of these hospitals, the New York Infirmary in New York City, was founded in 1853 by Dr. Elizabeth Blackwell and her friends. For a short period, this hospital also provided medical instruction for women. Since then, hospitals for women have appeared across the United States, extending even to 1905, with the opening in New Orleans of the Sara Mayo Hospital for women and children.[5]

The need for special hospitals for women physicians no longer exists today, as evidenced by the closing in 1969 of the New England Hospital for Women and Children in Boston, Massachusetts. This facility—founded in 1862 by Elizabeth Blackwell's friend Dr. Marie Zakrzewska—provided medical education for both female doctors and nurses.

By the beginning of the twentieth century, many medical schools were accepting women students, although incentives had to be provided in some cases. The Johns Hopkins Medical School received a sizable endowment with the provision that women be admitted on the same terms as men (when I enrolled in this school in 1944, women comprised 10 percent of the freshman class, double the number admitted to other American medical schools). Today, every medical school in the United States is coeducational.

In the United States in 1905, women students comprised 4.1 percent of those enrolled in medical school; that same year, 4 percent of those graduating with an M.D. degree were women. Only a few more women were admitted to schools in the years that followed. In 1926 women comprised only 5 percent of the first-year class, and approximately the same number graduated.[6] In 1960 the enrollment of women remained essentially unchanged—5.8 percent. After 1960 the trend continued slowly but steadily, with an increased enrollment of women to 9 percent in 1970.

The Public Health Service Act was passed in November 1971.[7] That same year, women comprised 13.7 percent of the first-year class. The increased acceptance of women each year thereafter is impressive. In 1972 women comprised 16.8 percent of the first-year class; in 1973 and 1974, 19.7 percent; in 1975, 22.2 percent; and in 1976, 24.7 percent.[8]

By 1980, therefore, it was expected that one of every four physicians entering a residency training program would be a woman, and in approximately seven years, one of every four physicians entering practice will be a woman. Women physicians will be playing an increasingly important role in the health care of the United States.

WHY DO WOMEN CHOOSE MEDICINE?

Women considering medicine as a career are influenced by several factors. The three factors of primary importance are the personality makeup of the woman herself; the medical schools—their aims, goals, and specific admission policies; and society, through socioeconomic and cultural pressures. These forces may change as the result of powerful influences such as wars and depressions. Wars reduce the supply of male doctors and increase the need for women physicians. Depressions, by contrast, have a negative effect on women's applications to medical school. Until now American families suffering financial hardship have favored supporting male members of the family for postgraduate education.

Perseverance to final accomplishment is related to the inner personality core of women entering a medical career. D. R. Mandelbaum analyzed the motivation and career persistence of seventy-one women physicians by a study of taped records, interviews, and questionnaires and found one primary factor to be of great importance: motivation sustained through early influences, often before the age of fifteen years. This motivation was usually the encouragement from family members and teachers and exposure in the early school years to scientific and social material, especially that related to nurturing and healing—the essence of the medical profession.[9]

Once motivation is established, the success of the female applicant depends on guidance from family, friends, teachers, and college vocational counselors. Until recently, however, the latter have tried to dis-

courage women from becoming physicians, usually citing difficulties
women will face in resolving conflicts between their future role as wife/
homemaker/mother and the demands of a medical career.

Women historically have also been discouraged from becoming physicians by the scarcity of loans and scholarships to finance their medical
education. Before 1950 the majority of bankers doubted that women
would complete their medical education; these reservations were based
on assumptions that such education would be interrupted by childbearing and child rearing.

The positive evidence is now convincing, but recognizing the difficulties
that most women face in obtaining loans to finance their medical education, the American Medical Women's Association in 1933 began a modest
loan fund. This fund is currently almost half a million dollars. Liberaliza-
tion of financial assistance comes from the increasing evidence of women's
persistence and success in pursuing medical careers.[10]

In addition, medical schools—and the particular choice of school by
the woman herself—can be a critical factor influencing the decision to
study medicine. (In 1944, for example, I entered the medical school of
my choice, deliberately selected for its high academic standards, but I
was also influenced by its recognized favorable attitude toward women
medical students.) In some medical schools, admission committees have
undoubtedly discriminated against women in the past in certain areas,
questioning their motivation and judgment in wanting to pursue the
chosen career, and seeking the type of woman not to be deterred by
marriage and so forth, but still not too aggressive or "mannish." In some
schools, women were referred to by their male colleages as "hen medics";
in addition, some faculty members deliberately embarrassed their female
students by telling unseemly jokes.

Finally, additional important deterrents were the limitations for
women in opportunities for internships, residencies, and fellowships.
Between 1930 and 1940, housing space in hospitals was limited, leading
to a restriction in house staff positions (this is still true in some hospitals).
Some specialties were restricted as well; for example, rarely has a woman
been accepted on a surgical service. Even today a discrepancy exists in
proportional representation of men and women in various specialties.
Is this a matter of choice or a lack of opportunity?

Women are not well represented in membership or leadership roles
in county, state, or local medical societies, nor are many women found

in top administrative positions in medical schools. As of 1977, none of
the deans of medical schools were women, although 221 assistant deans
were women. Only 3 women are currently heads of departments in
medical schools; each one is in pediatrics.

In the chosen career goal for academic medicine, promotion for
women has been slow. The low percentage of women on faculties today—
only 4 percent of professorial rank and only 2.1 percent as full professors—
indicates the slow rise. In contrast, however, even in the 1930s and
1940s, women were accepted into communities as private, practicing
physicians. Even so, a preference in the community for male doctors,
even by women, is not unusual.[11]

Women physicians receive lower incomes than men physicians. The
number of hours of work may be one factor. B. H. Kehrer found that
women physicians work fewer hours a week than men,[12] but longer
hours by women do not necessarily increase income; in fact, the opposite
may be true. Is this lower income the reflection of a smaller fee for
service requested by women in practice combined with their shorter
working hours, or is it the result of discrimination, especially in salaried
jobs? In academia, positions for women have been at the lower levels,
such as in fellowships and research assistantships and as laboratory
directors. Salaried incomes in these positions have been lower regardless
of specialty choice. The specialty choices made by women have been
fairly constant, namely, pediatrics, psychiatry, general or family practice,
and obstetrics and gynecology, with the recent additions of public
health, radiology, and anesthesiology.

WHO IS THE WOMAN PHYSICIAN TODAY?

The question has been repeatedly asked, "Is it a 'fact,' as many allege,
that women physicians, once trained, tend not to practice and therefore
training them is a waste of time and money?" Marilyn Heins, M.D., the
associate dean of students at Wayne State University School of Medicine,
and Lois Martindale, Ph.D., researched the life and practice patterns of
male and female physicians. Their results offer an answer to that question.

Heins and Martindale cited a 1960 study that stated that in contrast
to men physicians, women physicians "lose" two-fifths of their potential
working time. Using 1974 data, however, these researchers found that

women physicians work nearly 90 percent as much as men physicians.[13]

The "model woman physician" of their study was forty-seven years old, Caucasian, Protestant, and statistically as likely to be a Democrat as a Republican (unlike males, who are likely to be Republicans). She was married, often to a physician, and had 2.5 children. She had worked continuously since graduation from medical school and currently worked full time. She was board certified, and her main task was patient care in one of the primary core specialties.[14]

The women physician who did miss work time did so because of her children, but also, more than half of the women physicians with children had no interruption. Many of the other women had lost less than two years. Despite their demanding profession, more than three-quarters of the women physicians were responsible for cleaning, cooking, child care, marketing, and laundry. They were no more likely to have domestic help than the housewife spouses of male physicians. Mean income of the women physicians was $36,785; of the males, $59,230 (both in 1974 dollars).[15]

ROLE OVERHEAD AND ROLE CONFLICT

In the Heins and Martindale study, 60 percent of the men and 54 percent of the women physicians believed they experienced too many demands on their time and energy; three times as many men as women thought that pressures of work were the reason. The women related work overload to children and domestic responsibilities; 50 percent of the women thought they needed more help at home, either domestic paid help or assistance from spouse and family. More women than men thought they needed to improve themselves in some way, for example, to become better organized or more flexible. Both men and women physicians believed they did not have sufficient time for their families or themselves.[16]

CONCLUSION

Both men and women physicians work too hard and do not have enough time for personal growth or for their families. Working women physicians particularly bear an added strain. Women physicians, studies have shown, work hard in their dual roles. They rely less on domestic help than might be expected, and they assume the primary responsibility for child rearing and household management. Yet few women physicians seem to recognize the almost superhuman requirements of the dual role. Women in medicine appear to be high-energy and highly motivated physicians who have achieved a compromise (albeit not an ideal one) between the role of physician and that of wife/homemaker/mother and have found satisfaction and fulfillment in both.

NOTES

1. Maryland Pennell and Shirlene Showell, *Women in Health Careers,* Publication No. HRA-75-55 (Washington, D.C.: U.S. Government Printing Office, 1975).

2. *Wall Street Journal,* quoted in *Better Times Weekly,* August 31, 1978, p. 5.

3. Estelle Ramey, "Women in Medicine: An Overview" (Address to the Eighty-Eighth American Association of Medical Colleges [AAMC] Annual Meeting, Washington, D.C., November 7, 1977).

4. G. F. Alsop, *History of the Women's Medical College, Philadelphia, Pennsylvania, 1850-1950* (Philadelphia: J. B. Lippincott Company, 1950).

5. R. L. Nemir, "Women in Medicine during the Last Half-Century," *Journal of the American Medical Women's Association* 33, no. 5 (May 1978): 201.

6. Ibid.

7. Titles VII and VIII of the Public Health Service Act of 1971 prohibit discrimination on the basis of sex by health training institutions receiving federal financial support.

8. D. R. Mandelbaum, "Toward an Understanding of the Career Persistence of Women Physicians," *Journal of the American Medical Association* 31 (1976): 314.

9. Ibid.

10. R. L. Nemir, "American Medical Women's Association Scholarship and Loan Funds for Medical Education," *Journal of the American Medical Women's Association* 16 (1961): p. 777.

11. Vincente Navarro, "Women in Health Care," *New England Journal of Medicine* 292 (1975): 398.

12. B. H. Kehrer, "Factors Affecting the Incomes of Men and Women

Physicians: An Exploratory Analysis," *Journal of Human Resources* 11 (1976): 526.

13. Marilyn Heins and Lois Martindale, "Current Status of Women in Medicine" (Address to the Eighty-Eighth AAMC Annual Meeting, Washington, D.C., November 7, 1977).

14. Ibid.

15. Ibid.

16. Ibid.

PART II

Women's Private Lives:
The Personal as Political

6.

Knots in the
Family Tie

MARILOU BURNETT

One immutable truth in our reality as persons is that we must each experience our own life. Any effort, even on the part of a loving parent, to stand between us and our experience in meeting what life presents us becomes a knot in the family tie. If we do not experience the flow of our life process moment to moment, we experience the knots. For many people, life is a series of knots, and many of the knots are in the family tie. The pressure to untangle the knots comes from the will to live one's life. Indeed, the fear of death is not so much the fear of death itself; it is the fear that one will die having not yet lived.

A human being is an amazing creature. No matter how many times the birth process is successful, it always seems like a miracle. Each person is an enormously complex organism holding within itself a blueprint for the kind of person it may become and also owning an infinite plasticity that will be called upon to accommodate to a particular situation.

This situation usually includes both a mother and a father person, although it must always include a mothering person, since emotional nurturing is as essential as food, shelter, and physical care. These significant adults represent not only themselves and their experience, but also the cultural beliefs they have pulled into their life fabric. Such beliefs are used to manage their life process.[1] The newcomers must find a way to fit into the belief structures they encounter. Being powerful little creatures, they may bend the structure in surprising ways.

Whatever set of beliefs they encounter, children will learn the language and the essential tenets of the culture as represented by the family. This too is a miracle, for never again in their lifetime will they learn so much in so little time. As one begins life, the potential exists to develop, learn, and grow in all directions, without imposing an external system of judgment about good-bad, right-wrong, or should-ought not. Direct contact between self and experience through the use of freely operating senses makes accelerated learning a given.

The shutting down of this early, accelerated learning potential is a function of the need to "fit" a specific model of human interaction presented by the family. To play one's part in the family, it is necessary to inhibit certain of the sensory channels one previously had used to take in and organize a perception of the world. "Rules" come to stand between children's potential to learn and their free intake of experience. These system rules infringe on the free use of one's being able to see-hear-feel-think-do in regard to any experience.

Touch and its inhibition is an excellent example of a rule that diminishes the organism's capacity for feeling. In this culture, children are gradually weaned from touching others and themselves. Children learn to inhibit this freedom to take their world in by touch, sloughing off what is not useful and keeping what is socially valuable to their organism.

This selection process from their vast potential is guided by a wish-need to fit into the existing belief system, to become acceptable and approved. With each sacrifice, the integrity of the internal blueprint is compromised. To blind the self to see only the family perception of possibility, some aspects of the organism's capacity to see-hear-feel must be restricted.

In addition to picking up the major belief systems offered by the family, children have resolved, in some livable fashion, the deepest philosophical issues of life and death by the age of five. They may continue to refine their resolution, but the basics are in. Whether life is to be embraced and savored or feared and defended against will be the outcome of self meeting world. The strength and integrity of their constitution, plus the rigidity and degree of restriction demanded by the family, form the working elements each must use to write the book their days will record. Paul Reps said so beautifully: "Make a mark, on paper, wall, in the air. Aren't we making such marks with each moment we live?"[2]

Although some specific wrinkles do exist in a given family belief system, the family fits in some complex way into the larger systems of the community, country, and planet. An amalgamation of these systems' messages and forces is manifested in the language, communication, behavior, organization, and architecture of all people. Children, whether born in the United States, China, Russia, or Africa, will begin almost immediately to select some aspects of themselves to show and others to hide. Each family carries the message of the culture and thereby places limitations on the development of this incredible potential represented by the human being.

In tandem with cultural perspectives, each family system imposes certain functions in the form of roles that maintain the equilibrium of the family system. A family with a good child needs a bad child. A family with an aggressive child needs a passive child. Roles are parceled out like parts in a drama.

Most parents grasp the abstract image of the person they want their child to become, thus missing an awareness of the significance of birthing and childhood. Those two experiences are our best teachers of what it means to be a person. Even among professional people helpers, it is rare to find a person who is comfortable with children and rarer still to discover someone who opens herself to the birth experience. We are anesthetized during such opportunities lest we become aware of what they could teach us.[3] Adults say, "I don't know what to say to them, I feel helpless to relate to children, so I work with adults only." In fact, they have not lived their own childhood. It is as if they were born grown up.

The mothering person entrains a child in intricate and subtly covert ways into the rhythms needed to maintain the accepted perspective.[4] Entrainment into the cultural and family structure begins immediately through the voice tones of the communicating mothering person. These rhythms and tones embody so much more than we imagine.[5] The communication of touch and other nonverbal signals helps to begin the claiming and imprinting of this child by the culture through the hands of the mothering person. This transaction conveys to the child her worth and provides the basis for self-esteem.

Over time, a contract is made between the child and the significant

other that in essence is a bargain: "If I give up seeing-hearing-feeling
what I do see-hear-feel and adopt your perception, then sometime, if
not now, you will love me and approve of me, for this is the object of
my greatest longing. I am willing to sacrifice the integrity of my deeper
'self' for the security of your love." Added to this bargain is a promise:
"I further promise to 'forget' that I made this bargain. This lapse in
memory will help me to keep my bargain, for if I come to believe that
the perception I now buy into is the only perception, I will not be
tempted to reconsider. In that way I will remain safe and sure to get my
reward. It is a guarantee against my weakness." This bargain becomes
such an integral part of the individual that all future relationships are
affected by it. Until resolved, it can do nothing but repeat itself in marriage, friendships, and professional associations—indeed, in all human
transactions.

Neither parent nor child consciously makes the choices embodied
in the bargain, and whatever remnants of memory remain are carefully
covered by fear. Part of the self becomes a guard against that knowledge
escaping. The quality of the defense and fear encountered in therapy
(of crises) when those walls might crumble is intense, as it threatens to
leave the "bargain" revealed. Any challenge to the "arrangement" is a
threat to the commitment made by the organism early in its organization. The loss of the embraced perception about how things have to be
is anchored to the potential loss of love and belonging. In the sense that
the person has identified or led herself to believe that she *is* the perception, it is a fear of loss of self. Keeping the bargain is tantamount to keeping control. Loss of control is often given as the most threatening
experience people in this culture can have. I suspect that it is related to
the "bargain" and its safekeeping.

When individuals give up believing the bargain will pay off, they find
no reason to live. Suicide is then an out, for these persons have forgotten
that they can return to the drawing board, to the enormous potential
still waiting within; that, indeed, their perception of whom they are,
how they are limited, and so on is only one of many potential perceptions.

To fit into the family system and maintain the "bargain," a girl child,
for instance, agrees to forego development of her left brain or masculine
principal potentials.[6] Her "selection" from many personal potentials is
arranged to fit with a man who has in turn agreed to sacrifice the development of his right hemisphere, or feminine principal potentials. Qualities
such as tenderness, intuition, free-flowing creativity, and emotional ex-

pression are favored over the drive for achievement, rational endeavors, aggression, and so on. When a man has the opportunity to find "the other half," an expression conveying more truth than fiction, he takes on the expression of human qualities or traits traditionally attributed to men and leaves the others undeveloped for his wife. Together they are one full person, and they need each other to survive as persons—or so they think.

In time they may get bored or frustrated living half lives. One may express the frustration for both of them while the other holds back in fear. A change in the equilibrium leads them into confrontation with unknown aspects of themselves. If the courage of their integrity allows them to continue exploring new ways to communicate and relate, they will likely discover that no one really dies from change. With each confrontation, new territory opens up. More of the self is available for living life. One would like to believe this is a one-time effort. Alas, this is not the case. Mark Twain knew this when he said that life is like an onion. You peel a layer and cry, peel another layer and cry some more.

Some people obviously make their peace with dead structures and relationships. They acknowledge being trapped and unable to put life back into their relationships. Many of them will show you their scars and ask for sympathy. A few are utterly oblivious to their unlived lives. They are like robots, interesting for a while, then deadly boring. Generally, they do not tolerate being alone. They bore themselves as they bore others. They feel impelled to use what energy they have to attack those who are "different" from themselves and their choices. The analogy of war is called to mind. Sensing that "sameness" may offer some solace, they fight for conformity. Peace, on the other hand, celebrates difference and uses energy creatively to enrich life by finding ways for differences to be honored and so included for the "whole." To be perfect is to be whole, including all parts. This is true of person, community, and universe.

The strength to pursue the growth of self comes from a mix of the will of an individual to live a personally authentic life with the rigidity internalized from the family system rules. The more rigidly the family system has demanded sacrifice of the full self, the tighter the knot in the family tie. Much of our life work is spent trying to loosen that knot so we can be whom we are—to allow our seed self, the inner "knowing," to guide us in our unfolding.

This "internal knowing" may be interpreted as a mystical, unscientific thought, and indeed it may be. Such a criticism would, however, be expected from one who had developed critical, rational, abstracting parts of self and defended against developing other aspects of self. A flower, a tree, a blade of grass, "knows" what to become. No one need advise a tree on what mixture of air, earth, water, sun, to use to become a tree instead of a dandelion. It seems a minimal gift to give man/woman the same freedom as we give lesser forms of life.

The internal part of the self is very patient with the cultural and family rules. It will wait a long time for the "bargain" to pay off. For many persons, patience begins to wear thin when they pass the forty-year mark. What had heretofore been willing to lie quietly begins to introduce itself in conscious awareness. People grow desperate to be counted as legitimate offspring. They fear waiting—for nothing. Time is running out, and either they must decide that the bargain was a double-cross, or they must decide to adjust to an entire lifetime under the burden of the "promise." And they are *so* tired. Another fear grows to meet the existent fear, and that is that they may live their whole lives according to someone else's plan and never really live at all. A sense of panic may develop, and in that burst of energy—for fear has energy—they risk all that they have tried to build of that "other life"[7] they thought was required for the "reward."

To look at the current scene of apparent disintegration in relationships—the leave taking from anesthetizing jobs, from communities where the facade has grown too heavy—as manifestations of people searching for a way to express more of whom they are in more honest systems is to change the gloom-and-doom forecasts. All of those who take their leave in search of themselves and healthier, more honest environments are not "bad people." They are people who want more than plastic relationships. They are willing to risk the loss of old perspectives on the chance that they might live a new life born of their own plan.

Some persons struggle with genuine craziness and a few continue to search in emptiness for they know not what. The latter are likely to repeat with new partners their old themes until they can no longer blame their misfortunes on another. For many individuals, making such changes represents their wish to live and to have the courage to act on messages from their deepest self; they long for freedom in relationships.

If at this pivotal point of realization, individuals opt for risking the expression of parts of themselves they had hidden away—risk all they had invested in family, friends, profession, community—it may not indicate that they have suddenly gone out of their mind. They may simply be going for broke, to get some air time for the unintegrated parts of themselves. Their deep longing to live their own blueprint may have spoken so clearly that they no longer could avoid the voice.

The fear that one might die and never have lived is a message men and women of wisdom have echoed through the ages. Few have been able to hear. More are now able to hear. It is a call to return to the integrity of the organism, to listen and take into account the cultural voice, but to move from an external to an internal authority in making choices for how one lives life and how one relates to others. The wish is to be honest with the self and others. The price of wearing a facade to gain approval is thought to be too dear.

Change most frequently occurs at a time of crisis: a death, loss of job, friend, house, money, limb. Any one of these events may stop individuals in their evolution as people, or it may be a step, a learning opportunity, as they move on into their life process. A crisis need not be as bad as anticipated unless the person persists in trying to regain the same balance or translates the loss of equilibrium into resentment, revenge, and anger and uses the energy for those purposes rather than to evolve into new vistas of personhood.

It is from the grounded position that people may find their way to a new balance. That territory previously unknown is now almost like an old friend. The learnings therein are valuable. This second time up is under their own power, not that of their parents.

What is learned about getting up and reintegrating uses more of the potential strength. Such strength, demonstrated, is like money in the bank for future ventures, for once people survive an ordeal, they know more of their capability and depend upon it. Self-worth is made of these experiences. However, some spend the energy of an entire lifetime focusing on their loss, but "if you cry because you have lost the sun, your tears will prevent you from seeing the stars and the moon." Loss and change are difficult, but each offers an opportunity to stretch the potential of self and use one's energy in new directions.

Certain styles of relating, such as the authoritarian and paternalistic, do not enhance our potential for authentic human contact, for compassion, or for making bridges of understanding to others. Without the balance of the feminine principle, within and between persons, we will continue to gallop off to the end of the polarity represented by masculine principle behaviors, in this case the end of life on this planet. The hard-won technological gains must now be tempered with human values, or the "machine" mentality that served our survival on the Western frontier will become the instrument of our demise. Use of power, force, threat, and winning strategies to the exclusion of an awareness and articulation of organic relatedness, compassion, humanness, and creativity with differences will destroy us. Either these pompous childlike adults must get together and appreciate each other, or the game is over.

Some of the disintegration all of us see and participate in now is a leaving of old forms, indicative of a going forward to new forms. In contrast to the 1960s, which was a shaking of all structures in anger and frustration, what can be seen now is not attack and anger. In most cases, it is a genuine going forward rather than a sense of being pushed in reactive rebellion. In being pulled toward the future forms, we are going toward something we touch with our fingers but do not yet grasp. This process creates an excitement greater than the anxiety about the as-yet unknown. Like a snake having outgrown its old skin, we leave behind our old forms, our illusions of how we thought we had to be, and have no need to attack. What has happened? We can use the learning experiences as ingredients for the new skin. Many of us did not even know we were growing until rudiments of the new skin appeared. The new skin gives us more room for being human, honest, whole, and integrated.

Although these resources and potentials for balancing and including reside in each person, they are most accessible to women, especially those who have claimed their room to grow but who have not tried to become men. Women, as a group, have been dealt cards by the culture that allowed them to stay alive to their feelings. Although they are often miserable, they know they are alive, know that things are not as they should or could be. Men, for the most part, have been both unaware of and frightened of becoming aware of their tender, feeling, intuitive, creative, and metaphoric qualities. If we are to survive on this planet, input from women is critical, on all levels of human relationships.

Men must learn how to honor these principles in themselves and as they are offered as insights by others. We are called upon to keep the lines open among all of our differences. To be whole is to have all of the parts included. Exclusion is easy compared to inclusion. The latter requires more creativity.

It is hard to grow into a sense-self separate from the model we were asked to assume. Family rules and the skins we fashioned from them have much to do with power and authority, external authority based on fear and sometimes called respect. Internal authority born of the integrity of the full self is more a longing than a reality for most of us.

In authentic contact, the integrity of the self is greatly pressed to express itself. In fact, holding a facade between self and others in those positions of human encounter is practically impossible. People have such an intense hunger for human contact that they can hardly bear to keep intact the wall that allows them to observe the inhuman rules they bargained to hold so many years ago. If anything could jog their memory of the bargain they promised to forget, it would be the warmth of human contact, for that is the "reward" they have been holding out for. But, they do not dare risk losing "control," for that was a promise on which they now believe their life depends.

Reaching a time and place where crises or intense personal experience announce a need to tap more of our potential, to be more than we think we are, and to find that what we do-say does not work means simply that we have hit a knot in the family tie. This is an opportunity to untie the knot within the self and if appropriate to straighten out the knot with others. More than we had ever imagined, it is possible to trust and honor the capacity of our significant others to receive and adapt to the truth of our being and our experience. To "protect" persons who we decide cannot "tolerate" some fact of life is to dishonor them as whole persons and to deprive them of an opportunity to grow. When we withhold something from them that influences the quality of their lives, we invite them to live in a fantasy world rather than encounter and learn from real experience. As a family therapist, I hear some say, "We mustn't tell Mother about this, it would just kill her. . . ." or "We try to keep this from the children, there is no need to upset them." Life transactions become a game, a lethal game. These games are not very entertaining.

The security that is needed from the family is not in the form of family knots, but support from members so that a free, internally directed person may be actualized. In an open system that counts all humanness as bearable, anything that has happened can be discussed. No matter what has happened, a person needs someone who will not be "shocked," who will offer her full presence. That *is* what love is. To be present fully is to be in dialogue with others without judgment or effort to control them.

An honest message is that people's lovability is assured and that all else is merely evidence of their struggle to meet life. All people "fail," make mistakes, and slip. What is important is to learn from those experiences.

At times it is necessary to move off the marked trail into the uncharted forest. We rely on intuition and all of the strengths inherent in our personhood, trusting that what is needed from the creative self will be there. No maps are available in this new territory of the internal landscape, but the organism is enormously complex and elegant, with incredible resources. Some resources have been tested. Others are waiting to be formed by experience. The plasticity of the person engaging in meeting her life is infinite. The meetings of potential with life on new paths form something deep and beautiful and meaningful, much as a seed becomes a plant, a tree, and so on.

Long ago this plasticity allowed the child to form herself into a mold prescribed by a situation encountered in family and culture. All that was there is still there, waiting. To tap this creativity and flexibility to let in more of life, it is necessary only to let go of the tenacious grip on the perspective built by the infant-child out of early experiences. The strategies pieced together by that infant-child with so little experience in this world have brought the child this far. This man or woman has forgotten that the view of self and the world of others has served well in the past but is no longer equal to the task of the evolving self. That perception was selected from an infinite number of impressions, only a few of many possibilities.

It is possible to go back now and look with adult eyes. So much more can be seen. Looking forward with eyes and ears open brings in more data to be organized. As these sensory inputs are combined, what is needed becomes known. All that is really needed is enough to put one foot in front of the other with the whole organism awake, alert, alive. The entire body can see, fingers can hear.

Intuition integrated with experience and incorporation of more parts of the growth self leads to a trust in the wisdom of the self. When the self can be trusted, that sense of self-worth, so coveted, is automatic. Information comes in from the external source, but when it is centered in the self, the body, mind, and spirit are in accord and offer the best guidance possible to this unique and incredibly beautiful being. Upon encountering a knot from the family tie, it is possible to entertain that discovery as an invitation to grow. With guidance from the self, that knot becomes experience that can be used in the next step into the wider world.

NOTES

1. Virginia Satir, John Grinder, and Richard Bandler, *Changing with Families* (Palo Alto, Calif.: Science and Behavior Books, 1975).

2. Paul Reps, *Ten Ways to Meditate: No Need to Kill* (New York: John Weatherkill, 1969).

3. Robert Samples et al., *Where All Things Belong,* a film about rebirth (Tiburon, Calif.: Essentia, 1975).

4. John Pearce, *Exploring the Crack in the Cosmic Egg* (New York: Simon and Schuster, 1975).

5. William Condon, unpublished work (Boston: Boston Medical School, 1979).

6. Robert Ornstein, *The Psychology of Consciousness* (New York: Harcourt Brace Jovanovich, 1977).

7. Stanley Keleman, *Living Your Dying* (New York: Random House, 1976).

7.
Continuing Education:
A Vital Process for Women
ADELLE F. ROBERTSON

Women have moved in the 1970s from the "fear of success," identified
by Matina Horner[1] as a key factor in the achievement of women, to a
concern about how to handle and maintain success after their initial
achievement. Although numbers do not guarantee depth, women have
broken occupational barriers in many professions during the past decade.
By 1978, two women were governors and two were serving in the president's cabinet. A woman had been appointed to the Federal Reserve
Board, and another had become the president of a major university.
Women were students at West Point, Annapolis, the Air Force Academy,
and the FBI Academy.

But once successful, women face some of the same questions that
successful men face. "Is success my top priority?" "How do you remain
successful—intellectually current and professionally competent—in the
midst of rapid social and technological change?" "What happens to success
in the aging process?" Two concepts, lifelong learning and life stage development, provide a framework in which to examine these issues.

Lifelong learning, continuing education, and *adult education* are often
used interchangeably but with little understanding. Cyril Houle of the
University of Chicago explained the term *adult education* in words that
are equally appropriate for all three terms: "Adult education is the
process by which men and women (alone, in groups, or in institutional
settings) seek to improve themselves or their society by increasing their
skill, knowledge, or sensitiveness."[2]

This statement differs from the usual definition of education because
it is age free, time free, and location free. In other words, learning is not
confined to the ages between six and twenty-one years, or to traditional
education, or to daytime hours, or to the classroom. Another key word
in the definition is *process,* which means that learning is ongoing or non-
terminal. If this concept is plotted on an age line such as the one shown
in figure 1, it is apparent that the time remaining for lifelong learning is
nearly twice the time encompassing kindergarten through graduate school.

FIGURE 1

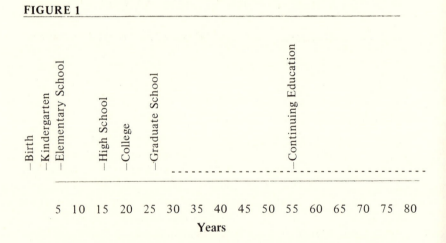

It is unlikely, therefore, that the high school-college-graduate school
progression can sustain the learning needs of a career woman during the
remaining years of her life. As a result, the needs of women for learning
activities that will help them complete an undergraduate or graduate
program, update training that has become obsolete, secure new knowledge for career advancement, move into one of the formerly "male"

career areas, or assume civic responsibilities have provided a major impetus to the growth of continuing education programs at universities. These programs differ from the traditional undergraduate and graduate programs: (1) the format, time, and location for learning are determined by the needs of part-time, adult learners; (2) the content of the course, program, conference, or learning experience develops from an assessment of the needs of the learner; and (3) all pertinent disciplines rather than one perspective are considered in the development of the content.

The response of women to continuing education opportunities also has forced change in undergraduate and graduate programs on some campuses. Just as the returning veteran from World War II changed admission standards, curricula, and attitudes toward part-time study and campus residence, the entry and reentry of women into the job market in large numbers have forced examination of credit for experiential learning, admission-by-performance, and the introduction of women's studies as a new curricular option. The rapid rate of social change in the past decade has also mandated a forum and access to experts who can respond to the issues faster than the five to six years it may take to change a curriculum. Drug use and abuse, affirmative action, minority counseling, assertiveness training, single parents, death and dying, personal negotiation, human sexuality, and attitudes toward aging are only a few of the topics that have been debated and discussed under continuing education sponsorship.

One of the aims of continuing education is to develop individuals who can cope with change, whether it be technological, geographic, economic, moral, or social. Since change often provides great potential for personal and professional growth, women need to develop their abilities to handle new situations effectively. Coping skills for these kinds of major adjustments result from an evolving education experience that develops exploration, objectivity, experimentation, separation of fact from inference, and the ability to think analytically. Although many of these qualities are the presumed result of a four-year undergraduate experience, reports and recommendations by the Carnegie Commission on Higher Education[3] and the examination of the time line suggest that regular practice and reexamination are essential for women to maintain these abilities at a functional level.

Because of the absence of many women from the mainstream of intellectual activity, continuing education units of universities are finding it necessary to provide services to accompany their reentry to academia. These services frequently include counselors who encourage women to set personal and professional goals and help them define educational objectives within the framework of their abilities, interests, and home responsibilities. Interest and aptitude testing have been used as a preliminary step in planning a full- or part-time program of study. However, continuing education is a more useful concept to women who already have valid self-concepts.[4]

What is a valid *self-concept*? The term is used to express what a woman knows about herself. Three concepts of self are frequently cited: the self you think you are, the self others perceive, and the self you actually are. When these three concepts or images are the same or "congruent," as psychologists say,[5] the self-concept is considered valid. A self-concept is important in continuing education, because to the extent a woman understands herself, her values, her priorities, her aspirations, her strengths, and her weaknesses, she is able to say with some assurance what she needs or wants to know or learn.

One of the basic problems in the continuing education of women is that many women have allowed society or other persons to give them their self-concept. Few women have taken the time to think about themselves, to examine values such as risk versus security, tradition versus innovation, intimacy versus isolation, freedom versus order, or idealism versus pragmatism and to establish priorities for the things that are important to them. Socrates said that the unexamined life is not worth living. That statement has special significance for women. John Gardner in *Self-Renewal* stated,

Human beings have always employed an enormous variety of clever devices for running away from themselves. We can keep ourselves so busy, fill our lives with so many diversions, stuff our heads with so much knowledge, involve ourselves with so many people, and cover so much ground that we never have time to probe the fearful and wonderful world within. More often than not we don't want to depend on ourselves, don't want to live with ourselves. By middle life most of us are accomplished fugitives from ourselves.[6]

We cannot understand the world without us until we comprehend the world within us. An anonymous Oriental proverb states this succinctly: "she who knows others is wise; she who knows herself is enlightened."

Continuing education and particularly counseling programs for women help women take this inward look. The combination of services for women and a variety of learning options designed to meet their needs has led to growing numbers of women on campus for part-time as well as full-time study. Twenty years ago, 35 percent of all American college students were women. Ten years ago, the figure was 40 percent. By 1978 women constituted 49 percent of the college student population, accounting for 46 percent of full-time students and 52 percent of part-time students.[7]

Another factor is important for the woman who recognizes continuing education as a requisite for maintenance of a successful career: an awareness of the change that has occurred in the function of education during the twentieth century—a change from the transmission of culture or preparation for life to the development of techniques for self-learning. Ideally this development should begin in child care centers and be reinforced in kindergarten and the elementary school years. However, until this happens, the encouragement of continuing educational development will be primarily the responsibility of continuing education units of colleges and universities, and the majority of self-learners will be found in the adult population.

What characteristics define a self-learner? A self-learner is one who, according to John Gardner, has developed "skills, attitudes, habits of mind, and the kinds of knowledge and understanding that will be the instruments of continuous change and growth."[8] Self-learners will be able to see themselves as independent and self-directed persons; share and receive educational ideas freely from their peers; diagnose their own learning needs; relate to teachers, professors, and others as learning resources and take the initiative in making use of these resources not only during their time on campus but throughout their lives; and identify human and material resources that are appropriate to different learning needs and select effective strategies to make use of these resources.[9] This means that women who decide to continue their education must change from a content model that encourages reliance on teachers to a process model that requires a significant amount of self-direction.

One of the analyses that explores this concept of self-direction and leads to a recognition of the valuable role that continuing education can play in women's lives is Erik Erikson's work on the "eight ages of man."[10] Erikson's description in 1950 of eight sequential stages of psychosocial development laid a foundation for subsequent research by others concerning adult development. Although it is not possible to treat these life-cycle theories in depth, a few examples indicate the potential of the relationship of education to developmental stages.

Using Erikson's eight sequential stages of psychosocial development as the framework, age ranges can be assigned to each stage, recognizing that the ranges are only approximate. The age or period required for the developmental stage varies with the individual and is dependent on the time required for resolution of tasks associated with that period of growth.

Erikson suggested "trust versus mistrust" as the developmental crisis in the first stage. This initial relationship of the infant with the mother creates the basis for the individual's development. In this period, the infant also experiences social attachment to another individual (the mother) and simultaneously the withdrawal of that attachment through separation. The polarity of attachment versus separation pervades the life cycle, and the way in which the individual initially learns to cope with this dilemma helps form her identity. Roger Gould stated that

A separation situation ranges from a physical separation to withdrawal of love, being misunderstood, being mislabeled, slights to our importance, being made to feel small and helpless, and other disturbances of empathy on the part of our parents. Every time these separation situations occur we feel impotent and we feel that we have been unnecessarily injured by someone we trusted.[11]

Failure to negotiate this psychosocial crisis successfully in the first stage of development may be one of many factors that leads to the need for interpersonal counseling and group therapy to establish confidence and self-identity as an adult. Many continuing education programs for women have recognized this developmental gap and have created seminars or group sessions to meet this need in women.

Between the ages of two and four years, a child begins to develop language and to experiment with self-control—running, skating, swimming, and practicing gross body movements that lead to muscular control. Erikson labeled this period as one of "autonomy versus shame and doubt." The psychosocial crisis Erikson described includes basic dichotomies such as love and hate, cooperation and willfulness, freedom of self-expression and its suppression. In Erikson's words, "from a sense of self-control without loss of self-esteem comes a lasting sense of good will and pride; from a sense of loss of self-control and of foreign overcontrol comes a lasting propensity for doubt and shame."[12]

As a child enters preschool and then school, she is faced with an emerging sex-role identity and the beginnings of moral development. In the previous stage, the child was engrossed with her own identity; in this period, between ages five and seven years, the child examines her environment with regard to pattern and stability. Called "initiative versus guilt" by Erikson, this stage is marked by intellectual curiosity at a high point. No subjects are taboo. Through enthusiastic questioning and testing, the child begins to internalize cultural prohibitions and taboos such as incest and infantile sexuality. This stage, as Erikson stated so well, "sets the direction toward the possible and the tangible which permits the dreams of early childhood to be attached to the goals of an active adult life."[13]

If educators, parents, and significant others could help the child sustain the ebullient "need to know" of this developmental stage in even modified form in the subsequent stages, she would have the basic skills to become a self-learning adult. It is perhaps at this stage that the greatest potential exists for initiating the habits of mind and patterns of thought related to the characteristics of the self-directed learner described earlier.

The middle-school age of eight to twelve years is a period of latency or quiescence before puberty, according to Freud.[14] In Erikson's view, it includes a serious introduction to work through the school setting. This experience calls on social skills to accomplish many of the assigned tasks that in turn create competition and a sense of achievement or failure. "Industry versus inferiority" is the term Erikson used to identify this development.

The fear of success that Matina Horner identified as a problem for women from school age through college has its beginnings in this stage of the life cycle. While a child is learning the basic skills of reading, writing, and counting, she is also absorbing the sexual stereotypes and observing behavior that is rewarded or ridiculed by her peer group and adults. The middle-school experience adds a layer of achievement or inadequacy to the evolving self-concept that is now transmitted through friends instead of only self and family.

"Identity versus role diffusion" is the hurdle Erikson described in the adolescent stage of ages thirteen to seventeen years. In this period, serious decisions are often made unwittingly by young women. At this juncture, boys are focusing their school activity around vocational choice.[15] This choice determines their entrance into the working world after high school graduation or their entrance into extended education at a vocational

school, college, or university. Females, on the other hand, concern themselves primarily with interpersonal relations during this adolescent period.
Even when they focus on vocational choice or further education, they
approach it "in a way that converts this world into a vehicle for express-
ing predominantly feminine interests"[16] (such as marriage and family
life).

It is logical for women who expect to marry early and to gain their
life-style and support secondhand from their husbands to give little attention to a career. However, in the introspection and self-examination that
accompany the vocational decision, one gains an important sense of
identity. Women who miss this step, and many do, are seriously handi-
capped in sequential self-development.

The young girl who decides before she finishes high school or directly
after completing high school to marry and have children is clearly limit-
ing or at least delaying her options for further education or employment.
If she were aware of the opportunities available through continuing education and part-time study, this delay or limitation could be shortened.
At this developmental stage, when pivotal decisions concerning marriage
and work occur, an awareness of alternatives provided by continuing
education is extremely useful.

Early adulthood, which stretches over the years from eighteen to
thirty, has as its central contradiction "intimacy versus isolation."
Women who have delayed the marriage decision until this period have
more social and peer pressure exerted to make that decision during this
stage. Simultaneously, women find the career options available after
business school, college, or graduate school competing with the options
available through marriage. If marriage is chosen, the next decision is
the childbearing choice. The decision to have children is one that has
obvious effects extending through other life stages. A woman who
finishes childbearing at age twenty-four can plan to return to work or to
further education at age thirty or thirty-one, if she decides to wait until
the child is of school age. On the other hand, the woman who finishes
childbearing at age thirty may plan to return to work or further education
at age thirty-six or thirty-seven.

Again, the availability of continuing education and part-time study
in day or evening provides alternatives to women who are making these
decisions. In the "identity versus role diffusion" stage, women often
have less knowledge of their identity than men because of the failure to

work through a career choice; This absence of self-knowledge is a handi-
cap in marriage and often creates more anxiety for women than men.
The dependence of women on their husbands for social status and economic level can be frustrating to the woman who is able and ambitious.
The period of middle adulthood, from ages thirty to fifty, presents
the choice of "generativity or stagnation," according to Erikson. *Generativity* implies concern for the influence your life has had on others. This
influence may be through the values a woman has transmitted to her
children, in the thread of continuity and promise they represent, or in
the quality of life she has developed for herself. But it may also be viewed
as a form of creativity, of the way she responds to failure, of the way
she adjusts and perhaps seeks out new relationships.

For women, it is the time of the empty nest, the time when the
marriage becomes a partnership rather than a family, the time when a
woman may decide to get that delayed degree, open that shop, or become a realtor. In many ways, it is a period of second chance, when discre-
tionary income and increased leisure may come together in a happy relationship. Knowing that this part of the life cycle is ahead and
understanding its potential can help women control their frustration
during the homebound, married, child-rearing eras.

Realizing the support available from continuing education programs
that are especially designed to help women return to work, to adjust to
divorce, and to recover from widowhood is invaluable. In this period,
women who have kept their intellectual skills current reap the benefits
when they have the opportunity to put them to full-time use. Also, many
older students register for college or university courses at this age because
of the social opportunities and chance for personal expression the classes
provide. The ability to articulate one's own values and follow them rather
than accept those society appears to dictate is a significant achievement
in this life-cycle stage.

If middle adulthood has been a period of generativity, it is more likely
that from age fifty-one onward, a woman will relate more to the integrity
aspects rather than the alternative despair that Erikson described. Recent
research has developed new approaches to this part of the life cycle. Contrary to previous conclusions, growth does not stop. Women who maintain their physical and psychological or emotional selves in a healthy
state and continue to renew their education can expect a dynamic rather
than a static old age. Increasingly, aging is being recognized as an atti-

tudinal rather than a chronological process. As a result, the benefits of continuing education in learning new skills, in absorbing new ideas, and in building personal relationships around knowledge or learning rather than work or physical appearance are being discovered.

In examining the conflicts facing women who must deal with "success" in the external world, two ideas have been explored: (1) the relationship of lifelong learning to the ability of women to sustain their personal growth and professional achievement, and (2) the value of understanding life stage development for women who are planning a professional career. Women who develop responsibility for their own learning may improve their ability to maintain intellectual activity at a fairly stable level. Women who understand their own identity may find questions concerning success and its priority in their lives easier to resolve. Critical inquiry, decision making, and objective analysis are skills women must continually renew and practice if they are to be current in their professions. Continuing education programs and services can provide an effective and efficient process for preventing career obsolescence.

Women who are aware of the pattern of adult development may be more successful in balancing the pursuit of personal versus professional goals. An understanding that the decisions made at age twenty or thirty-five will affect the quality of life at sixty-five or seventy, as well as the knowledge that these decisions can be mitigated by subsequent choices and actions, is important. The contemplation of the various crisis, eras, or phases that women experience during their lifetime can be useful in planning or selecting the professional activities they choose. In summary, continuing education can be a resource to aid and direct the personal and professional development of women throughout their lifespan.

NOTES

1. Judith M. Bardwick, Elizabeth Ann Douvan, Matina S. Horner, and David Gutmann, *Feminine Personality and Conflict* (Belmont, Calif.: Brooks Cole Publishing Company, 1970).

2. Cyril O. Houle, *The Design of Education* (San Francisco: Jossey-Bass, 1973), p. 32.

3. Carnegie Commission on Higher Education, *Less Time, More Options* (New York: McGraw-Hill Book Company, 1971); and Carnegie Commission on Higher Education, *Toward a Learning Society* (New York: McGraw-Hill Book Company, 1973).

4. Rose Marie Roach, "Honey, Won't You Please Stay Home," *Personal and Guidance Journal,* October 1976.

5. *Psychology Today* (Del Mar, Calif.: CRM Books, 1970), p. 477.

6. John W. Gardner, *Self-Renewal* (New York: Harper and Row, 1964), p. 13.

7. Jack Magarrell, "Women Account for 93 Percent of Enrollment Gain," *Chronicle of Higher Education,* January 9, 1978.

8. Gardner, *Self-Renewal,* p. 21.

9. Malcolm Knowles, *Self-Directed Learning* (New York: Associated Press, 1975).

10. E. H. Erikson, *Childhood and Society* (New York: Norton, 1950).

11. Roger L. Gould, "Adult Development Stages" (Address to National Association of Psychological Counselors and Educators/American Education Association Conference, New York, November 1976).

12. Erikson, *Childhood and Society,* p. 254.

13. Ibid., p. 258.

14. Ibid., p. 260.

15. Elizabeth Ann Douvan and Joseph Adelson, *The Adolescent Experience* (New York: John Wiley and Sons, 1966).

16. Ibid.

8.

Toward Freedom and Self-Determination: New Directions in Mental Health Services

EDITH BREEN

Since 1950 significant changes have taken place in the theory and practice of mental health as it relates to women. Especially in the 1970s, new theories of mental health, more relevant to the psychology of women, have appeared to challenge the monopoly of Freudian thought. Coinciding with the development of the new theories, several new publications related to women and mental health have also appeared. Furthermore, changes have occurred in the personnel delivering health care. But even more improvements are needed to make mental health services more relevant and helpful to the female populations they serve.

In the 1950s, the predominant theory about emotional health and mental health was one of mental illness. Most therapists were trained primarily in Freudian theory, which meant that the predominant idea was that all women's emotional problems could be reduced to envy of the male penis. Theory said that unless women were able to work through their sexual problems in psychotherapy, they could not solve their emotional problems.

The neo-Freudians defined emotional conflict somewhat differently but retained the dominant idea that men fear castration and women believe they have been castrated. Both men and women were therefore unhappy about having or not having a penis. This capsule summary is, of course, an oversimplification of a brilliant and complex theory about the functioning of human emotions. Freud deserves much credit for valid observations, but his understanding of women left a great deal to be desired.

Some more modern therapists, in examining the psychology of women, have agreed with Freud that women often envy men. But their analyses suggest that women do not envy male sexuality or the male sex organ but rather the male's superior position of power and privilege within the society. The envy may start early, with young girls who are often quite aware that boys have more fun, that boys are encouraged while girls are discouraged from active play, that boys are given preferential treatment in many ways in families and at school. Fathers typically seem to pay more attention to their sons than to their daughters; boys are encouraged to be active and to assume and use power; girls are taught to be passive, nurturing, and self-sacrificing.

Another change since the 1950s has been in the personnel involved in mental health care. The biggest change seems to have come about with the growth of the community mental health centers, the local outpatient facilities that offer therapy to the public on a once- or twice-a-week basis. These centers came into being in the late 1950s and early 1960s, subsidized with public funding, with most of the staffing being different from that in previous existing facilities.

For example, according to a study by F. Redlich and S. R. Kellert,[1] the number of social workers and psychologists increased by 700 percent in one eastern metropolitan area between 1950 and 1975. During this same period, the increase in the number of psychiatrists was significantly less. Psychologists and social workers have also moved into administrative positions in the mental health system, allowing them to affect policy in the agencies in which they work.

Presently, women account for nearly 70 percent of social workers and 25 percent of clinical psychologists. Many of them have entered the various therapy professions. This has had a tremendous impact on the services available in the community, as female therapists are more likely to understand the frustrations women face in their daily lives. Since two-thirds of those receiving outpatient services are women, one result of the increased number of female therapists has been a shared experience and perhaps greater empathy for those seeking help.

Another major source of change in the practice of therapy in the last twenty-five years has been the increasing influence of new theoretical approaches to understanding human behavior. Some of these new theories seem to have much greater relevance for women than Freudian theory. For example, a behavioral approach to mental health takes an environmental view of the client's problems, paying little attention to inner motivations. Events happening currently in the person's life, interpersonal relationships, past history of behavior, and social environment are seen as factors that influence a person's emotional state.

Another more recent approach to emotional problems is one based on learning theory. Seeking a key to understanding depression, M. A. Seligman developed a model that suggests that much depressed behavior can be explained as a state of learned helplessness.[2] Seligman drew parallels between the behavior of animals in response to trauma and frustration and the behavior exhibited by depressed persons. He concluded that traumatic events *over which the individual has no control* can produce depression, accompanied by a continuing concept of self as helpless. Even in the absence of impediments, the depressed individual continues to believe that she is helpless to act in her own behalf. Such theories seem to offer much more promise for understanding emotions than the earlier views based on unresolved sexual conflicts.

Other theories that seem more useful in working with women are the growth and development models, which focus not on illness and emotional problems but on healthy behavior. These models delineate common stages of development that occur throughout a person's life. Therapists using this model emphasize helping people to develop their lives to their fullest potential.

One other important theoretical viewpoint that is beginning to affect mental health services for women comes from the growing number of social workers, psychologists, psychiatric nurses, and a handful of psychiatrists who call themselves "feminist therapists." A feminist therapist works with clients to help them achieve equality in their lives using many different techniques of therapy. Feminist therapy itself is not a new technique. Rather, it is simply a philosophy or point of view on the nature of the social, economic, and political condition of our society.

In the last decade, women (many of them feminists) have published books and articles on subjects relating to the psychology of women. To mention a few of the important recent works, Phyllis Chesler's provocative *Women and Madness*[3] was published in 1972. *Women in Therapy: New Psychotherapies for a Changing Society,*[4] a collection of papers about the vital issues facing women in modern society, was published in 1974. *Psychotherapy: The Hazardous Cure,*[5] by Dorothy Tennov, was published in 1975; the American Psychological Association's new journal, *Psychology of Women Quarterly,* began publication in 1976.

Until the last decade, most of the published research on the psychology of women had been done by men. In recent years, increasing numbers of women have been making contributions in the field. Sandra Bem,[6] for example, has developed a scale for measuring psychological androgyny, the acceptance of nonstereotypical masculine or feminine behavior. Since then a number of explorations of this topic have been published.

One of the recent studies that has had an impact on the mental health community is "Sex-Role Stereotypes and Clinical Judgments of Mental Health," by I. K. Broverman and associates (1970).[7] This study examined the question of bias in terms of rigid sex-role definitions among mental health professionals. The researchers asked a group of psychiatrists, psychologists, and social workers to describe the behavior and personality characteristics of the emotionally healthy adult, the healthy male, and the healthy female. The study indicated that behavior and character traits seen as healthy for the mature adult male—such as independence, objectivity, ability to make decisions easily, self-confidence, and ambition—were not seen as healthy traits for females by the therapists. Conversely, few of the traits and behaviors said to describe the healthy female—such as awareness of the feelings of others, tactful speech, gentleness, and enjoyment of the arts and literature—were seen as healthy for men. Most of the therapists thought that healthy women should be submissive and less independent, less adventurous, and less competitive than men. They also believed that women were more likely to have their feelings easily hurt. As the authors suggested, this is an odd description of a mature, healthy person.

The Broverman study and several other similar studies sparked the attention of a segment of the professional community. More therapists are now reexamining their views on sex-role stereotyping. Although it might have been expected that the female therapists in the study would show less bias than the men, the findings applied equally to male and female therapists. Perhaps this is due to their professional training as well as to the possibility that all therapists are influenced by their own socialization and by the social context in which they practice.

Another development that is helping to change viewpoints about what constitutes healthy behavior for women is the number of assertiveness training courses that are springing up all over the country. Colleges, businesses, and federal agencies are offering these courses to teach women that they do not have to remain passive, quiet, and meek—that it is healthy to be assertive. The assertiveness training courses have been well attended and continue to be popular.

Finally, some of the most important changes in the last few years in regard to improving mental health services for women have come about as a result of pressure from groups of concerned citizens, primarily concerned women, working for change in their local communities. Two of the issues brought to public attention by the hard work of many dedicated women outside the mental health profession are battered women and children and rape. Women have formed volunteer, nonprofessional counseling groups to provide services such as supportive counseling for victims of rape, information and referral resources for women, and emergency housing for battered wives and children. Only after such volunteer groups became active on these issues did the public mental health agencies take an interest in them. Recently, greater cooperation has occurred between the community mental health centers, hospitals, police, and other public agencies and the nonprofessional organizations.

Although these changes indicate a positive trend, they have been slow to filter down to individual therapists and public service organizations. One of the reasons is that many of our training institutions, our colleges and universities, are about fifteen years out of date in their teaching. A tremendous lag can be seen between what is happening in the community and what is happening in the classroom. Even programs with heavy emphasis on training in field settings seldom narrow the gap between what students observe and do in their agency placements and the theory taught in the classroom.

The issues that clients bring to therapy are continually changing. The concerns of today are not the same as those of five or ten years ago. One way of keeping the therapist training programs more up to date might be to have a large percentage of the university faculty teach only half time and devote the other half to working directly with clients or in community agencies. Now most of those teaching new therapists are full-time instructors who have little recent experience in dealing directly with clients. This kind of time split would enrich both the universities and the public agencies.

Another problem related to the quality and diversity in the training of therapists is the lack of representation of minorities and women on college and university faculties. Despite pressure from the federal government, many universities have hired only a few women or minorities and have promoted and given tenure to even fewer. Legally, the threat of cuts in federal funding support exists if universities are found to be discriminatory in hiring and promotion decisions. In practice, a large backlog of discrimination cases is awaiting government attention, and even when cases receive attention, the enforcement mechanisms are weak.

Beyond attempts to change the training of new therapists entering the profession is the issue of therapists already providing services. The new literature on the psychology of women, workshops, and continuing education courses are available for those who want to understand current trends, but it is hard to predict how many will take advantage of them. Indications are that many female therapists are interested in the topic, but few males appear concerned.

The community service agencies, such as community mental health centers, family service agencies, alcohol rehabilitation programs, and hospitals, can and should try to update the skills of their staff through in-service education and training. Many of the best agencies devote an hour or two of staff time per week to in-service education. Often the agencies have a person designated as coordinator or director of in-service education. Where the system for in-service education already exists, the problem involves convincing the administration that the agency would benefit from exploring the new literature on the psychology of women.

Apart from hoping that the professional community will reeducate itself, the best means of improving mental health services will be through a strong consumer movement. Only a small portion of the professional community is leading the way in improving services for women. Instead, improvements are being made in response to pressure from volunteer organizations who set up their own services for women. The rape crisis centers and the shelters for battered women and children that were begun entirely through the efforts of volunteers are now starting to receive some government funding and sometimes staff support from government-funded mental health agencies.

Even the individual consumer can have an impact on the services offered in her local area. Anyone seeking counseling or therapy ought to "shop" for a therapist. It is pertinent to ask the prospective therapist about background, biases, and beliefs. For example, it is important to know whether the therapist has strictly traditional views about women's and men's roles in society, or whether he or she is open to a more androgynous point of view. It is relevant to ask whether a therapist who offers help with a marital problem has ever been married. For a lesbian or gay man seeking counseling, it is especially important to know how the prospective therapist regards homosexuality. If the therapist views homosexuality as an illness, as social immaturity, or as immoral, the therapist will be of no help to the client. A biased therapist may actually harm a lesbian by further supporting the guilt she may already feel about being different from other women.

In conclusion, it is important to stress that freedom and self-determination are important for mental and emotional well-being. Concerning the theory that much depression is learned helplessness, one of the ways we can effectively combat depression, which affects women at twice the rate it affects men, is for women to gain more control over their lives. Much of the depression that I see in the clients with whom I work relates not to their inner psyche but to problems involving their lack of freedom to do what they would like to do with their time. Being caught between pressures from family, child care, expectations from relatives, and social lives that they often do not control, these women are frustrated, discouraged, and depressed.

In addition to their very real burden of household and child care responsibilities, many of these women also have impossible expectations of themselves. They are not satisfied to be average or good mothers and wives; they believe they should be Super Mom, Super Wife, and Super Housekeeper all rolled into one. With such a set of expectations, one's work is never done. For the increasing numbers of mothers who are employed outside the home in full-time jobs, the burdens are especially severe. In most cases, women work for very low wages, earning on the average 40 percent less than men with comparable education. Because they earn so little, they often cannot afford to pay for help with household and child care duties and consequently end up working two full-time jobs. The working mother in our society is one of the more extreme examples of a person with little control over life.

Is it any wonder so many women suffer from chronic depression?

Depressed women often feel trapped by the pressure of circumstances that they perceive to be beyond their control. By contrast, the woman who recognizes the pressures she is under and decides to make changes to bring more of her life under her own control loses her depression and begins to function as a happy, healthy individual.

The implications of the learned helplessness theory of depression extend will beyond the domain of psychotherapy. Since women suffer from serious depression at twice the rate of men because they have far less freedom and control over their own lives than men do, it has become evident that measures other than psychotherapy are needed to help women overcome depression. Helping women to gain greater control for themselves in their lives is not simply a matter of changing their perceptions of their situation. Rather, it is frequently necessary to change some of the external circumstances that create frustration. For example, no amount of the best psychotherapy is going to relieve the frustration, anger, and depression that come from working hard for an employer who pays women substantially less than he pays men for doing the same job. No amount of therapy can alleviate the misery and frustration of a young girl or woman who unintentionally becomes pregnant but does not want to marry, and whose only alternatives are to raise the child by herself or to give up the baby for adoption because abortion is illegal or unavailable.

To the extent that the United States is a land of freedom and equal opportunity for individuals to grow and develop their full potential, it will nurture a more productive and happy citizenry. But where freedom of choice and equal opportunity extend more to some and less to others because of their sex, sexual preference, color, ethnic background, or age, the nation perpetuates and creates circumstances that lead to emotional disturbance, depression, alcoholism, drug addiction, and other forms of mental and emotional illness. In the largest political sense, efforts designed to eliminate various forms of discrimination against women and minority people should be of vital concern to everyone in the mental health community.

NOTES

1. F. Redlich and S. R. Kellert, "Trends in American Mental Health," *American Journal of Psychiatry* 135 (1978): 22-28.

2. M. A. Seligman, "Depression and Learned Helplessness," in *The Psychology of Depression: Contemporary Theory and Research,* ed. Raymond J. Friedman and Martin M. Katz (Washington, D.C.: V. H. Winston and Sons, 1974).

3. Phyllis Chesler, *Women and Madness* (New York: Doubleday, 1972).

4. Violet Franks and Vasanti Burtle, eds., *Women in Therapy: New Psychotherapies for a Changing Society* (New York: Brunner Mazel, 1974).

5. Dorothy Tennov, *Psychotherapy: The Hazardous Cure* (New York: Abelard-Shuman, 1975).

6. S. L. Bem, "The Measurement of Psychological Androgyny," *Journal of Consulting and Clinical Psychology* 42 (1974): 155-62.

7. I. K. Broverman et al., "Sex-Role Stereotypes and Clinical Judgments of Mental Health," *Journal of Consulting and Clinical Psychology* 34 (1970): 1-7.

9.

The Menopause in Changing Times

PAULINE BART
and ELLEN PERLMUTTER

Women who survive long enough will experience either a surgical or a natural menopause. Unfortunately, little is known about this common and significant experience. But the lack of information is not surprising in that both sexism and ageism have long shrouded topics such as this in indifference and mystery. It is hard to imagine that an event as universal for men as menopause is for women would ever be so neglected.

Although we still know too little about all aspects of the menopause, even its most fundamental physiological effects, the past decade has brought a surge of interest in it. The work of feminist academics, of the women's health movement, and of some medical researchers has begun to provide information that can help women directly and to reclaim the menopause from the male-dominated institution of medicine, which has too long defined those things that make women different from men as causing them to be deviant, diseased, or, at the very least, undesirable.

MEDICAL VIEWS OF THE MENOPAUSE

Physicians have long written about their views on menopause. Rarely
have their essays contained any systematic data, and for the most part,
the medical literature has consisted of physicians' "clinical opinions,"
which generally reflect a great deal of bias. In these papers, it is rarely
acknowledged that only 25 percent of women see their physicians for
menopausal symptoms[1] and that therefore the clinical papers do not
account for the experiences of the majority of women. Even more disturbing, however, are the powerful misogynist views expressed throughout the history of medical literature on women. Historian Ann Wood
pointed out that reading the medical literature from the nineteenth century tells us less about medical advances than about cultural attitudes,[2]
and Diane Scully and Pauline Bart documented sexism in modern textbooks.[3] The literature on the menopause shows no lack of demeaning
views of women.

In the nineteenth century, women were seen as little more than reproductive creatures. One physician pontificated that it was "as if the
Almighty in creating the female sex had taken the uterus and built up a
woman around it."[4] It is no surprise then that the loss of this function
would be observed as a catastrophic event bearing "evil effects,"[5]
which is "always a time of trial, often of suffering and danger,"[6] and is
generally a reflection of decay.[7] In fact, the menopause was held responsible for insanity,[8] nervousness,[9] loss of feminine appeal,[10] and, in 1870,
120 "morbid liabilities."[11] It was common practice then, and for some
physicians even now, to blame the menopause for nearly any problem
that occurred at midlife.

Of course, appropriate sex-role behavior was also an issue for these
doctors. If a woman had committed prior indiscretions, had lived a fast
or luxurious life, or had not abided by the laws of hygiene, she was expected to suffer at menopause.[12] In addition, some physicians seemed
to be more concerned with their patients' husbands, who had to tolerate
conditions such as "intolerable garrulity," suspiciousness, self-centered
behavior, lying, angry outbursts, jealousy, and the refusal to do house-
work.[13] An advertisement that appeared in medical journals a few years
ago indicated that this sentiment is still shared—the ad suggested the
prescription of medication for the menopausal woman "for the symptoms
that bother *him* most"![14]

Negative views of the menopausal woman are not only a nineteenth-

century phenomenon. It might surprise some readers not familiar with
the pervasive sexism in recent gynecological textbooks and the traditional
antifemale ambiance in medical education to learn that as recently as
1971, at a conference on menopause and aging sponsored by the U.S.
Department of Health, Education, and Welfare—a conference uncon-
taminated by the presence of a single female participant—Johns Hopkins
gynecologist Howard Jones characterized menopausal women as "a
caricature of their younger selves at their emotional worst."[15] To many
people, menopause is still a "deficiency disease" that is debilitating if
untreated. For instance, K. A. Achte stated, "The assumption has been
put forward that women's ability to work reduces to a quarter of the
normal by menopause."[16] Little research has been done on the effects of
menopause—none that can support statements like these—and Mary Brown
Parlee noted that it is the male physicians' bias against menopausal women
that leads them to make statements having no empirical grounding.[17]

The two most destructive ideologies about the menopause in the
twentieth century have been the biological approach of Robert Wilson
and his supporters and the psychoanalytic perspective heralded by Helene
Deutsch in the 1940s. The former blamed a large array of physical and
psychological symptoms, as well as the loss of femininity and youthful-
ness, on the diminished supply of estrogen in the menopausal and postmenopausal woman. The psychoanalytic approach focused more on the
inevitability of psychological distress as a result of the loss of reproductive capacity and femininity. Although many physicians have also been
aware that real stresses and role changes could affect the experience of
menopause, most relied upon these theories in their understanding of
their patients. Both approaches were well publicized in the popular press
and were influential with the general public.

The work that came from the Wilson Research Foundation (which
had actually received funding from drug companies)[18] described the
menopause as a disease for which women should take estrogen for the
rest of their lives. Wilson's very popular book, *Feminine Forever,*[19]
was excerpted in *Look* and *Vogue,* and as a result, his belief that estrogen
could cure twenty-six symptoms[20] (from anxiety and thoughts of suicide
to chronic indigestion and backache) received wide circulation. He furthermore suggested that menopause was so bad that statistics and research
could not tap the real extent of the problem: "The untold misery of
alcoholism, drug addiction, divorce, and broken homes caused by these
unstable, estrogen-starved women cannot be presented in statistical

form."[21] Although he was criticized by other physicians and by the Food and Drug Administration, Wilson's work had quite an impact on the increase in the use of estrogen replacement therapy as well as on a heightening of women's fears about this transitional period in their lives. The redefinition of a natural event, such as menopause, into a disease is an example (like childbirth) of the increasing medicalization of normal events in women's lives. This process is both a cause and an effect of the enormous power that American physicians have to define and manipulate our reality.

Deutsch's work is a strong example of the phallocentric views that came from orthodox psychoanalysis. Deutsch described the menopausal woman as having "reached her natural end—her partial death—as servant of the species"[22] and saw the menopause as a blow to vanity, because "with the lapse of the reproductive service, her beauty vanishes, and usually the warm, vital flow of feminine emotional life as well."[23] Few options other than a stereotyped form of "femininity" were seen as possible for fulfillment for women. She believed that "feminine, loving" women would fare best at menopause, and Miguel Prados, a more contemporary psychoanalyst, took this idea further, saying:

Reproduction and motherhood are essential for both complete physical maturity and emotional development of the woman. Everyday observations show that the woman who has reached the climacteric period without having fulfilled her reproductive function . . . will find it much more difficult to adapt herself to this phase than the woman who reaches her menopause after having fulfilled her motherhood drives.[24]

This theory focused upon the intrapsychic meaning of menopause and rested upon a series of notoriously erroneous concepts about the nature of womanhood.

The past decade has seen some progress in changing attitudes toward menopause. Several authors, mainly women, have written positive, instructive books that expose medical sexism, explore myths and historical ideas about menopause, provide information on what women say menopause is like, criticize current medical treatment, and provide some news about alternatives to estrogen replacement therapy.[25] Two books in particular provide interesting suggestions for nutritional approaches to menopausal symptoms, one by Barbara Seaman and Gideon Seaman[26] and the other by Rosetta Reitz.[27] Contrary to the articles and books we have been discussing, these two books take a nonsexist approach to menopause. Fortunately, they are published in paperback and are as readily available as Wilson's book was in the 1960s.

Strong critiques of the existing research have come from within the fields of the social sciences. Sonja McKinlay and John McKinlay[28] and Mary Brown Parlee[29] did trenchant reviews of the literature that shed light upon the biases, errors, and omissions throughout. Sociological and and psychological studies by Pauline Bart,[30] Leonore Levit,[31] and Leslie Marilyn Meltzer[32] disproved some psychoanalytic hypotheses and found that "feminine" women and women who are highly invested in the role of motherhood fare worse at menopause. The Interdisciplinary Research Conference on Menopause[33] in 1979 included papers from the fields of anthropology, physiology and medicine, sociology, psychology, history, and the humanities. The conference involved mostly women researchers and participants, and it offered information on a wide range of topics, including the hot flash, attitudes toward menopause, the depiction of the menopausal woman in fiction, menopause in a cross-cultural and historical perspective, and the physiology of the menopause. It is a very hopeful sign that women academics are becoming more concerned about the experience of menopause.

Changes have occurred even within the field of medicine. Some progress has been made regarding alternatives to estrogen replacement therapy, and women are beginning to be given more say in their treatment. Medical researchers are responsible for the important studies showing the connection between estrogen replacement therapy and cancer[34] and the methodologically sophisticated studies showing that estrogen is only effective in the treatment of vasomotor symptoms and vaginal atrophy and is not the cure-all that had been suggested.[35]

Two physicians, Howard Osofsky and Robert Seidenberg, were astute in their analysis of mental health practitioners' views of menopause:

It becomes obvious that a type of confused, fuzzy, and prejudicial thinking has existed in the minds of psychologists, psychiatrists, and physicians in general toward the female. Whereas it is clearly recognized that male psychology must be differentiated from male biology . . . no such differentiation has been allowed for females. Males are not governed by biologic maturation processes related to aging. They can be abstract, external, and worldly, and are concerned with jobs and events of the day. For whatever reasons, little attention has been given to the obviously similar dichotomy in the psychology and biology of women. Emotions and cognition both have been viewed as being a part of, and controlled by, biology. . . . It is no wonder that so many women become depressed around the time of menopause; professionals and society have helped to ensure this reaction.[36]

Several medical textbooks published during the 1970s show that changes in knowledge are slow to take effect. A few present well-balanced views of the menopause that question some of the assumptions held in previous medical texts.[37] They present information about estrogen replacement therapy that was accurate at the time they were published and they usually report pertinent data. Others, however, read as if they came from the 1960s. Their tone is often condescending, and they too often hedge on the issue of the dangers of estrogen replacement therapy.[38] At least one recent text continues to catastrophize the menopause as previous ones did,[39] and still another claims that depression can be caused by estrogen deficiency and can be treated with estrogen replacement therapy.[40] We have far to go in changing medical attitudes about the menopause.

THE TREATMENT OF MENOPAUSE:
MEDICAL ATTITUDES AND THE PROFIT MOTIVE

The development of various "treatments" has come hand in hand with the identification of the menopause as a medical event. Historically, these treatments have at times been worse than the reported ailments. For example, in the nineteenth century, women were treated with potent and debilitating drugs,[41] enforced rest,[42] and the application of leeches to parts of their bodies.[43] Now women are treated with the conjugated estrogens, the fourth or fifth most commonly prescribed type of medication in the United States.[44] Although not as barbaric as earlier treatments, these drugs have been linked to the development of cancer in the menopausal and postmenopausal woman. Indeed, estrogen replacement therapy has something for everyone—patients for physicians, profits for the drug companies, and cancer for women.

The use of estrogens grew rapidly during the period when the "feminine forever" philosophy was popular, and over 300 articles promoting its use have appeared in popular magazines. This promotion occurred even though researchers reported increases in uterine and breast cancer in women taking estrogen as far back as the 1940s,[45] and even though animal studies showed that estrogen can induce cancer in estrogen-dependent organs (breast, uterus, cervix, and vagina) almost twenty years ago.[46] More recent studies have shown that women who take estrogen have an increased risk of developing cancer of the lining of the uterus.[47] Although the methods and results of the studies vary somewhat, it appears that the risk for estrogen users is two to fifteen times that of women who have not used estrogen replacement therapy. Larger dosages have been found to increase this risk,[48] and long-term users are in more danger of developing cancer than are short-term users.[49] Another study showed a possible link between taking estrogen and developing breast cancer.[50]

Ayerst (the company that markets Premarin, the most frequently prescribed form of estrogen replacement therapy) was well prepared for the alarm that followed the publication of the first two of these studies in 1975. Immediately after their appearance in the *New England Journal of Medicine,* Ayerst sent physicians a letter recommending "business as usual" and did not even mention the cancer studies, an act that FDA Commissioner Alexander Schmidt called "irresponsible."[51] In addition, a public relations firm developed some ideas about how Ayerst could reach the public and "preserve the identity of estrogen replacement therapy as effective, safe treatment for the symptoms of menopause." An employee of one of the firms involved intercepted a letter from Hill and Knowlton to the president of Ayerst and sent it to the *Majority Report,* a women's newspaper in New York.[52] In the letter, dated December 17, 1976, Hill and Knowlton advised Ayerst to undertake an ongoing program of communication that would plant articles with major women's magazines, general magazines, syndicated columnists, science editors, editorial services for small-town newspapers, and television. The articles would deal with menopause and would contain discreet references to "products your doctor may prescribe." Subtlety was required so as not to jeopardize delicate negotiations with the Food and Drug Administration for new patient labeling for Premarin. A second component of the communications program would provide quick, powerful counteraction to potentially dangerous developments such as analysis of Food and Drug Administration decisions and an expected negative report from the Mayo Clinic. This component would include press releases and intensively schooled Ayerst spokesmen who could comment confidently and convincingly.

Physicians have done little to resist the drug companies' siren song. According to sociologist John McKinlay, in 1977 estrogen was still being prescribed as frequently as it was before 1975.[53] This behavior is not startling, since some of these same professionals in 1975 wrote about 11,000 prescriptions for diethylstilbestrol (DES) for prenatal care, even though the Food and Drug Administration had banned its use for this problem in light of its clear danger to the fetus.[54] The result is that a cohort of young women are at risk for cancer of the vagina, and it is clearly a case of an iatrogenic, or doctor-caused, illness.

Medical practitioners have also been warned by their own publications to avoid "hasty or ill-conceived termination" of estrogen replacement therapy. The American College of Obstetrics and Gynecology newsletter asserted ten months after the publication of the cancer studies in 1975 that there was "no conclusive evidence to indicate an increased risk of malignancy."[55] Although it was true that the studies had some methodological problems, the data were strong enough not to be dismissed glibly or out of hand. The most recent study by Carlos Antunes and associates[56] corrected for previous methodological weaknesses and still found a strong connection between estrogen replacement therapy and cancer of the uterine lining.

It is important to understand why this neglect of the research occurred. When people talk about medicine and women, they usually focus upon the negative attitudes that the institution holds about women. Although many physicians no doubt do hold such views, the attempt to cover up the importance of the research on cancer and estrogen replacement therapy shows it is also a question of profits. The drug industry is based on profits, and companies believe it is important for them to get people to use their medications and to convince physicians to prescribe their products. As long ago as 1854, Joseph Parrish understood the way the role of economic concerns entered into the treatment of menopause:

In these times when specialties are becoming the order of the day in medicine; when physicians are apt to select some particular subject upon which to display their talent, and exercise their skill, there is a great deal of exaggeration, both as to the nature, and treatment of the particular diseases that may claim attention . . . and the physician is too often tempted . . . to subject her [the patient] to treatment, sometimes the most unscientific in character, and in its results, most unsatisfactory, except to the pecuniary taste of the prescriber.[57]

This reality exists today, and the behavior of Ayerst and gynecologists regarding estrogen replacement therapy cannot be reduced to negative attitudes toward women at midlife. This kind of activity is not limited to the United States; four major drug companies in England have recently funded the Association of Women's Health Care, which has established special information services for women and doctors to provide estrogen replacement therapy for women in menopause.[58] They also hope to increase the demand for such drugs at the National Health Services clinics, since they will be speaking with doctors in medical staff rooms with a large female work force.

The news is not all bad, however. On July 22, 1977, the Food and Drug Administration published a regulation stating that estrogen drugs should contain patient package inserts detailing what estrogen does and does not do. They recommended a candid and hard-hitting model insert, and the drug companies petitioned the Food and Drug Administration and sued in federal court to block the regulation. They were joined in this action by the American College of Obstetricians and Gynecologists, the American Pharmaceutical Association, the American Medical Association, and the National Association of Chain Drug Stores.

The medical and pharmaceutical groups claimed that the information brochure inserted in packets would interfere with the traditional doctor-patient-pharmacist relationship. In a paternalistic tone consistent with patriarchal institutions, the American Pharmaceutical Association claimed:

The officially composed leaflet is far from understandable—to many patients, it will be utterly incomprehensible. And much of the information mandated for the leaflet is not only in no way pertinent to *the proper concerns of the patient*, once therapy has been determined, but it is wholly unsuitable for lay persons without medical or scientific training.[59]

These groups have lost their suit, and women getting estrogen replacement therapy find a package insert with their pills. The section on menopause in the pamphlet briefly describes what the menopause is, what symptoms are associated with it, what estrogen replacement therapy can help with, and what its dangers are. It strongly states that estrogen replacement therapy is not helpful for nervous symptoms or depression (unless they are associated with hot flashes) and that it will not keep skin soft and supple or keep women feeling young. It is clear progress that women are now being given accurate information (with or without their physician's sanction) and can become more active in making this choice about their health. The activities of the Women's Health Network (the lobby in Washington) and a general increase in consumerism and health consciousness have made a major contribution to the well-being of women at midlife.

WOMEN'S EXPERIENCE OF MENOPAUSE

It is not surprising that what little we know about the experience of menopause for most women (those who do not end up in doctors' offices) comes almost exclusively from research done by women. In the past decade, several large-scale studies of women in the community have been done in the United States and abroad.[60]

Although most of the studies that directly asked women about symptoms found the incidence of vasomotor symptoms to be high (between 60 percent and 93 percent for menopausal and postmenopausal women), one recent analysis of health records of Caucasion and Japanese women living in Hawaii found that only approximately one-quarter of them reported traditional menopausal symptoms like hot flashes or sweats.[61] Sonja McKinlay and Margot Jefferys surveyed over 600 women between the ages of forty-five and fifty-four who lived in and around London.[62] They found that three-quarters of the menopausal women were experiencing hot flashes and that one-quarter of the postmenopausal women continued to have hot flashes for five years or more. The six other symptoms that were specifically inquired about—headaches, dizzy spells, palpitations, sleeplessness, depression, and weight increase—were each reported by one-third to one-half of the women. Although having these symptoms was not related to whether a woman was pre-menopausal, postmenopausal, or currently menopausal, a woman who reported any symptoms was likely to report more than one. Two other studies also found that one-quarter to one-third of the women reported depression, but no clear connection was found between being depressed and menopausal status.[63] McKinley and Jefferys found that even though three-quarters of the women who had hot flashes found them embarrassing or uncomfortable, only about one-fifth sought medical treatment.

Because of the lack of sound research on the menopause, women's self-help groups have begun to study it. Two groups, one in Seattle and one in Boston, used mail-in questionnaires in an attempt to survey women's physical and emotional experiences at menopause.[64]

The Seattle group, Women in Midstream, originally set out to investigate what the experience of the menopause was like for middle-aged women *before* estrogen replacement therapy was available. They sent out 1,000 questionnaires to nursing homes but received only 70 replies. These older women were also unwilling to talk about the subject in face-to-face interviews. This experience is of interest, because it shows to what extent women are socialized to regard normal bodily processes and life experiences with shame and to hide them from public scrutiny. People in nursing homes are usually eager to talk to anyone, because they are lonely, but menopause seems to have been too embarrassing to them. The poor response also suggests that most, if not all, earlier studies of menopause may well suffer from the respondents' unwillingness to reveal to researchers the full extent of their actual feelings and experiences. It may be that only now, when support is available in our culture for women to share these formerly private areas of their lives with other women, can we really learn about these experiences in a systematic way.

Clearly, women are interested in sharing this information now. Women in Midstream received over 700 completed questionnaires from a highly motivated sample of women from groups who wrote asking to receive the questionnaire. However, they have been able to analyze only 250 because of a lack of womanpower and funding. As a result of the method of sampling used, the Women in Midstream researchers think their respondents probably are largely from the middle and upper classes and have had a relatively difficult experience in the menopause (although half of the group described it as easy or moderately easy). Approximately 60 percent came from the state of Washington, the rest from elsewhere in the United States. The majority of the women were white, married, had three children on the average, and lived only with their husband at the time they answered the questionnaire. They ranged in age from twenty-eight to seventy-three, with two-thirds of the group between forty-five and fifty-five.

One of the most striking findings was that three-quarters of the women had been prescribed hormone therapy, although no more than 60 percent of the group had sought physician help for hot flashes and/or thinning or drying of the vaginal walls. Fifty-five percent of this group was prescribed tranquilizers, and one must wonder how much of this was in response to the women's needs and how much in response to those of their husbands and physicians, especially since psychiatric therapy was recommended for less than 10 percent of the women. Only 15 percent of the women received dietary supplements. This is important, because, as Reitz and the Seamans[65] pointed out, one can mitigate some of the symptoms of menopause by judicious use of various dietary supplements and exercise.

Only slightly more than half of the women reported satisfaction with their doctor's attitudes and found the doctor helpful. Of the one-fifth of the group who sought help from nonmedical sources, three-fifths of these women found the sources helpful. The Women in Midstream group believes social supports are important for women going through menopause, and they asked the women if they would like to talk with other women about the health and social problems of older women. More than half were interested. The desirability of such discussions is borne out by an incident Paula Weideger talked about in her book *Menstruation and Menopause.*[66] During a menopause consciousness-raising group, one of the participants was surprised to find that her hot flashes, once considered uncomfortable, had become pleasurable as a result of her group experience.

The Boston Women's Health Collective attempted an ambitious survey of women's experiences and attitudes. Mail questionnaires were sent to friends and relatives of the collective's members as well as to all of the clinics and counseling centers that ordered the 1973 edition of *Our Bodies, Ourselves.*[67] Replies were received from about 500 women. Most of the women lived in large northeastern or Middle Atlantic cities or suburbs. Less than two-thirds were married, about one-fifth were divorced or widowed, and one-tenth were single. Slightly more than one-third of the total group was menopausal or postmenopausal. As in the Seattle sample, two-thirds of this group was employed outside the home.

Slightly more than three-fifths of the Boston menopausal sample received estrogen replacement therapy. Although this is less than the Seattle group, it is surprisingly high for a group that probably was experiencing many fewer "menopausal" problems (given the ways the respective samples were gathered). Five-sixths of the women talked with friends about their menopausal experiences, and over two-thirds talked to husbands. One-sixth talked to therapists, and one-sixth talked to women's groups. About two-thirds of the menopausal or postmenopausal women felt neutral or positive about the changes they experienced.

Bernice Neugarten and her students investigated menopause from a developmental and social psychological perspective. They found that women who had already experienced menopause were less likely to consider it a significant event than were pre-menopausal women.[68] The students found that menopause was not a particularly important or difficult experience for the women,[69] but since their experience was over before the rise of the women's movement and its encouragement to women to "speak bitterness"[70] about the limitations of their socially prescribed roles, an underreporting of negative feelings may have occurred.

Some of the interesting findings from these studies resulted from subdividing the women interviewed in various ways. For instance, Leonore Levit found no difference in general in the anxiety menopausal women suffered compared to postmenopausal women.[71] However, women who were very invested in their role as mother were more anxious going through menopause than they were after it. Thus the transition is harder for women who are giving up a role they value highly. Although middle-class women did not differ in anxiety whether in menopause or postmenopause, working-class menopausal women were more anxious than postmenopausal women. This finding was replicated in a recent large-scale study of Belgian women.[72] The researchers found that subjects in the lower socioeconomic group scored more highly on an index of "nervosity" than did women from the higher socioeconomic group. A particularly intriguing finding was that among the subjects from the lower socioeconomic group, women who worked outside the home fared worse on this index than did the housewives. In the higher socioeconomic group, this trend was reversed, and the women with jobs reported the least "nervosity." Perhaps this finding reflects the relative richness or paucity of available roles for women in these social classes. For advantaged women who may have more options than their poorer counterparts, a job may provide significant gratification. For women in the lower socioeconomic group, however, a job may offer little interest and may be more of a burden that intensifies other stresses at menopause.

Ruth Kraines studied 100 women divided about equally among menopausal, pre-menopausal, and postmenopausal women.[73] Using interviews, self-report forms, and checklists, she did not find differences among her three groups (although menopausal women did check more of the symptoms associated with the menopause). She did find that women who were low in self-esteem and life satisfaction were most likely to have difficulty during menopause and that the relationship seemed to be circular, that is, low self-esteem led to difficulty during menopause, which in turn led to low self-esteem, and so on. Kraines also found a continuity between a woman's previous reactions to bodily experiences (such as health problems, menstruation, and pregnancy) and her reaction to menopause. She concluded that, contrary to the medical studies, menopause in itself is not experienced by most women as a critical event. She suggested that women who seek medical help are different from most middle-aged women in their physical and emotional reactions to stress.

A clear discrepancy exists between the views of these psychologists and medical practitioners—the former suggest that most women do not regard menopause as a difficult stage of life, and the latter see it as a major change, often requiring treatment. As we stated earlier, both approaches reflect bias. How then can we figure out what is really happening to women and how much physiological and sociocultural factors influence women's experience of menopause?

One way to tease out the sociocultural from the physiological is to look at cross-cultural studies. Nancy Datan worked in Israel studying five subcultures, which she arrayed on a continuum of modernization, from traditional Arab women at one end to European-born Israeli women at the other, with Jews from Turkey, Persia, and North Africa in the middle.[74] The relationship she found between social change and difficulty during the menopause was not linear. The transitional women, midway between traditional life-styles and modernization, suffered most. They had lost the privileges afforded traditional women, while not receiving those benefits that modernization confers upon women. They had the problems of both groups but the advantages of neither. Marcha Flint studied Indian women of the Rajput caste and found that they did not have menopausal symptoms. She suggested that menopause for these women may have been easy because of the increase in social status and freedom they experienced at that time.[75]

Two researchers used the Human Relations Area Files and ethnographic monographs to study menopause. Joyce Griffen[76] found the literature limited, but she did note that no behavior change took place for postmenopausal women in eight cultures, it was seen as a disorder or a cause for withdrawal from previous social activities in five cultures, women gained freedom in the postmenopausal years in ten cultures, and an increase in social and perhaps supernatural power occurred in seven other cultures. Pauline Bart[77] found that certain structural arrangements and cultural values were associated with women's changed status after the childbearing years. These are summarized below.

CHARACTERISTICS OF SOCIETIES IN WHICH WOMEN'S STATUS CHANGES AT MENOPAUSE

STATUS RISES	STATUS DECLINES
Strong tie to family of origin and relatives	Marital tie stronger than tie to family of origin
Extended family system	Nuclear family system
Reproduction important	Sex an end in itself
Strong mother-child relationship; reciprocal in later life	Weak maternal bond; adult-oriented culture
Institutionalized grandmother role	Noninstitutionalized grandmother role; grandmother role not important
Institutionalized mother-in-law role	Noninstitutionalized mother-in-law role; mother-in-law does not train daughter-in-law
Extensive menstrual taboos	Minimal menstrual taboos
Age valued over youth	Youth valued over age

An increase in status probably would increase the likelihood of feelings of well-being, so even if physiological stresses are experienced at this time, they are well buffered. This appears to be the case in kinship-dominated societies. When this system begins to break down, as it is now doing in some Third World countries, problems arise similar to those faced by some women in our culture. For example, one (Asian) Indian mother who brought up her children to live in the modern manner, that is, independently, felt lonely and commented, "I sometimes feel, 'What is the use of my living now that I am no longer useful to them [her children]!' "[78]

In our society, it is easy to see why some women find middle age stressful. Except for the mother-child bond, which in our society is strong but *non*reciprocal, we fall on the right-hand side of the table, with the cultures in which women's status drops in middle age. It is true that for women whose lives have not been child centered and whose strong marital tie continues, or for those whose children have set up their own residence near the mother, the transition to middle age may be buffered. However, for women who have emphasized the maternal role or the glamour role, middle age may be a difficult stage in the life cycle. Our emphasis on youth (particularly for women) and the stipulation that mothers-in-law should not interfere can make middle age stressful for many women who have not had the opportunity to invest themselves in anything beside wife and mother roles. By examining the question in a cross-cultural perspective, however, we can observe the multiplicity of possible roles for middle-aged women and appreciate the fact that middle age need not be a difficult time. Indeed, it can and should offer women its own unique rewards.

Although the cross-cultural evidence strongly suggests that the phenomenon of menopausal depression is not related to physiological changes but rather to social factors and cultural structures, a study of individual depressed menopausal women in our society could shed a great deal of light on how these factors operate in American culture. One of us[79] studied such women, using the hospital records of over 500 women between the ages of forty and fifty-nine who had had no previous hospitalization for mental illness. These records were drawn from five mental hospitals, ranging from an upper-class private institution to two state hospitals. The records were used to compare all of the women diagnosed as depressed with those women who had received other diagnoses. Twenty intensive interviews were also conducted to flesh out the picture obtained from the records.

Statistical analysis of the hospital records indicated that depression was associated with current role loss and even with the prospect of loss. Housewives were particularly vulnerable to the effects of losing other roles, such as those of wife or mother. Ethnicity is another relevant variable, with Jewish women having the highest rate of depression. When all women having overinvolved or overprotective relationships with their children are compared with women who do not, however, the ethnic differences almost wash out. Thus you do not have to be Jewish to be a Jewish mother, but it helps a little. Overall, the highest rate of depression was found among housewives who had overprotective or overinvolved relationships with their children who were currently or soon leaving home. Thus the lack of meaningful roles and the consequent loss of self-esteem, rather than any hormonal changes, seemed largely to account for the incidence of menopausal depression.

This hypothesis received further support from the results of the interviews. All women with children, when asked what they were most proud of, replied, "My children." None mentioned any accomplishment of their own, except being a good mother. When they were asked to rank seven roles available to middle-aged women in order of importance, the mother role ("helping my children") was most frequently ranked first or second. When children leave home, however, the woman suffers a consequent loss of self-esteem, because she is frustrated in attempting to carry out this role she values so highly. To the extent that a woman "buys" our society's traditional norms and seeks vicarious achievement and identity she is vulnerable when her children leave. Moreover, many of these women then experience their life situation as unjust and meaningless, because the implicit bargain they had struck with fate did not pay off. In the words of one of the women,

I'm glad that God gave me . . . the privilege of being a mother . . . and I loved them [my children]. In fact, I wrapped my love so much around them. . . . I'm grateful to my husband since if it wasn't for him, there wouldn't be the children. They were my whole life. . . . My whole life was that because I had no life with my husband, the children should make me happy . . . but it never worked out.[80]

Statements such as this poignantly portray middle age as a time when reality overtakes women's dreams for the future, when some women are confronted with the meaninglessness of their lives. Women have been taught to believe that they can achieve "true happiness" through self-abnegation and sacrifice for their husbands and their children, that to do anything for themselves is selfish. Some women are able to evade or overcome this script. Some continue to receive the vicarious gratification for which this life-style prepared them—their husbands are still alive, well, and attentive, their children have made "proper" marriages and/or embarked upon "proper" careers, grandchildren have arrived, and significant others congratulate them on a job well done. Other women are bewildered by their children's life-style, which rejects the values the mothers have worked so hard to attain, indeed not so much for themselves but for those very children. They cannot understand why their daughters do not want to have the children they were taught were their destiny and why they are denied the grandchildren they so joyfully anticipated and whom they expected to give new meaning to their lives. Their husbands may have left them for younger women to bolster their own waning egos and diminished potencies (on average, the second wife is younger than the current age of the first wife).[81] For these women, to seek a younger mate would be considered ludicrous, since they are no longer considered sexual (although of course physiologically, unlike men, they are as capable of sex as they ever were).[82] Because so many of these events coincide with menopause, their effects are attributed to this physiological change.

Alice Rossi, analyzing recent census data, noted that maternity has become a very small part of an adult woman's life: a woman who marries at twenty-two, has two children two years apart, and dies at seventy-four will spend one-quarter of her adult life without a husband, two-fifths with a husband but no children under eighteen, one-third with her spouse and at least one child under eighteen—but only one-eighth of her life in full-time maternal care of preschool-age children.[83] This projection dramatizes how poor the standard script is. It is important that women be given this message, and early, so that they will not become casualties of the culture in middle age.

CONCLUSION

As feminists, we believe that societal problems cannot be dealt with only on an individual basis. Although some women may slip through by chance or special privilege, the economic situation of many women at midlife does not allow them the freedom to make many life choices (Elizabeth Kutza reported that among women aged forty-five to sixty-five, about one out of twenty white married women, one out of two black married women, one out of four white single women, and one out of two black single women live in poverty).[84] What is necessary for the situation of most women to improve is sweeping social change.

For now, the only changes we can count on are those that can be brought about by the organized efforts of many women working together to confront the system and to structure alternatives for themselves and others. The research, books with feminist analyses of menopause, and opposition to the medical practices we have discussed are important steps in this process.

Older Women's Liberation (OWL) and the task force on older women of the National Organization for Women are examples of organizations offering support for women in their middle years.

Rap groups for middle-aged women are increasing both here and in other countries. These groups help midlife women break through the isolation they often experience by offering a place for women to share their experiences. As a result, women learn about menopause, share remedies for problems, and together confront some of the destructive myths about aging and menopause so prevalent in our society.[85]

We must expand these types of support systems if we are ever to accomplish the broader social change we seek.

NOTES

1. Edmund R. Novak, Georgeanna Seegar Jones, and Howard W. Jones, *Textbook of Gynecology,* 9th ed. (Baltimore: Waverly Press, 1975).

2. Ann Douglas Wood, " 'The Fashionable Diseases': Women's Complaints and Their Treatment in Nineteenth-Century America," *Journal of Interdisciplinary History* 4, no. 1 (Summer 1973): 25-52.

3. Diane Scully and Pauline Bart, "A Funny Thing Happened on the Way to the Orifice: Women in Gynecology Textbooks," *American Journal of Sociology* 78 (1973): pp. 1045-50.

4. Carol Smith-Rosenberg and Charles Rosenberg, "The Female Animal: Medical and Biological Views of Woman and Her Role in Nineteenth-Century America," *Journal of American History* 60 (1973): 332-56.

5. Edward Tilt, *The Change of Life in Health and Disease,* 4th ed. (Philadelphia: P. Blakiston, Son, and Company, 1882), p. 19.

6. John Merson, "The Climacteric Period in Relation to Insanity," *West Riding Lunatic Asylum Reports*, vol. 6 (London, 1876), p. 85.

7. Peter Stearns, "Interpreting the Medical Literature on Aging," *Newberry Library Family and Community History Colloquia: The Physician and Social History*, October 30, 1975.

8. George Savage, "The Mental Diseases of the Climacterium," *Lancet*, October 31, 1903, pp. 1209-13; Frances Skae, "Climacteric Insanity," *Edinburgh Medical Journal* 10, no. 8 (1865): 703-16.

9. J. H. Kellogg, *Plain Facts for Old and Young Embracing the Natural History and Hygiene of Organic Life* (Burlington, Ia.: I. F. Segner, 1886); George Frink, "The Menopause," *International Clinics*, 9th series, 1 (April 1899): 247-55.

10. M. C. M'Gannon, "The Menopause," *Transactions of the Tennessee State Medical Association* (1902), pp. 85-107.

11. Edward Tilt, *The Change of Life in Health and Disease*, 3rd ed. (London: John Churchill and Sons, 1870).

12. Frink, "The Menopause"; Gustavus Eliot, "The Disorders of the Nervous System Associated with the Change of Life," *American Journal of the Medical Sciences* 106 (1893): 292-97.

13. Gustavus Eliot, "The Disorders of the Nervous System"; Merson, "The Climacteric Period"; Skae, "Climacteric Insanity"; Savage, "The Mental Diseases"; Henry Sutherland, "Menstrual Irregularities and Insanity," *West Riding Lunatic Asylum Medical Reports* 2 (1872): 53-92.

14. This ad is quoted in the Boston Women's Health Book Collective, *Our Bodies, Ourselves* (New York: Simon and Schuster, 1976), p. 327. Emphasis added.

15. Howard W. Jones, Jr., E. J. Cohen, and Robert B. Wilson, "Clinical Aspects of the Menopause," in *Menopause and Aging*, ed. John K. Ryan and D. G. Gibson (Washington, D.C.: U.S. Government Printing Office, 1971), p. 3.

16. K. A. Achté, "Menopause from the Psychiatrist's Point of View," *Acta Obstetrica and Gynecologica* 1 (Supplement, 1970): 13.

17. Mary Brown Parlee, "Psychological Aspects of the Climacteric in Women" (Paper presented to the Eastern Psychological Association, New York, April 1976).

18. Morton Mintz, *The Pill: An Alarming Report* (New York: Fawcett, 1969).

19. Robert Wilson, *Feminine Forever* (New York: M. Evans, 1966).

20. Robert Wilson, "A Key to Staying Young," *Look*, January 1966.

21. Robert Wilson and Thelma Wilson, "The Fate of the Nontreated Post-Menopausal Woman: A Plea for the Maintenance of Adequate

Estrogen from Puberty to the Grave," *Journal of the American Geriatrics Society* 11 (1963): 355.

22. Helene Deutsch, *The Psychology of Women,* vol. 2 (New York: Bantam Books, 1973), p. 479.

23. Ibid., p. 481.

24. Miguel Prados, "Emotional Factors in the Climacterium of Women," *Psychotherapy and Psychosomatics* 15 (1967): 237-38.

25. Boston Women's Health Book Collective, *Our Bodies, Ourselves;* Sheldon Cherry, *The Menopause Myth* (New York: Ballantine Books, 1976); Vidal Clay, *Women: Menopause and Middle Age* (Pittsburgh: Know, 1977); Jane Delaney, Mary Jane Lupton, and Emily Toth, *The Curse: A Cultural History of Menstruation* (New York: Mentor Books, 1976); Jane Page, *The Other Awkward Age: Menopause* (Berkeley, Calif.: Ten Speed Press, 1977); Paula Weideger, *Menstruation and Menopause* New York: Alfred A. Knopf, 1976).

26. Barbara Seaman and Gideon Seaman, *Women and the Crisis in Sex Hormones* (New York: Bantam Books, 1978).

27. Rosetta Reitz, *Menopause: A Positive Approach* (Radnor, Pa.: Chilton Book Company, 1977).

28. Sonja McKinlay and John McKinlay, "The Menopausal Syndrome," *British Journal of Preventive and Social Medicine* 28, no. 2 (1974): 108-15.

29. Parlee, "Psychological Aspects."

30. Pauline B. Bart, "Mother Portnoy's Complaints," *Trans-Action* 8, no. 1-2 (1970): 69-74.

31. Leonore Levit, "Anxiety and the Menopause: A Study of Normal Women" (Ph.D. diss., University of Chicago, 1963).

32. Leslie Marilyn Meltzer, "The Aging Female: A Study of Attitudes toward Aging and Self-Concept Held by Pre-Menopausal, Menopausal, and Post-Menopausal Women" (Ph.D. diss., Adelphi University, 1974).

33. Interdisciplinary Research Conference on Menopause (Third Annual Menstrual Cycle Conference), University of Arizona, Tucson, Arizona, April 26-27, 1979.

34. Carlos M. F. Antunes et al., "Endometrial Cancer and Estrogen Use," *New England Journal of Medicine* 300, no. 1 (January 4, 1979): 9-13; Thomas M. Mack et al., "Estrogens and Endometrial Cancer in a Retirement Community," *New England Journal of Medicine* 294, no. 23 (June 3, 1976): 1262-67; Donald Smith, Ross Prentice, Donovan Thompson, and Walter Herrmann, "Association of Exogenous Estrogen and Endometrial Carcinoma," *New England Journal of Medicine* 293, no. 23 (December 4, 1975): 1164-67; Harry Ziel and William Finkle,

"Increased Risk of Endometrial Carcinoma among Users of Conjugated Estrogens," *New England Journal of Medicine* 293, no. 23 (December 4, 1975): 1167-70.

35. G. C. W. George, W. H. Utian, P. J. V. Beumont, and C. J. Beardwood, "Effect of Exogenous Oestrogens on Minor Psychiatric Symptoms in Postmenopausal Women," *S. A. Medical Journal,* December 15, 1973, pp. 2387-88; Melinda Schneider, Patricia Brotherton, and Jean Hailes, "The Effect of Exogenous Oestrogens in Depression in Menopausal Women," *Medical Journal of Australia,* July 30, 1977, pp. 162-63; Joan Thomson, "Double Blind Study on the Effect of Oestrogen on Sleep, Anxiety, and Depression in Peri-Menopausal Women: Preliminary Results," *Proceedings of the Royal Society of Medicine* 69 (1976): 17-18.

36. Howard J. Osofsky and Robert Seidenberg, "Is Female Menopausal Depression Inevitable?" *American Journal of Obstetrics and Gynecology* 36, no. 4 (1970): 613.

37. Mary Anna Friederich, "Psychophysiology of Menstruation and the Menopause," in *Gynecology and Obstetrics: The Health Care of Women,* ed. Seymour L. Romney et al. (New York: McGraw-Hill Book Company, 1975), pp. 605-17; Georgeanna Seegar Jones and Anne Colston Wentz, "Adolescence, Menstruation, and the Climacteric," in *Obstetrics and Gynecology,* 3rd ed., ed. David Danforth (New York: Harper and Row, 1977), pp. 163-86; Edmund R. Novak, G. S. Jones, and H. W. Jones, *Textbook of Gynecology.*

38. D. A. Davey, "The Menopause and Postmenopause," in *Integrated Obstetrics and Gynaecology for Postgraduates,* 2nd ed., ed. C. J. Dewhurst (London: Blackwell Scientific Publications, 1976), pp. 635-49; Langdon Parsons and Sheldon C. Sommers, *Gynecology* (Philadelphia: W. B. Saunders Company, 1978).

39. Parsons and Sommers, *Gynecology.*

40. Sherwin A. Kaufman, "The Menopause," in *Gynecology and Obstetrics,* ed. John J. Sciarra (New York: Harper and Row, 1979).

41. Frink, "The Menopause"; Skae, "Climacteric Insanity."

42. Kellogg, *Plain Facts;* Skae, "Climacteric Insanity."

43. Tilt, *The Change of Life* (1882).

44. Seaman and Seaman, *Women and the Crisis.*

45. S. B. Gusberg, "Precursors of Corpus Carcinoma Estrogens and Adenomatous Hyperplasia," *American Journal of Obstetrics and Gynecology* 54, no. 6 (1947): 905-27.

46. W. V. Gardner, "Carcinoma of the Uterine Cervix and Upper Vagina: Induction under Experimental Conditions in Mice," *Annals of the New York Academy of Sciences* 75 (1959): 543-64.

47. Antunes et al., "Endometrial Cancer"; Mack et al., "Estrogens and Endometrial Cancer"; Smith, Prentice, Thompson, and Hermann, "Association of Exogenous Estrogen"; Ziel and Finkle, "Increased Risk."
48. Antunes et al., "Endometrial Cancer"; Mack et al., "Estrogens and Endometrial Cancer."
49. Antunes et al., "Endometrial Cancer"; Ziel and Finkle, "Increased Risk."
50. Robert Hoover, Laman A. Gray, Philip Cole, and Brian MacMahan, "Menopausal Estrogen and Breast Cancer," *New England Journal of Medicine* 295, no. 8 (1976): 501-05.
51. Sharon Lieberman, "But You'll Make Such a Feminine Corpse...," *Majority Report,* February 19-March 4, 1977, pp. 3-4.
52. "New Discovery: Public Relations Cures Cancer," *Majority Report,* February 8-18, 1977, pp. 9-10.
53. John McKinlay, personal communication (June 10, 1977).
54. *National Disease and Therapeutic Index* (Ambler, Pa.: IMS America, Ltd., 1975).
55. "ACOG Warns against Removal of Estrogen," *ACOG Newsletter,* October 1976.
56. Antunes et al., "Endometrial Cancer."
57. Joseph Parrish, "The Change of Life in Women," *New Jersey Medical Reporter* 7 (1854): 13.
58. L. H. Edmunds, "Change of Thinking about the Problems of the Menopause," *London Daily Telegraph,* February 28, 1977.
59. *F-D-C Reports,* September 5, 1977, pp. 10-12. Emphasis added.
60. Boston Women's Health Book Collective, *Our Bodies, Ourselves;* L. Jaszmann, N. D. van Lith, and J. C. A. Zaat, "The Peri-Menopausal Symptoms: The Statistical Analysis of a Survey," *Medical Gynaecology and Sociology* 4 (1969): 268-77; Sonja McKinlay and Margot Jefferys, "The Menopausal Syndrome," *British Journal of Preventive and Social Medicine* 28 (1974): 108-15; Page, *The Other Awkward Age;* Lisbeth Severne, "Psycho-Social Aspects of the Menopause" (Paper presented to the Interdisciplinary Research Conference on Menopause, Tucson, Arizona, April 26-27, 1979); Barbara Thompson, Shirley Hart, and D. Durno, "Menopausal Age and Symptomatology in a General Practice," *Journal of Biosocial Science* 5 (1973): 71-82; Pieter A. van Keep and Jean M. Kellerhals, "The Impact of Socio-Cultural Factors on Symptom Formation," *Psychotherapy and Psychosomatics* 23 (1974): 251-63.
61. Madeleine Goodman, Cynthia Stewart, and Fred Gilbert, "Patterns of Menopause," *Journal of Gerontology* 32, no. 3 (1977): 291-98.
62. McKinlay and Jefferys, "The Menopausal Syndrome."

63. Jaszmann, van Lith, and Zaat, "The Post-Menopausal Symptoms";
Thompson, Hart, and Durno, "Menopausal Age."

64. We would like to thank the Boston Women's Health Book Collective and Women in Midstream for generously sharing their data with us. For reports on their studies, see Boston Women's Health Book Collective, *Our Bodies, Ourselves,* and Page, *The Other Awkward Age.*

65. Reitz, *Menopause;* Seaman and Seaman, *Woman and the Crisis.*

66. Weideger, *Menstruation and Menopause.*

67. Boston Women's Health Book Collective, *Our Bodies, Ourselves* (New York: Simon and Schuster, 1973).

68. Bernice L. Neugarten, Vivian Wood, Ruth Kraines, and Barbara Loomis, "Women's Attitudes toward the Menopause," *Vita Humana* 6 (1963): 140-51.

69. Bernice L. Neugarten, "A New Look at Menopause," *Psychology Today* 1 (December 1967): 43-45, 67-69.

70. The term comes from the Chinese revolutionary groups that gathered to talk about the "bad old days" to purge themselves of the feudal mentality so that they could create a new society. Women's consciousness-raising groups function similarly to help women free themselves from their constricting role socialization.

71. Levit, "Anxiety and the Menopause."

72. Severne, "Psycho-Social Aspects."

73. Ruth Kraines, "The Menopause and Evaluations of the Self: A Study of Middle-Aged Women" (Ph.D. diss., University of Chicago, 1963).

74. Nancy Datan, "To Be a Woman in Israel," *School Review* 80 (1972): 319-32.

75. Marcha Flint, "The Menopause: Reward or Punishment?", *Psychosomatics* 16, no. 4 (1975): 161-63.

76. Joyce Griffen, "A Cross-Cultural Investigation of Behavioral Changes at Menopause," *Social Science Journal* 14, no. 2 (April 1977): 49-55.

77. Pauline B. Bart, "Why Women's Status Changes in Middle Age," *Sociological Symposium* 3 (1969): 1-18.

78. Ibid., p. 11.

79. Pauline B. Bart, "Depression in Middle-Aged Women: Some Sociocultural Factors" (Ph.D. diss., University of California at Los Angeles, 1967); Bart, "Mother Portnoy's Complaints"; Bart, "Depression in Middle-Aged Women," in *Women in Sexist Society: Studies in Power and Powerlessness,* ed. Vivian Gornick and B. K. Moran (New York: Basic Books, 1971).

80. Quoted in Bart, "Depression in Middle-Aged Women," p. 99.

81. Inge P. Bell, "The Double Standard," *Trans-Action* 8, no. 1-2 (1970): 76-81.

82. Zoe Moss, "It Hurts to Be Alive and Obsolete: The Aging Woman," in *Sisterhood Is Powerful,* ed. Robin Morgan (New York: Vintage, 1970).

83. Alice Rossi, "Family Development in a Changing World," *American Journal of Psychiatry* 128 (1972): 1057-80.

84. Elizabeth Kutza, "Passed Over by Progress: Women at the Bottom," in *Women in Midlife–Security and Fulfillment,* ed. Ann Foote Cahn (Washington, D.C.: U.S. Government Printing Office, 1978).

85. For instance, Holland has menopause rap groups. Since few Dutch married women work outside their home, the automatic problems of transition are exacerbated by the lack of alternative sources of self-esteem. Although the women originally join the groups to discuss problems around menopause per se, broader life-style and life cycle issues emerge. Although the group members feel that Dutch society does not offer them many options for changing the realities of their lives, the existence of these rap groups (as well as those in other countries) is bound to make the physical and social experience of menopause more positive for more women.

10.

The Lost Cause: The Aging Woman in American Feminism

NANCY DATAN

Today's aging woman is caught at a crossroad in social consciousness.
She is at the intersection of two movements of major social importance:
the feminist movement and the "aging movement"—the increasing political activity of our aging population. Yet she does not belong to either of
these two movements.

The women's movement has a young constituency, and its concerns
are those of young women. The politically active aging groups are concerned with the elemental issues of the survival of the old. Today's aging
woman looks forward to greater freedom, better health, a longer life—
and does not yet know how to make the best use of this potential.
Neither the women's movement nor the "aging movement" addresses the
questions that are central to the life of the aging woman. Nevertheless,
the current activities of these two movements suggest a convergence that
will bring about a better future for tomorrow's aging woman.

Sexism and ageism are two disorders that have only recently been
diagnosed and have still more recently begun to receive treatment.

Sexism describes the tendency to devalue women, and it is far from cured: the United States granted women a political voice hardly more than half a century ago; Switzerland has only conceded the right to women within this decade. Numerous examples of other forms of discrimination against women, all based on their capacity to become pregnant and give birth, can easily be identified.

Our steadily growing control over our reproductive biology has meant that pregnancy and motherhood have become women's choice—not their fate. With the diminished tyranny of the reproductive cycle have come increased personal independence and an increased awareness of choice. This awareness has brought with it some questions about the value and viability of traditional women's roles. These questions, in turn, have led to the women's movement, which seeks to expand choices for women beyond the traditional roles of wife and mother.

A *sexist* is a person who refuses to consider women eligible for anything other than traditional roles. I cannot endorse this position, but I can be sympathetic to it. I have often come home after work and wished that a "wife" would greet me with love, patience, understanding, and a warm dinner. So it does not surprise me at all that men, who unlike myself can indeed hope to find wives who will look after them, might resist any social change that would make such women less available. Moreover, men today may be at a disadvantage in seeking jobs, for in an effort to correct the injustices of the past, present affirmative action programs favor the equally qualified woman applicant. Finally, this disadvantage is biological as well as historical: no program for political and social equality will ever make it possible for a man to quit his job to stay home and be pregnant.

Thus feminist movements are expanding the horizons of women at what men perceive as their immediate expense. However, men also have something to gain: a dual-career family can earn twice as much money; less tangibly but more importantly, women are becoming partners and comrades, rather than a fragile subspecies set apart for the protection and support that men have had to provide in the past. Nevertheless, although men gain something, women gain more, and sometimes a woman's gain is a man's loss. Sexism, then, may be more than simply stubborn resistance to change; it may reflect, in part, a man's realistic assessment of his gains and losses, in turn a reflection of a genuine potential conflict of interest between the sexes.

Ageism, like sexism, is the categorical disqualification of a group of people on biological grounds. Like sexism, ageism has gained attention as a consequence of a constellation of medical, economic, social, and historical changes. More people are now living longer, and thus age-based discrimination is affecting increasing numbers of people. With present trends in the population, this proportion can be expected to increase further. Therefore, a certain parallel exists between ageism and sexism.

However, the parallel soon ends: the old have not met discrimination until recently, since as a group they have not been sufficiently numerous to evoke categorical restrictions. Women, on the other hand, have always made up half of humanity, and nearly all human societies have imposed some measure of social differentiation, in addition to the sex-based differentiation in the reproductive process, to the disadvantage of women.

A second fundamental difference between ageism and sexism is that old age—we hope—is for everyone. But only half of us are women. It is possible to conceive of a conflict of interests between the sexes that does not admit of resolution. It is less easy to see a conflict of interests that might lead to discrimination against old age—and thus against one's own future. Indeed, the successful political activity of the aged is based, it seems, on this awareness. By contrast, the women's movement cannot count on the support that might come from a unified identification among women. Thus despite its potential numerical strength—over half of the population—it has had less success.

Consider some of the political impact the aging population is currently enjoying. The Gray Panthers, a group that takes its name from the Black Panthers, who are militant advocates for minority rights, are a highly visible and militant organization seeking, in large part, to raise the consciousness of the population as a whole to the needs of the aging minority. A more moderate but no less effective group is the large American Association of Retired Persons (AARP). The newly elected president of the AARP described her induction as president—and the power of this organization: "And the governor of West Virginia was there, boys and girls, and he gave me a big kiss. And do you think he kissed me because he likes old ladies? Oh, no, boys and girls, he kissed me because he thought it might get him six million votes."

In the United States, voting activity is heavily skewed in the direction of the elderly: 90 percent of the old vote, a higher proportion than for any other age group. Thus although they are a minority, the old are far

from powerless. They are actively involved in shaping government response to issues that affect them, such as social security and Medicare.
As their numbers grow, we can expect to see their influence grow as well.

The converse is true of the women's movement. Women are a numerical majority in the United States, but they do not have the political unity
that the aged, as a group, enjoy. Feminist groups such as the National
Organization for Women have not yet been able even to marshall sufficient strength to turn the Equal Rights Amendment into law. Women
politicians are scarce. Former President Carter claimed that it was difficult to find capable women for his cabinet (to which Juanita Kreps, when
she was secretary of commerce, replied that he evidently was not looking
very hard). When Shirley Chisholm declared her candidacy in the 1972
election campaign for president, the national response was to ask whether
the country was ready for a woman president. The answer, obviously, was
negative. But if women had voted as a bloc in support of their own sex,
the answer would have been positive. Clearly, no consensus on women's
issues is in any way comparable to the consensus on issues that affect our
aging population.

On the other hand, the women's movement has made inroads into
American social consciousness. On issues such as abortion, affirmative
action employment programs, tax relief for the child care expenses of
working mothers, and day care centers for young children, a general
pattern of response reflects the increasing awareness of women's right to
self-determination—independent of their roles as wives and mothers.

One of the less happy paradoxes of our time is that the women's movement, which, like preceding women's movements, has had a history of
sensitivity to oppression of all sorts, is surprisingly insensitive to one of
the most oppressed groups in American culture today: the aging woman.
Although the aging woman stands to gain from the general goals of the
"aging movement," these gains are not directed to the particular needs
of today's older woman, who looks forward to increased good health,
a longer life, and inadequate personal and economic resources for the
years ahead. The aging woman, therefore, is at a double disadvantage,
facing the narrowing horizons of old age, compounded by the traditional discrimination against her sex.

The aging woman is located at the intersection of two political waves,
without belonging to either. The special concerns of the aging woman
are no different from the general goals of the women's movement:

women of all ages are increasingly seeking their own personal fulfillment through roles other than the traditional ones of wife and mother.
These goals have particular potential importance for the aging woman,
since in the normal course of her life cycle, she can expect the role of
mother to diminish sharply as her children leave home, while she is still
in middle age. Moreover, she is likely to lose the role of wife, since it is
probable that her husband will predecease her.

The primary thrust of the women's movement, however, is directed
at the early portion of the adult life cycle, at the time when choices are
made concerning career and family or the timing of children. The constituency of the women's movement is young. Abortion, affirmative
action, and day care are the concerns of young women. The women's
movement has not, I believe, intentionally neglected the older woman.
Rather, the movement simply fails to represent her, because she is not
represented in the constituency of the movement.

The special needs of women go unrecognized in the general political
activity of the aged for different reasons. The concern of the American
aging population is a more elemental and primitive concern: survival in
an increasingly harsh economy on the fixed incomes of pensions, savings,
or social security. The old—women and men—are threatened by poverty,
with its brutal consequences of hunger, untreated sickness, and inadequate
shelter. The winter of 1977 left behind many frightening memories;
among the worst was the story of an old woman who froze to death when
the utility company closed her account because she was unable to pay
her bills. Stories such as these are a disgrace to American society. The
American economy—even when Americans believe it is less than strong—
is an economy of affluence, and provision for its old people, who have
contributed a lifetime of productivity, should be among its primary concerns. Indeed, economic security is the priority concern in the political
activities of our aging population—and it will undoubtedly remain so
until economic survival can be taken for granted by the old.

The aging woman then is caught at a painful crossroad of consciousness. Behind her are the decisions currently being debated in the women's
movement: marriage, children, career. Ahead of her are the consequences
of her own past decisions—which are likely to have been marriage, to a
man older than herself, and children, at the expense of a career. The consequences of these decisions are likely to be a combination of social and
economic poverty.

If her childbearing history is typical, today's aging woman will have borne one or two children in her early twenties and will have been out of a job as a mother by the time she reached forty. Before very long, she will have been out of a job as a wife as well. Marriages today have a high probability of ending in divorce. If her marriage did survive, her husband most likely did not, and she has had to anticipate a decade or more of widowhood. In every decade since the fifties, women have outnumbered men in the general population, and the proportion of unmarried women to unmarried men has been still more uneven. The differential in life expectancy has been compounded by the persistent expectation that women should marry men older than themselves—an outdated expectation reflecting the economic dependency of women, a dependency that is the target of action by the women's movement.

Thus the aging woman is particularly vulnerable to the economic privation that is the target of the political activities of the aged, and she is also vulnerable to a social isolation that may come about as a consequence of earlier life decisions made on the basis of traditional role expectations. In addition, she is "cursed" with good health and a lengthening life expectancy. She has more years to look forward to and less to do with her time than ever before. She is very much in need of the economic advantages the "aging movement" seeks to insure, but she is no less in need of room for the personal growth that is one of the goals of the women's movement.

I have been suggesting that aging women today are caught at a historical and political crossroad, suffering a double disadvantage: the narrowing horizons of old age compounded by the traditional discriminations faced by women. This double discrimination is rendered more poignant because the potential of the aging woman—in health and longevity—is greater than that of the aging man. However, this double injustice is likely to have a short future. As we have seen, social injustices to women and to the aging seem to have found expression in movements that are not only the mirrors but also the instruments of social change. The pessimistic present will likely soon give way to an optimistic future.

My optimism is not a simple, naive belief that justice triumphs. On the contrary: my optimistic perspective on the future is entirely Machiavellian. The basis of this optimism is threefold: first, the aging woman of tomorrow is the feminist of today. Thus she brings to her maturity and old age her political self-awareness, a personal self-confidence, and the professional resources and career experience that are lacking for so many of today's aging women. Although the feminist movement has had little direct effect on the life of the aging woman, it has had a measure of sensitivity— and it is growing—to the unmet obligations of feminists to their "older sisters."

The second source of my optimism is the educational effect of the current political activity of the aged. Like the political activity of feminists, this is a movement that is not only growing in force but is creating new growth. That is, the political activities of the aged affect not only social policy but also our social consciousness. Tomorrow's aging woman will have grown up in and will be growing into a climate of political activity. Unlike the traditional woman of yesterday, who could do no more than hope that society would not ignore her needs, the aging woman of tomorrow increasingly will be able to shape society to her needs.

The final source of my Machiavellian optimism is the simplest: the unused potential of women today—their numbers, their health, their longevity—is a remarkable latent force. When these latent sources of power are activated by the growing political consciousness of women, they will no longer be a social burden but a social force. All political movements have taught their members to make their own destiny; before long, aging women will be claiming their rights too and creating for themselves a new and better future.

PART III
Women Facing the Future: Political and Social Developments

11.

Education, Girls, and Power

MARY ELLEN VERHEYDEN-HILLIARD

> The underlying notion that if a male finds the female
> worthy, she need not worry about her future has not
> changed. It is the one belief, carefully nurtured in
> secondary schools as the hidden agenda, which kills
> the potential of American girls.

Forty-eight percent of all of the families living in poverty in the United
States are headed by women. The divorce rate is up 127 percent since
1962 and continues to rise. "Women's work"—homemaking, teaching,
secretarial duties, nursing—is given one value on the lip-service scale with
regard to honor and worth and another value on the economic scale. On
the economic scale, women make fifty-nine cents for every dollar men
make, when their work is given any economic value at all.

Despite these and similar facts presented in the newspapers and on television news with monotonous regularity, the educational system continues to socialize young girls to prepare themselves to become wives and mothers, to expect to be "taken care of" financially by a husband, and to train themselves in overwhelming numbers for those careers in the female job ghettos. Why should this continue to be so?

Title IX of the federal Education Amendments of 1972 mandated only that girls and women in our democracy be treated with equal consideration in educational institutions receiving federal financial assistance— provided by the tax dollars of both men and women. This civil rights law met with much resistance. In general, American schools did not rise up en masse to speak of democracy and equal opportunity for both sexes. Initially, most school administrators ignored the law or rose to speak of the need to keep girls and women out of athletics, which can lead to strong bodies and scholarships; out of father and son banquets, where rites of male bonding are in progress; out of male choirs, with the "perks" of recognition and travel; or out of the male-intensive vocational education courses, which can lead to better paying jobs. Often this overt resistance was accompanied, ironically, by a statement that Title IX was not needed, since sex discrimination did not exist anyway.

Why should this have happened? Perhaps because it is only with great effort that many educational policy makers are able to see girls in the same way they see boys as potential adult human beings. This limited vision is not necessarily malicious. The policy makers have been socialized too. For example, even among the programs for the disadvantaged, the target population is usually "youth," which most often effectively translates into "boys." Girls get into the assistance picture only when they become teen-aged pregnancy statistics. Programs for minority "youth" often wear the same blinders—yet unemployment is higher for teen-aged minority women than for any other category in the nation.

Could it be that American public schools, through subtle but nonetheless pervasive messages, train the female half of the school population to choose a less potent education and thereby a secondary and serving role in society? It seems that, on anyone's block, regardless of the number of families in which both adults work outside the home or which are headed by women, teachers, counselors, and administrators are loath to encourage girls to understand this reality. Suggesting that girls should plan for independent, ongoing careers with a ladder to the top is almost taboo. Rather, career preparation for girls is approached as giving them "something to fall back on" if the prince does not appear or, having appeared, departs early. Cinderella is a completely dependent creature who never takes charge of her own life.

Clearly, the educational system actively trains girls for a secondary role. The driving, dynamic, boisterous, creative, intellectual, even arrogant schoolgirl is not the one who is supported and encouraged. Most often, teachers, counselors, and parents worry about such a girl. They try to tone her down and make her conform to a more "feminine" ideal. The driving, dynamic, athletic, creative, intellectual, even arrogant boy is more likely to be singled out by adults and recognized for the potential he is demonstrating. Compared to a girl exhibiting similar behavior, he is more likely to be guided to reach for his star. The girl is taught to reach for the boy.

Although the American dream asserts that everyone can go as far as and as high as his or her capabilities allow, the school system supports a different dream for girls. A girl's worth in high school is evaluated not so much on the basis of whom *she* is and what *she* accomplishes as on the degree to which popular, talented, clever, and athletic *boys* anoint her with attention. Many educators call this "peer pressure" and shrug their shoulders helplessly in the face of a problem "beyond their influence." Not so!

High school girls and boys do not independently and outside the school structure provide the mechanism for popularity contests resulting in crowned beauty queens. High school girls and boys do not provide the mechanism offering years of athletic training for boys and nothing but cheerleading tryouts for girls. High school girls and boys do not provide the mechanism for deciding that valedictorians should be boys and salutatorians should be girls. Teen peer pressure does not determine what the research has revealed: that counselors believe girls who want to be engineers *should* be considered "deviant," and those who want to be home economics majors *should* be considered "normal."

A powerful socialization factor underlies school activities. If a girl is not an athlete, not an academic success, not a creative person—it matters scarcely at all as long as boys with those qualities seek her out and by their attention convey that she is "all right." On the other hand, if a girl is a super athlete, brilliant, or creative, but not popular with the boys, her family and many adults in her school will worry about her future.

Perhaps in the past few years some of these notions have changed.

A little. In some places. However, the underlying notion that if a male finds a female worthy that she need not worry about her future has not changed. It is the one belief, carefully nurtured in secondary schools, as the hidden agenda, that kills the potential of American girls. As long as a girl believes she has the option of being "taken care of" through someone else's abilities and capabilities rather than her own, she is relieved of the responsibility of making serious educational and career plans of her own. This belief is the single most devastating factor in the socialization process that influences the choices of American girls and thus the course of their lives as women.

The school system conveys the belief that girls should take a secondary role in a variety of ways. Elementary readers frequently portray girls as stupid, limited in their activities, and constantly admiring of boys. In other textbooks, the discrimination is not so blatant and can be more easily recognized as a sin of omission rather than commission. Math and science texts show far fewer girls than boys. In the upper grades, where the illustrated role models are adult women and men, the women disappear from the textbooks almost entirely. Even educational audiovisuals more often than not have male voice-overs as the givers of wisdom, and school libraries have long been notorious for their lack of biographies of women or even fiction about strong girls and women. Boys, so the theory goes, will not read stories about girls and women. Boys—apparently the schools' most important concern—must be attended to. That boys grow up to become men with stereotypical ideas about women's place should be a surprise to no one. Boys have read the same textbooks and have listened to the same audiovisuals; they have observed the results of extra money spent on their athletic activities and have noted the supportive cheers for their accomplishments from the girls on the sidelines. Boys, too, are trained in what to expect from girls.

Thus schools—far from being the educators of the next generation in the sense that "education" means to lift up—serve as powerful communicators of the sexual status quo. But as educators claim, outside influences also promote sex-stereotypic behavior and the outcome we see in the behavior of girls and boys is not the sole responsibility of the schools they have attended. Parents, peers, television, movies, books, and records continue to make grossly sexist assumptions about the roles of women and men. However, it is also clear that the schools—if they choose—can make a major effort to present a different view of social roles to the girls and boys in attendance for the ten years of their lives when our children are obliged by law to be in school.

To accomplish the intervention that is needed requires a concerted, ongoing, in-depth effort. The research tells us that girls have been so heavily socialized that they do not easily change their perception of their potential from that which has traditionally been available to them. Most girls need overt encouragement, support, and constant reinforcement to break free of the stereotypes and to dare to aspire. Because the research also indicates that boys at every age level are less willing than girls for women to take more part—particularly a prestigious part—in the world of work, it is clear that boys also need assistance to change their expectations for girls and women.

Elementary school, junior high school, and high school are critical experiences. Courses not taken in high school—math, science, vocational training for the well-paying skilled crafts—are very difficult, expensive, and time consuming to make up once a student leaves the public schools. School is a place where children try out their social roles and learn what brings rewards and what does not. The foundation of self-confidence and self-worth must be strong and must be built early. At present, this foundation needs reinforcement and constant tending if a girl is to progress to high school graduation with a dream of self-sufficiency intact.

Accomplishing this massive educational change has required committed federal interest and the power that only the federal government can muster to counteract the educational discrimination, both blatant and subtle, influencing the socialization of American girls. In the early 1970s, congressional hearings were held to document the extent of discrimination against girls and women in educational institutions. The range of testimony extended from kindergarten to postdoctoral experiences, and the list of organizations and individuals testifying to the discrimination was lengthy and varied. As a direct result of the documentation of discrimination obtained by these hearings, Title IX of the Education Amendments of 1972 was passed by both houses of Congress and signed by the president.

The federal law went into effect on June 21, 1972. The regulation detailing how the law would be interpreted was circulated by the U.S. Department of Health, Education, and Welfare (HEW), which received 10,000 comments from various segments of the education community, the women's movement, and individual citizens. The document submitted by the National Organization for Women (NOW) alone contained 600 pages of comment on the proposed Title IX regulations. After two years of study of all comments from all sources, HEW adopted the Final Regulation effective July 21, 1975.

Before, during, and after the passage of Title IX, various segments of the women's movement paid a lot of attention to sex stereotyping, sex bias, and sex discrimination in elementary and secondary schools and the effect of such attitudes on the students. New York NOW published a study on sexism in the schools. A group from New Jersey called Women on Words and Images carefully reviewed nationally used elementary school textbooks for sexism and developed a book and a slide show on the subject. The Peoria chapter of NOW reviewed career education materials. Citizens' coalitions in Kalamazoo and Ann Arbor studied their communities' schools and compiled additional reports on sexism in education. A coalition of Texas women reviewed every school book on the state textbook committee list and provided proof of sexism, line by line and picture by picture.

The Project on Equal Education Rights (the PEER Project), a creation of the NOW Legal Defense and Educational Fund, was funded by the Ford Foundation to monitor HEW efforts to implement and enforce Title IX. The Women's Program staff of the U.S. Office of Education funded the first nationally coordinated training program for counselors on sex equity. This training effort, called the Sex Equality in Guidance Opportunities project, held over 300 workshops for 7,000 educators during its eighteen months of operation.

The Women's Educational Equity Act program of the U.S. Office of Education was established by congressional legislation to award grants and contracts for innovative demonstration projects and materials to assist educators in doing a more effective, unsex-biased job. The Equal Educational Opportunity Program of the U.S. Office of Education began funding sex desegregation training institutes and centers across the country to work directly with public school educators in eliminating sex discrimination through technical assistance, resource development, and training in sex equity. The National Institute of Education, the research arm of the U.S. Office of Education, developed projects focusing on women and work and on women and math in addition to a multimillion-dollar television series called "Free Style," which offers upper elementary school students programs on nontraditional career options.

Nationally, millions of dollars are being spent to achieve sex equality, and things are moving in a positive direction through efforts undreamed of less than ten years ago. However, only the tip of sexism iceberg has been touched by these efforts. Of the millions of public school teachers in this country, few have had any quality, direct training on Title IX or sex equity. Collectively, these millions of teachers work with additional millions of students, who may or may not be getting an education unaffected by sex bias, sex stereotyping, or sex discrimination.

An education unaffected by sex discrimination, as Mary Wollstonecraft recognized some 200 years ago, is one that renders a girl "independent." With that criterion, much obviously remains to be done. Girls are still not sufficiently encouraged to prepare themselves to be responsible financially for their own lives, whether or not they choose to join their lives with another. Girls need physical education and athletic training opportunities to insure that they are as independent as a strong body can make them. Girls should be encouraged and cajoled, as boys are, to struggle with advanced math and science—those "critical filters" that have been identified as opening the way to so many high-paying jobs in our increasingly technological world. For those who will live most of their adult lives in the twenty-first century, the lack of knowledge in math and science will be not so much a filter as a lockbox, imprisoning those who do not have the mathematical and scientific keys to escape. Schools need to do much more to reward girls with high academic and athletic achievement—achievements that depend heavily on independent commitment to excellence and that are different from the rewards of popularity contests.

As a final bench mark of school mores that need to be changed, consider the cheerleading squad. Title IX requires that boys as well as girls be allowed and encouraged to participate in cheerleading squads, a change already instituted in some localities. However, few schools see to it that the cheerleading squad, whether comprised of females or males or both, is cheering for the girls' and women's athletic teams. Is this an insignificant issue? Not when we understand the powerful socialization message behind these activities. The schools expect girls to display themselves as supportive, to cheer the boys on to victory, to look up to and admire the winners, and to seek to be recognized by them. With respect to girls' athletics, however, schools do not expect boys to be supportive, to cheer the girls on to victory, to look up to and admire the winners, or to seek to be recognized by them. The message concerning who cheers and who gets to *be* cheered is indeed powerful.

Educational sexual imperialism has much in common with the colonial model of political domination. The colonial ruling class has priorities and rights and is certainly never expected, by itself or by its victims, to do for the colonized what the colonized group is expected to do for the ruling class. In the educational milieu, it is, of course, not the boys in the schools of America who institute sexist role assumptions. Rather, just as children internalize attitudes of racial superiority when they have before them an active adult model, so the boys—as well as the girls—internalize male sexist superiority by following a sexist educational model, by expecting girls to be dependent, supportive, and secondary. What is the cognitive cost of training girls to dependency?

According to recent research on gifted children, it is the independent girl whose IQ continues to rise. It is the independent girl who wants to control her own life whose IQ does not fall in high school. It is the independent girl who is willing to postpone marriage and who is more likely to pursue a nontraditional career goal in college. It is the independent woman in middle age who is likely to be reaching beyond her home for broader fulfillment.

But we really already know this, if not through the research then because we have all seen girls who do not fit the stereotypes and yet grow up to be achievers. What we also know is that powerful, independent girls do not grow up in a vacuum. They have received the message that it is all right to achieve.

The school systems—with the help of feminists in the government, in equity projects, and in the roles of mother, father, or teacher—are beginning to move in a positive direction. Sexist books are not as acceptable as they once were. Athletic programs for girls are improving. Vocational classes, formerly restricted to males, are open to all students, and some vocational schools are even making serious recruitment overtures to girls.

But much more is needed. To accomplish that task, school systems need to begin remedial programs for girls in math, science, physical education, athletics, and spatial relationships in the same way that remedial programs currently exist to help boys with their reading, writing, and verbal scores, which are, on the average, lower than those of girls. Superintendents, principals, and athletic directors should be required to expend a school's resources—whether large or small—equally between girl and boy athletes. Indeed, in this remedial period, it would be socially desirable for athletic budgets to tip toward more expenditures for girls. Heavy funding and staff time should go into recruitment of girls into math, science, and the vocational programs, which have been traditionally male. Recruitment programs should spend time not only with the girl but with her parents as well, explaining what the realities of their daughter's adult life are likely to be.

"Jokes" or put-downs of girls and women should be as forbidden as racist "jokes" are. School-by-school retraining should be undertaken to assist administrators, counselors, and teachers to understand how their own personal biases may undermine quality education for the girls in their school. Most importantly, the underlying assumption of Cinderella-hood and its secondary social role for women must be addressed head on in these changes.

Everyone should learn not to worry about the girl who is a super achiever, a great athlete, and a leader of both girls and boys. Instead, attention should be given to assisting both boys and girls who are uncomfortable with the fact of girls as achievers. For example, if a girl says that going out with the star basketball player, who is also an honor student and the class president, makes her uncomfortable because he is "better" at everything than she is, most adults would think that odd. Yet if a boy comments that he feels uncomfortable about going out with the star basketball player, who is also an honor student and president of the class, because *she* is "better" at everything than he is, some people would probably encourage the girl to play down her abilities so as not to upset the boy. That is the classic example of taking a secondary role regardless of the reality of the situation.

Schools and our society must encourage girls to ask themselves what kind of boy or man needs someone else to be less to make himself more and whether that kind of person should be taken seriously, let alone respected or loved. Boys need to understand that they do not have to be "better" than girls at everything or be considered less "masculine."

These changes in basic assumptions about the respective social roles for the two sexes take time, effort, and commitment. It certainly appears simpler when one sex agrees to take a secondary role and lets the other take the lead role regardless of where the real capabilities lie. Everyone then knows what is expected even if such expectations are not congruent with individual preferences and abilities.

But although the stereotypical roles may *appear* simpler, without overt discussion or open difference of opinion, the result is often a morass of complications. We have all seen women trapped in homes that no longer need them, trapped in dead-end, low-paying jobs regardless of interests and abilities, because they considered their work life during the early years of their marriage as a fill-in job rather than a planned, long-range career. In the 1970s, such women often became statistics in a new category—displaced homemakers—when their husbands left them. We have all seen too many men incapable of bearing the day-to-day responsibilities of family life, acting out middle-aged dreams of adolescent, never-ending sexual and professional conquest.

A school system that recognizes preparation for life as one of its major concerns would teach boys that homemaking and child care are their on-going responsibilities if homes and children are part of their life plans. Girls would be taught the cost of taking secondary roles in a life pattern and the importance of being all they can be and of remaining financially independent, regardless of whether or not they have homes and children.

The schools ideally would help girls to attain power in the physical sense of being strong and able to take care of themselves and in the intellectual sense of achieving independence and self-confidence. Educational objectives would assume that when a girl grows up, she will have an ongoing career that will allow her to be independent financially all of her life. The socialization process would teach her to plan to take care of herself when she grows up—in exactly the same way that boys in school expect to learn to take care of themselves. Both boys and girls would learn that loving and caring and sharing do not require taking on a dependent, helpless, or childlike status.

Is this task the work of the schools? Yes, in the same way that it has been the work of the schools to convey the message that girls are expected to cheer for boys and that boys expect to be cheered, now the message must be that boys are expected to cheer for girls as well and that girls expect to be cheered. In healthy relationships, the giving of emotional support and respect is a two-way street.

Girls educated in such a way are more likely to become women capable of standing on their own two feet—strong, powerful, assured, and independent. They will know that they can take care of themselves physically, intellectually, and financially—lovely picture.

Yet a worry raises its head, deep in the socialized recesses of our minds. Regardless of how fine a person she is, the still small voice of our own socialization wants to define her by whether a male will find such a person acceptable. Try as we may, we cannot hush the worrisome question: who will want to marry a girl like that?

"Only the best," I answer.

12.

Challenging Curricular Assumptions: Teaching and Studying Women's Literature from a Regional Perspective

JUDITH STITZEL

We feel confident that an institution has changed only when we see changes in the behavior and attitudes of the individuals within it. In an educational institution, change must ultimately be sought and measured in the lives and work of the students it is meant to serve. For this reason, I begin this chapter with two lists: a list of student projects and a list of student evaluations. Together they are indicative of the work accomplished during three years of an important national project: Teaching Women's Literature from a Regional Perspective.[1] They also point to the emotional, intellectual, and political contexts in which that work was accomplished and which made it possible.

PROJECTS

- *A biographical sketch of Grace C. Carver.* Mrs. Carver was born and reared in the mountains and owns a restaurant in Maggie Valley, a tourist town in North Carolina. She talks about her experiences growing up in southern Appalachia and her present views about women's roles.

- *Midwives in southern Appalachia.* The student writes about past and current practices and interviews one midwife who has been practicing for fifty years.
- *An analysis of the writings of Wilma Dykeman, including an interview* with her about her writing and her views on Appalachian women.
- *Food preparation methods in southern Appalachia.* The student researches old cookbooks, newspapers, and magazine articles and does some interviewing to learn how food was preserved. In the appendix of her paper, she compiles an excellent list of old cookbooks.
- *A study of the writing of women in prison at Nashville Women's Prison.* The materials include journals, short fiction, and poetry.
- *The fictionalized autobiography of a woman who from the age of six has lived in one town in North Carolina.* Her materials deal with her growing up and marriage, memories of people she knew well, and experiences as a woman in southern Appalachia.
- *An edition and criticism of a series of letters and memoirs of a student's aunt written between 1896 and 1972.* The memoirs concern her schooling, family, and engagement. The letters are written to her sister and detail many feelings about politics, literature, and friends.
- *The influence of "Charleston summer people" on local residents of Flat Rock, North Carolina,* emphasizing the student's grandmother's experience as "hired help."
- *An interpretive essay based on in-depth interviews with women who emigrated from Czechoslovakia as young girls* to marry and settle in West Virginia coal towns.
- *"Four Women," a fictional narrative incorporating creative material written by three generations of North Carolina women,* based upon the student's collection of original letters, diaries, poems, songs, wall writings, and photographs.

EVALUATIONS

I think the research experience was invaluable. Besides learning in depth about my topic, I learned what doing "real" research meant and what it involved (which was a vast amount).

I came into the course with a deep love of Appalachia but with a stereotyped image. Now I totally disagree with the stereotyped image, but I am still not sure what sort of image to replace it with, if indeed one needs an image. I'm questioning things more now as a result.

Before, I had always looked torward the patrilineal descent of my family rather than the matrilineal.

I think the basic idea of this course is so important it is urgent. It should add something valuable to our knowledge and also to literature. Much more needs to be done. This region seems very rich in the personal experiences and history of women. The course has made me think and has truly enriched my life.

I learned more in a single course than I ever thought possible. . . . The hard work was well worth it.

The course had two effects on me: I now have better family relationships (because of the oral history work), and I can now call myself an Appalachian (I am happy about this).

This women's course is not against men. On the contrary, it is an attempt to reach a mutual understanding between the two sexes. Likewise, all the differences in our ages, the different generations, enriched our discussions. Whatever the barriers were, one feeling emerged—love, respect, and deep friendship.

These project descriptions and evaluations were taken from the final reports of courses taught in the Appalachian cluster, one of four regional clusters that shaped the project's work in its third year and the one in which I worked.[2] The project descriptions represent the wide variety of topics students throughout the United States chose to work on, topics that stretched both their analytical and their creative skills. The comments reveal that teaching and learning in the project were holistic endeavors, engaging students' emotions, values, and intellects. With few exceptions, the students found their work compelling and demanding; they developed and honed research skills because they had something important to discover—their own heritage and history as women.

What was the project about? The four words in the project's official title—*Teaching, Women, Literature,* and *Regional*—represent its key concepts; an elaboration of these concepts gives a sense of the challenges the project offered to the traditional curriculum. The general approach of the course was from the perspective of women's studies, and the analysis of the concepts was from a feminist perspective. The originators of the project used the definitions articulated by members of the Women's Studies Program at Brooklyn College and quoted in the summer 1977 issue of the *Women's Studies Newsletter:* "The 'perspective of

women's studies' . . . acknowledges the experience of women as a legitimate part of the classroom and research. A 'feminist analysis,' whatever
its particular ideology, begins from the assumption that inequities in
society upon women of all races and social classes have had harmful
effects."[3]

TEACHING

"Just as feminist pedagogy validates personal experience which the
student brings into the classroom, this project places the student rather
than the teacher at the center of the course." Feminists do not all teach
in one way, nor is there a school of feminist education. Nonetheless, the
introduction of women's studies materials into curricula has been accompanied by a reconsideration of the processes appropriate to the endeavor.[4]

It is important not to substitute one orthodoxy for another, one un-
questioned authority for another. Feminists want to teach not only a
certain body of knowledge, but an attitude toward the attainment of
knowledge; they want to provide contexts for the realization that knowledge is, in fact, not attained at all, but constructed, that knowledge involves an interaction between the knower and the known.

Feminist teachers want to assert the centrality of the person in the
process of knowing. In this project, feminist pedagogy was evident in
the entire structure of the course, from early exercises that encouraged
students to understand regionalism by thinking and feeling back to the
scenes and places that had been important in their early lives, to making
students' original research and presentation of that research the core of
the course. Making public presentations central to the project was one
of the major keys to its success, for in addition to giving students a professional sense of responsibility for the quality of their work, it reinforced
the importance of another responsibility—that of sharing knowledge, of
making it available and accessible.

WOMEN

Some of the premises of this course—the emphasis on material long
thought insignificant, the challenge to traditional notions of epistemology
and pedagogy—reflect a change in consciousness that has also affected

disciplines and educational endeavors that do not focus specifically on women. Men, no less than women, are in need of the fundamental re-questioning of economic, political, and aesthetic values that underlies the intellectual challenges of women's studies. But the focus in this project *is* on women. It represents "a conscious effort to recover women's literature and history" in the face of "the racist, sexist, and heterosexist biases in our society,"[5] biases that illuminate still others, such as those of age and class—biases that are still operative, however much projects such as these challenge them.

LITERATURE

One of the major results of the project was the expansion of the canon of works traditionally studied as literature to include genres and forms often trivialized by a male literary establishment—letters, diaries, journals, autobiographies, oral testimonies (especially when created by women). An experience shared by all of those involved is the sense of amazement at the extent of materials as yet unexamined. These materials not only add to our knowledge of women's lives and creative expression, they force some radical reinterpretations of literary history and the reevaluation of both literary and historical methods of analysis. Project participants become acutely aware that we must make efforts, through reading, through working with colleagues in other disciplines (especially history), to get in touch with the art and the acts of the women who have preceded us, both as victims and as survivors of oppression.

Working with out-of-print materials also provides the opportunity for participants to understand the politics of literary reputation. For most students, one of the most exhilarating, empowering experiences was becoming aware that choices other than those of pure and neutral aesthetic standards had shaped the curriculum that in turn had socialized them. Students confronted the question of why certain works, popular in their time, had been "forgotten"; they asked what and who determines literary reputations and therefore the literary canon. They speculated on whether works were perhaps neglected because they subvert the "established" order.

Students had a chance to challenge the dictim they had so often

heard—that the cream rises naturally to the top. True as this might be
on the farm, students became aware that no such "natural" process takes
place in the literary world. As Louise Bernikow wrote:

What is commonly called literary history is actually a record of choices.
Which authors have survived their time and which have not depends upon
who noticed them and chose to record the notice. Which works have become a part of the "canon" of literature, read, thought about, discussed,
and which have disappeared, depends, in the same way, on the process
of selection and power to select along the way. Such power to select, in
England and America, has always belonged to white men.[6]

REGIONAL

The regional approach was dictated by the conviction that "literature
does not exist in a vacuum." Among the goals of feminist critics has been
the attempt to place literature squarely in the historical and political
contexts from which it comes and which it can illuminate. Although
students were not always from the region being studied, an implicit goal
was to encourage those involved (students and faculty alike) to make
connections, to see literature not only as something they studied but
as something to which they were connected—to see that a continuum
exists between themselves and those whose works they read and about
whom they read.

We read literature not only to find ourselves but to move outside ourselves, but first we must have an authentic self—understood, acknowledged,
and valued—to move outside. One of the hopes of the project was that
"through shared experiences with women past and present of their region . . . students [would] attain a sense of self." The regional approach
also allowed participants to focus on the wealth of material, often unknown or uncataloged, that exists in university and community libraries,
in historical societies and private homes—diaries, letters, journals, clippings,
that are helping us to describe and interpret more accurately the continui-
ties and the changes in women's status, role, and experience throughout
the history of the United States.

The emphasis on region also provided a stimulus for the reevaluation
of critical standards, another project goal. Why has one writer been
called "regional" (that is, "local," "limited," "minor") and another
"universal"? "Regional" has often been used not as a means of neutral

description but as a deprecation of women authors. As Florence Howe, editor of the Feminist Press and past president of the Modern Language Association, put it:

All literature is regional or it wouldn't exist. It has to be regional first, whether the region is in Spain, in a part of West Africa, or in Eastern Tennessee. It has to be regional before it can be something else. To call a woman a regional writer usually relegates her to the category "interesting but minor." To call a woman a regional writer generally amounts, therefore, to a sexist slur. Yet, of course, there is no more regional [a] writer than Thoreau—or Faulkner.[7]

We were not satisfied to rescue the term *regional.* We wanted to stretch its boundaries as well and to ask, for instance, whether one's sex itself— or one's race, class, or sexual preference—is to be considered a region.

CONCLUSION

I began this chapter with evidence of change; I followed with a description of one program responsible for change; I end with a warning. We must not underestimate the profound effects associated with the introduction of women's studies into the curriculum, effects I have outlined in reference to the project I know best. Likewise, we must not underestimate the enormous tasks ahead for those engaged in recovering and reassessing women's words and women's worlds. What feminist critics, teachers, and students are doing is giving voices to women who have hitherto been silent, sometimes because they never thought to speak or write and document their lives, sometimes because what they did say, or sing, or write, was not heard or, if heard, was not attended to or valued.

No one writing today has made us more attuned to these women's silences than Tillie Olsen, a writer whose work and commitment were the spiritual center of my own course and whose connection to the women's movement, especially as it affects women's studies, is already legendary. Her words give us inspiration for new beginnings:

There is so much unwritten that needs to be written. . . . It does not matter if in its beginning what emerges is not great, or even (as ordinarily defined) "good" writing. "Whether that is literature, or whether that is not literature, I will not presume to say," wrote Virginia Woolf in her preface to *Life As We Have Known It, Memoirs of the Working Women's Guild,* "but that it explains much and tells much, that is certain. . . ." But there are other forms of expression which can do this, and more: the journal, letters, memoirs, personal utterances—for they come more natural to most, closer to possibility of use, of shaping—and, *in one's own words,* become source, add to the authentic store of human life, human experience. The inestimable value of this, its emergence as a form of literature, is only beginning to be acknowledged.[8]

NOTES

1. The project I am describing, Teaching Women's Literature from a Regional Perspective, was developed in 1976 by the Modern Language Association's Commission on the Status of Women in the Profession and has been supported by the Fund for the Improvement of Postsecondary Education. The project's director is Leonore Hoffman. Three moving and informative articles by faculty in the project have been published in the *Women's Studies Newsletter,* Spring 1976.

2. The other clusters were the Great Plains, the Deep South, and California. Earlier years included other regions.

3. Women's Studies, *Newsletter,* Summer 1977.

4. Articles on feminist pedagogy have appeared in *Female Studies* (Know/Feminist Press) and *Radical Teacher.*

5. "Teaching Women's Literature from a Regional Perspective," *Newsletter,* published by the Women's Commission of the Modern Language Association, Fall 1977.

6. *The World Split Open: Four Generations of Women Poets in England and America, 1552-1952* (New York: Vintage Books, 1974), p. 3.

7. "Teaching Women's Literature from a Regional Perspective," *Newsletter,* Fall 1977.

8. Tillie Olsen, *Silences* (New York: Delta/Seymour Lawrence, 1978), p. 45.

13.

De Jure Sex
Discrimination

JUDITH L. LICHTMAN
and CAROL BAEKEY *

Many people recognize that sex discrimination permeates every fiber of our society. But few people comprehend the pervasive roots of sex discrimination in our laws and, consequently, our lives. Historically, our legal system has perceived women as being essentially different from and inferior to men. Examining the ways in which our laws affect women provides critical insight into the contemporary status of women in the United States. The proposed Equal Rights Amendment would aid in overriding many of the laws that make institutionalized sex discrimination legal.

Most of our laws are based on one or both of two demeaning views of women. First, for legal purposes, women historically have been equated with the mentally ill and infants. Based on this view, women were con-

*Great appreciation and deep thanks are offered to Brooksley Landau and Marna Tucker, the authors of the original speech from which this chapter was developed.

sidered legally incompetent to handle their own financial and legal affairs. Today, this outmoded view is still reflected in many federal and state statutes. For example, in some states, a married woman must prove her competence to a court before she will be permitted to establish a business. In contrast, a man is presumed competent until his actions indicate otherwise.

The second view of women ingrained in our laws is that under most circumstances, they assume the legal status of property. The woman is considered an object—something to be used and taken care of. The *law of personal property* provides that the legal location of personal property, regardless of its actual location, is the place where its owner resides. For example, if an individual owns stock, the legal fiction provides that the stock is located where the owner is located, even though the stock certificates may be in a safe deposit box in another state or country. Similarly, the legal residence of a married woman—regardless of where she actually lives—is deemed to be the residence of her husband. Clearly, in this respect, a married woman is relegated to the status of personal property.

The origin of these concepts of women's legal status is in English common law. The tenets of the common law reflect legal and cultural traditions that have lived beyond their usefulness and do not represent swiftly changing contemporary reality. The *law of coverture* essentially stated that upon marriage, the husband and wife merged into one person by virtue of the legal fiction. As the late Justice Hugo Black stated, "The one is usually the husband." This concept denied the married woman the power to hold or transfer property and awarded her husband control of all of her goods and real estate. As a wife, the woman lost the power to enter into agreements with others and to sue or be sued in a court of law. In theory, the wife received a right to support from her husband. However, as a practical matter, this right to support was unenforceable unless the couple separated and the estranged wife sought support through the auspices of the courts.

A corollary aspect of the notion of a woman as property gave a husband the right to discipline his wife with physical violence, reflecting the fact that under English common law, women or wives had the same status as apprentices or children. With women and children viewed as property to be managed by the husband (or owner) and few laws protecting the rights of women, it is easy to discern the socially acceptable rationale for physical abuse against women and children that still persists in our society.

In the landmark decision of the United States Supreme Court in *Frontiero v. Richardson,* Mr. Justice Brennan stated:

Our statute books gradually became laden with gross stereotypical distinctions between the sexes, and indeed throughout much of the nineteenth century, the position of women in our society was in many respects comparable to that of blacks under the pre-Civil War slave codes.[1]

It is no accident that women and slaves were both relegated to the status of property. When slavery was introduced in the United States, legislators—in developing laws to apply to the slave—determined that the role of the slave was equivalent to that of women. Thus the common law doctrine viewing women as property or defective creatures (mentally ill or infants) served as the underpinning for the laws permitting the legal ownership of slaves as a form of personal property.

In the middle of the nineteenth century, some states adopted the forward view that the situation of the married woman under the common law should be redressed. The various statutes, generally entitled the "married women's property acts," varied in wording and content but essentially granted to married women the rights to hold property, to enter into contracts, and to sue and be sued.

Despite these statutes, many vestiges of the married woman's incapacity to act on her own behalf remain in the laws today. In some states, a married woman holding real property in her name only may not transfer or lease that property without the consent of her husband. Similarly, her right to act as a trustee may be restricted by her "marital incapacity." A few states that require court approval before a married woman may go into business for herself may require the woman's husband to give written permission to the court before the woman is allowed to proceed. Thus a woman who wants to start a dressmaking business must—before commencing business—convince the court that she is competent to organize, operate, and own the business and that such an enterprise is in her best interests.

Generally, under common law, marital property rights reflect the assumption that a husband is entitled to the services of his wife in the home, with no concomitant obligation by the husband to compensate his wife for the value of the services she renders. These "services" include maintaining the family home and caring for the husband and children. Clearly, the wife provides her husband with services of economic value. Nonetheless, the married woman has no control over and no immediate right to any portion of the husband's earnings or property. The wife has an unenforceable and, therefore, only theoretical right to support from her husband. Although the courts admit that such a right of support exists, a husband will be ordered by a court to provide for his wife only in the event of separation from the marriage or divorce.

A recent case illustrates the practical aspects of the predicament of women as well as the archaic notions about women still embedded in our laws. After being married to a male Foreign Service officer for thirty years, a woman was divorced by her husband because he had found a younger woman he wanted to marry. By specific Foreign Service regulations, this former wife had been prohibited from working outside the home. Furthermore, the wife's performance of her duties as a homemaker and hostess had figured prominently in the evaluations and promotions attained by her husband as a Foreign Service officer.[2]

During their marriage, the couple had purchased large quantities of silver and china, worth a substantial amount of money. When the marriage ended, the wife wanted an equitable distribution, with each party retaining half of the china and silver.

Although fighting over china and silver may seem petty, the issue was important, because the woman in her role as wife—through her efforts to advance her husband's career—had clearly contributed to the economic well-being of the marriage. Because of Foreign Service regulations, she had been prohibited from working outside the home, and like many women, she had contributed substantially to the family's well-being through her work within the family home. Nevertheless, the divorce court refused to recognize the economic contributions of this woman to her marriage, a decision subsequently upheld by the Maryland Supreme Court.

Although the lost china and silver were not inherently important, the critical principle—the economic contribution of the wife to the marriage— was lost. While she was arranging flowers, planning social events, and constituting the backbone of the marital home, her husband was moving forward in his career. When he decided to discard her, she was entitled to little or no compensation for thirty years of labor in his and their behalf. Although it will not redress the victim in this particular case, the remedy for this problem is a legislative rule directing divorce court judges that they *must* take into account the economic contribution of the wife in a marriage.

In community property states, the wife is granted a right to one-half of her husband's earnings during marriage. Yet the husband retains control and management of all of the community property. In some states, the husband has sole control over the earnings of his wife, and she has no power to spend money she has earned by her labor without her husband's permission. As a general rule, the wife's interest in the community property is essentially recognized by the law only when the marriage terminates through divorce or death.

The law provides that all single women and adult men may choose a domicile simply by establishing a permanent home. Married women, on the other hand, are conclusively presumed to take the domicile of their husband. If a woman who has always lived in Maryland marries a man from New York who is temporarily working and living in Maryland, while maintaining his New York domicile, the woman immediately loses her Maryland domicile and becomes a New York resident. In losing her Maryland domicile, the married woman forfeits her right to Maryland citizenship. In Maryland she may no longer vote, serve on juries, or run for public office. The courts in which she may sue, where she is taxed, the laws governing her property, and her right to use public facilities all depend upon the state of her husband's domicile.

In a particular case highlighting the absurdity of this domicile rule, a woman brought up in Maryland owned and resided in a house in Maryland inherited from her parents before marriage. While a graduate student in a publicly supported institution, she married a man working for the World Bank. Because of her husband's residency status and despite her actual residence, the state of Maryland informed her that she was no longer eligible for the lower in-state tuition and student status because she was no longer a resident of Maryland.

In another case, a woman who had lived in Virginia her entire life was a student at the University of Virginia. She married a man serving in the armed forces and stationed in Virginia but who maintained his domicile in Massachusetts. Although the woman had never left Virginia, upon her marriage, the University of Virginia advised her that she would henceforth be required to pay the higher nonresident tuition.

After a suit was filed by the Women's Legal Defense Fund, the state attorney general ruled that for in-state tuition purposes, a woman can maintain her own domicile. This decision was limited strictly to the tuition issue. Notably, she could neither vote nor serve on a jury in Virginia. None of the rights of state citizenship was retained by the woman.

The domicile rule creates many practical problems in contemporary society. The United States is an increasingly mobile society. Additionally, for myriad personal reasons, increasing numbers of married persons live apart. When a married woman lives in a state other than the domicile of her husband, she is almost always deprived of basic political and economic rights ordinarily inuring to citizens of the individual states and the United States.

Another issue related to the rule regarding the domicile of a married woman concerns the legal rule that a married woman must follow her husband wherever he chooses to go. If the wife does not choose to move with her husband and live with him, she is judged guilty of desertion. As an example, assume that a husband and wife live in California. The husband wants to move to New York; the wife wants to remain in California. After a family squabble, the husband packs his belongings and goes to New York. Legally, the wife who remains at home in California has deserted her husband.

The psychological impact of the stripping of rights of the woman upon marriage must be significant, even if subtle and unexplored. The economic and political rights of women are seriously infringed. However, single as well as married women are subject to the cutting edge of discriminatory treatment. Many laws purport to protect women, regardless of their marital status, from the burdens of citizenship. Women have always been exempt from compulsory military service and are often excused from jury service on the sole basis of sex. Although these laws seemingly relieve women of unwanted burdens, the underlying assumptions and explicit public policies reflected by these laws should be subjected to close scrutiny.

A number of direct and indirect benefits accrue from jury and military service. For instance, jury duty is often the only way citizens can participate in the judicial process, a governmental decision-making process second only to voting in its importance as a political right. In addition, compulsory military service has provided young men in this

country with a vast array of economic benefits, including the rewards of
on-the-job training and extensive veterans' benefits, particularly through
policies that prefer veterans in the hiring of workers into jobs in the
public service.

As a reward for serving their country, veterans have been accorded a
preference in perpetuity in federal employment (and in public employment in many states as well). In the federal government rating process,
veterans receive an immediate and irrevocable five-point preference for
any employment opening whatsoever. Nor is the preference limited in
its duration.[3] A nonveteran takes the civil service examination, and his
or her numerical score, be it seventy or ninety-two or ninety-seven,
stands. But the competitive score of an applicant who is a veteran is the
test result plus five points. This practice wreaks havoc for women seeking
federal employment since so few women are veterans (women having
been historically discriminated against in the military). Despite merit,
women are at a disadvantage with veterans who receive the five-point
preference without regard to merit.

The veterans' preference points can be, and often are, critical in the
determination of who receives a job. Thus affirmative action plans are
effectively curtailed by the veterans' preference points and subsequent
civil service ratings. This result is most obvious in a "company" town
like Washington, D.C., where the federal government is the major
employer.

Where the government employs a large portion of the population,
women suffer severe economic consequences, regardless of any individual
woman's intrinsic merit, skills, or ability. Repeatedly, lawyer and non-
lawyer advocates of affirmative action report being told by well-meaning
program managers in the federal establishment that their desire to initiate
and enforce affirmative action principles in the hiring process is frustrated
because of the veterans' preference.

The obligations of citizenship, apparent in jury and military service,
are prerequisites to full acceptance of the benefits and responsibilities of
citizenship. When women are exempted from these obligations in the
guise of protecting their sex, they are both realistically and symbolically
relegated to second-class citizenship. The nature and effects of this second-
class citizenship are revealed in a way that is both dramatic and subtle in
the application of protective legislation to women workers.

Such laws were enacted originally by the individual states to protect women from the rigors of the workplace. Typically, these statutes restricted the maximum number of hours women could work, prescribed maximum weight-lifting requirements for women, and otherwise regulated working conditions confronted on a daily basis. Although originally adopted to protect women from exploitation, these laws ironically permitted employers legally to discriminate against women in terms of the jobs and conditions available to women workers. Since the enactment of antidiscrimination in employment legislation as part of the Civil Rights Act of 1964, most of these discriminatory laws have been eliminated.

Even so, we are still faced with the irony of the modern version of protective labor legislation. The promise of the federal Occupational Safety and Health Act of 1970 (OSHA) was a clean and safe workplace for men *and* women. Nonetheless, the enforcement agency for the law, part of the U.S. Department of Labor, proposed regulations in 1977 that would have permitted employers to bar women of childbearing age from workplaces that contained more than a certain amount of airborne lead. The impetus for the regulation was the unproven premise that women were more susceptible to problems from airborne lead than men were and the employer fear of liability for deformities occurring in unborn fetuses. The proposed regulation would have barred from the workplace *all* women of childbearing age, regardless of their plans to have children.

The effects of airborne lead on men of comparable age or on the fetuses they fathered were unknown, and, worse, considered irrelevant. The only scientific research that OSHA had commissioned focused exclusively on the effect of lead in women of childbearing age. Although it is dangerous to be in a workplace with lead, OSHA did not contemplate stringent requirements to clean up the workplace for all persons. Rather, the effect of OSHA's proposed regulation was to protect women right out of their jobs, which in many instances were the only well-paying jobs in the community. Women workers needed those jobs and argued that they should make their own decisions about the risks they take with their health and their bodies.

Historically, the law has restricted the control women may exercise over their bodies. Men have been subject to few such controls. Until recently, the law treated abortion differently from all other medical procedures, making it a crime. Recent Supreme Court decisions have ruled unconstitutional most abortion statutes that deprive a woman of the freedom to choose this medical procedure. However, these Supreme Court decisions are under constant attack by Congress. Many of the rights won in earlier abortion decisions have been severely curtailed.

Another area illustrating the patent abuse of a woman's right to control her body is the complex set of laws surrounding the crime of rape. In most states, a husband who rapes his wife is guilty of no crime and cannot be prosecuted. Once again, the underlying legal premise is that the woman is the personal property of her husband.

In addition, a rape victim is treated differently from victims of all other types of bodily assault. In most states, she is treated like a guilty party or assumed to be lying, and her testimony must be corroborated before the jury can consider her words.

In a related area of the law—physical violence—spouses are barred in most states from suing one another for bodily harm caused by one to the other. Predictably, this has tended to insulate husbands from legal responsibility for abusing their wives. Reported incidences of violence to the woman by the man in a domestic situation are increasing rapidly. Frequently, the woman suffers social stigma in addition to psychological and physical damage and is generally left with no legal recourse against her husband, the abuser.

Often economically dependent on the man, she has no resources with which to escape an untenable situation. Police called in to settle disputes often regard the violence as a family affair and/or an acceptable means of settling disputes. In the states where the man can be prosecuted for violence against family members, prosecutors rarely follow through with the cases, because they are "messy" or it is believed that the woman provoked the situation and got what she deserved. In the absence of more adequate measures, the usual solution is civil redress through divorce.

The inadequacies of the laws in protecting women reflect, to some extent, prevailing notions in a society ambivalent about the propriety of governmentally mandated equality. But governmental institutions, as creations of the law, themselves play a fundamental role in the development and transmission of those very ideas. Probably no governmental institution is as significant to that process as the school, where the mode of operation and the curriculum presented both reflect a view that boys and girls, men and women, have distinctly different social roles.

Public schools serve as a mirror of outmoded cultural stereotypes, and girls are treated in a manner significantly different from boys in the educa-

tional process. Some schools, especially on the high school and college
levels, segregate the sexes in the same fashion and as completely as racial
segregation formerly separated the races. Far more common is the practice of separating boys and girls for some courses—barring girls from shop
and mechanical courses and requiring them to take home economics instead. Extracurricular activities also tend to be segregated. Athletic
activities are not only separate but of highly disparate quality and quantity.
Most school districts spend significantly more on boys' than on girls'
athletics. The precept enforced by our educational institutions from the
day children enter the school system is that females need fewer educational opportunities than boys.

Differing standards of acceptable conduct are often imposed by the
schools on the basis of sex. Girls are expected to be less active and less
aggressive. A girl's realization and actualization of her sexuality are pun-
ished more severely than those of a boy. Vocational programs and counseling in the schools shunt girls into certain types of "acceptable" employment and boys into others. Traditionally, employed males have expected
and reaped higher salaries and better fringe benefits than women—on the
faulty premise that men, not women, support families. These expectations about future employment are fostered by societal expectations
manifested in school curricula. The long-range economic and psychological impacts of such policies on the girls are overwhelming.

The result of this educational process is a secondary role for women
in society, a fact then used to bolster and justify other policies and
laws that discriminate against women. The treatment of women, particularly "housewives," under various federal social benefit programs is an
example. Even though the housewife (or homemaker) plays a significant,
productive, and economically necessary role in our society, the value of
her services is denigrated because she receives no pay for her work. For
her labors, the housewife is rewarded with ineligibility for government
disability payments, for unemployment compensation, and for social
security benefits. In strictly economic terms, her work has been considered of no monetary value to the society it helps support. Although
she may in certain circumstances receive benefits as a dependent of her
husband, our society—as represented by the federal government—has refused to recognize her as a worker entitled to the protections and benefits
of its social insurance programs.

Until recently, even the family of a woman working outside the home could be denied benefits under these social insurance programs merely because the worker was a woman and therefore not valued as highly as a man. This policy was based on the belief that a woman's economic contribution to a family was supplemental to that of a man, who was always considered the primary breadwinner. Comparatively, a man's family received benefits automatically as a matter of right, even if the family received no support from him. With respect to social security, the courts have recently substantially rectified this vast inequity.

Although this brief description of the current legal status of women is far from exhaustive, it serves to illustrate the extensive disparities in the way the law treats men and women. Few guarantees against sex discrimination are currently available by law. Although the Supreme Court of the United States, in several cases litigated during the 1970s, has ruled that laws discriminating on the basis of sex are unconstitutional, it has also ruled and reasoned that in some circumstances discrimination on the basis of sex is proper.

The Supreme Court's treatment of sex discrimination in *Gilbert v. General Electric Co.*[4] serves to pinpoint critical issues of concern. The General Electric Company provided a disability plan for its employees that paid for any disability suffered by an employee, whether it generated from a vasectomy or circumcision or, surprisingly, even if it occurred during the commission of a felony by the employee. The only exclusion under the disability plan was for disabilities resulting from pregnancy, childbirth, or any related medical condition.

The Supreme Court, in approving this exclusion, reasoned that because the differential treatment was based on pregnancy (even though a condition clearly unique to women), the exclusion did not constitute sex discrimination. The court argued that the valid comparison was not between men and women but between pregnant women and nonpregnant women. On that basis, the Court ruled that GE's plan showed no sex discrimination. In 1978 Congress amended Title VII of the Civil Rights Act of 1964 to define discrimination on account of sex as including discrimination on account of pregnancy, childbirth, and related medical conditions.

Strangely, women do not enjoy as strong a position as blacks under the United States Constitution. Although the Supreme Court has ruled discrimination on the basis of race presumptively invalid, discrimination on the basis of sex is not an inherently suspect classification. In contrast to race discrimination, which is constitutional only if closely related to an *overriding* governmental interest, discrimination on the basis of sex is evaluated at a middle-tier level of scrutiny—it is constitutional only if it is *substantially* related to an important governmental interest, clearly a less strict standard of review.

In addition to the Constitution, federal statutory law provides some remedies against sex discrimination. The Equal Pay Act, adopted in 1963, was the first statute aimed at sex discrimination and had the purpose of guaranteeing to women an equal pay scale for equal work. In 1964 Congress enacted Title VII of the Civil Rights Act, which forbade other types of discriminatory practices in employment. In 1972 Title VII was amended to extend its protection to employment in federal, state, and local governments, to educational institutions, and to certain small companies. Title VII has had a pervasive impact on employment practices and attitudes in the United States. Today Title VII is the most widely used law in the arsenal of weapons available for the ongoing battle against sex discrimination in the workplace.

Title IX of the Higher Education Amendments of 1972 forbids certain types of sex discrimination by federally funded education programs. The utility of this statute is dubious, since the U.S. Department of Health, Education, and Welfare has never adequately implemented the statute. Nonetheless, for the first time, Congress extended consideration of sex discrimination beyond the employment arena. Additionally, the Fair Housing Act of 1972 contains a provision prohibiting sex discrimination in housing. The Equal Credit Opportunity of 1974 prohibits discrimination based on sex by retail and banking industries.

The major problem with the many laws prohibiting various forms of sex discrimination is that they go largely unenforced. The federal bureaucracy ambles along, haphazardly enforcing laws, generally ignoring the intended beneficiaries of the various statutes. Specifically, seven years after the passage of Title IX, the U.S. Department of Health, Education, and Welfare had not instituted a single action or proceeding against any educational program, school district, or institution of higher learning. Nor has it even threatened to withhold funds for the failure of institutions to end sex discriminatory practices. Unfortunately, this is but one of a legion of examples of malign neglect of statutory duty.

Certainly, before women can obtain equality under the law in the United States, an enormous amount of work must be done. The Equal

Rights Amendment would give constitutional authority to the rights
and obligations of women as full, not second-class, citizens. Without
the will to enforce existing laws and to break new legal ground, the parade
of "horribles" for women will continue and increase.

In the past decade, women have won many legal battles, but this is
only the beginning of the struggle to gain an equal legal status. Women
still need strong enforcement of existing laws and creative, forceful action
to initiate litigation and formulate new laws and programs. Beyond the
legislative and litigation strategies, however, women of all ages and backgrounds must unite in the struggle to realize their full capacities as human
beings, willing to take great leaps of faith to fight the battles for economic
and legal independence. In the decades of the 1960s and the 1970s,
women won some important battles. To win the war against sex discrimination, be it in legal, economic, or psychological terms, women must continue the struggle to have the laws reflect the values and imperatives of
twentieth-century America.

NOTES

1. 411 U.S. 677 (1973).
2. The hierarchy among wives of Foreign Service officers was identical
to that of the officers themselves and reflected a distinct pecking order.
If a woman was the wife of a labor attaché, any initial communication
or response had to be directed to the wife of the person to whom her
husband responded. Topping the hierarchy was the ambassador's wife,
who enjoyed such "perks" as having the wives of lower ranking embassy
officials cut flowers and pour tea at the embassy. Recently—because of
suits instituted by wives of Foreign Service officers—these practices have
been terminated by internal Foreign Service regulations. However, women
may still experience internal pressures to comply in order to further
their husband's career.
3. A recent legislative effort to put a limit on the veterans' preference
failed dismally.
4. 429 U.S. 881 (1976).

14.

Resistance to the Women's Movement in the United States: The ERA Controversy as Prototype

MARY DUNLAP

> Equality of rights under the law shall not be denied or abridged by the United States or by any State on account of sex.
>
> > Proposed Twenty-Seventh Amendment to the U.S. Constitution, Section 1 (passed by U.S. Senate, March 22, 1972).

Rarely have so few words provided a catalyst for so substantial and nationwide an argument about the rights of so large a group: *women* constitute approximately 53 percent of the United States population. Yet as the years of setbacks and defeats following Senate passage of the Equal Rights Amendment (ERA) in 1972 have worn on, the minorityhood of women relative to political power has become clearer.

Perhaps the ERA is less a catalyst for dispute about its framing principle than a vehicle for a far broader and deeper phenomenon: women,
suffering centuries of oppression on account of sex, are not unified in
support of equality. In the tangled and complex roots of women's oppression, and to an undetermined extent in the diversity of women's responses
to that oppression, a partial answer to the ERA's nonratification may be
buried.

At the outset, it must be recognized that awareness of the history and
currency of oppression of women and consciousness of its major features
and symbols in a particular time and place—from foot-binding to ownership of wives to rape to occupational segregation—are no more universal
than, for example, present understanding of and support for equal rights
without regard to sex. Denial of the reality that women are oppressed
continues.

Once it is denied that women are oppressed today, *on account of sex,*
debate about the ERA becomes an exercise in tired abstractions and
legalistic technicalities. Once that denial is believed, its believers cannot
see the necessity of the ERA; the ERA is transformed into the subject
of a frivolous or even dangerous effort to change what does not require
changing—the "status of women."

In 1973 several members of the U.S. Supreme Court observed that
although "it is true, *of course,* that the position of women in America
has improved markedly in recent decades"[1] (emphasis added), the absence or paucity of women in positions of national political power—from
the Senate and executive branch to the Court itself—illustrates continuing sex-based discrimination against women.

The first part of the Court's reasoning is severely and dramatically
relativist; "progress" and "improvement" do not fully and accurately
describe present reality for women. For example, the characterization
of "improvement" defies reality for socioeconomically poor women in
the United States. Also in 1973, when the "improvement" of women's
"status" was proclaimed, a poor woman was deprived of Aid to Families
with Dependent Children (AFDC) benefits sufficient to buy a single
housedress.[2] To say that this poor woman's status *has* "improved," by
existence of a welfare system, is to ignore the existence of a strikingly
similar welfare system under the Elizabethan poor laws of England
centuries ago. Moreover, to say that the AFDC applicant's plight is explained by her poverty and not by reference to her female sex is to *deny*

the continuing, enforced link between poverty and womanhood in the United States.[3]

If poor women were the only group about whom the characterization of the status of women as "improved" were both factually and legally untrue, that untruth alone—touching the lives of persons who can *least* afford misrepresentations by and about law and government—should serve to unhinge that matter-of-fact assertion (*"of course*. . . the position of women in America has improved markedly in recent decades"). But the inaccuracy and dishonesty of the characterization that the status of women has improved touch, in fact, upon women of every socioeconomic class.

Women continue to be primary and numerous victims of rape and of domestic violence.

> Women all around the world,
> Every color, religion, and age,
> One thing we have in common,
> We can all be battered and raped.
>   Holly Near, "Fight Back"
>   (song lyric).[4]

The physical and sexual abuse of females mocks statements about the improvement of the "position of women" in the United States as of the 1970s. The reply, that men also can be victimized by beating and rape, ignores both the female-as victim psychology of *every* rape, regardless of the victim's genitally defined sex,[5] and the overwhelming reality of the menace of rapists and batterers in the lives of women.

Among the favorite arguments against the ERA, repeated by opponents such as ex-Senator Sam Ervin and reactionary leader Phyllis Schlafly, is that the ERA will take away the "benefits" and "privileges" that the current legal system bestows upon women on account of sex. This common argument in opposition to the ERA represents a high-water mark in the mechanism of denial of oppression of women and affirmation of women's mythical "progress" and "improvement" in legal status and power.

Beneath the "privileges" argument of ERA opponents—with its *legally* untrue assertions about the "right" of women because of womanhood to alimony, preference in custody, and other "benefits" of family law—churns the reality of women's treatment in both marriage and divorce. A stunningly small percentage of all women, who are idiosyncratically rich, powerful, and special in the eyes of the law, receive "privileges" and "benefits," in marriage and upon divorce, that the legal system enforces. Some of these super-rich women can be expected to oppose the ERA for other reasons as well. Their "privileges" include the use of a cheap, maltreated labor force of women and minorities to keep house for them, raise their children, and produce an endless array of objects for their material consumption. The ERA would threaten these beneficiaries of women's oppression.

Yet unquestionably, the female opponents of the ERA are of diverse socioeconomic statuses, including among them presumably thousands of women who have no realistic possibility of sharing in the "privileges of (super-rich) womanhood" that Schlafly and others persistently "offer" as incentives to preserve the inequality of women under law. By what manipulation of emotions and motives have those women, for whom equality of opportunity free from sex-based discrimination is indispensable to sharing in the purported "progress" of women, turned out to oppose the ERA?

In the propaganda disseminated against the ERA by groups such as "STOP ERA,"[6] two basic lies are told repeatedly. The first is that women who support the ERA are opposed to family, child rearing, and marriage. This lie, when believed, is especially effective in dividing mothers against daughters and in dividing "generations" from each other.

The second lie in the ERA opponents' propaganda is that women already share in the "great American dream" and that equality would only reduce women's share. This lie is closely tied to the argument, discussed above, that women's "privileges" will be swept away by the ERA.

In the ideological warfare that has been and is being waged upon the interstate platform of ERA ratification, capitalistic economic forces are hard at work. Those who continue to profit by the illusion that every person in the United States can be materially comfortable by personal devotion to the work ethic are menaced by any constitutional force that recognizes the falsity of the illusion for discriminated-against groups.

Discrimination against women remains massively profitable to those for whom profit equals money today, whatever the consequences for human and natural resources. For decades, women who work outside the home have earned and now earn only slightly over one-half of what men earn, working full time and year round. Occupational segregation maintains the "rationale" for sex discrimination in average female earnings; "men's work" is paid better, in terms of that "rationale," because it is worth more than "women's work." Meanwhile, the "free labor" of housewives provides a precious capital resource to the employer.[7] Finally, the half lie of procreative choice has enabled government and employers alike to contend that the capital outlay for producing tomorrow's labor force (children) fairly should be borne by parents.[8]

The ERA could provide a basis and a force for legal limitation or even redistribution of the profits of sex-based discrimination. Opponents of the ERA contend that the ERA will have no effect on areas of economic discrimination against women—such as employment—because antidiscrimination laws already exist to prohibit such discrimination. That argument has two chief fallacies.

First, the argument that the ERA will not affect such economic discrimination, where existing laws apply, erroneously assumes that existing laws are being fully enforced and forthrightly obeyed. For example, in the well-known case of Title VII of the Civil Rights Act of 1964, which prohibits sex-based discrimination by almost all employers, unions, and government agencies, the assumption about enforcement and obedience is palpably invalid. Courts and agencies have not consistently and firmly enforced Title VII, nor have employers busily and widely adhered to it. The Constitution contains no real legal force toward such enforcement and compliance, absent the ERA. Consequently, even the Supreme Court's shifting majority has acted in an ambivalent and sometimes overtly hostile manner toward full vindication of the right of women to equal employment opportunity.[9]

The second fallacy in the contention that the ERA will not make a difference in economic forms of discrimination against women is the assumption that all present forms of such discrimination are the clear and unambiguous targets of existing antidiscrimination laws. The best example of the naiveté (or malice) of the assumption consists in the behavior of the United States insurance industry. Presently, the insurance industry unabashedly profits at the multimillion-dollar level by sex-discriminatory policy designs, riders, waivers, limitations, and ratemaking. Until fairly recently, the insurance industry overtly excluded women from purchase of various types of insurance; today, women pay substantially more in premiums than men do for at least one crucial type of coverage, to wit, disability insurance.

If ratified, the ERA might be invoked as a prod to Congress and/or state legislatures to act to stop such practices. It is not surprising then that in insurance capitals such as the state of Illinois, the amendment remains unratified. The economic interests that might be jeopardized by ERA ratification are strong, politically powerful in the extreme, and capable of surreptitious influence. Thus the transactions by which those economic interests have secured nonratification of the ERA are difficult to trace, difficult to prove, and elude media and public understanding.

In summary, the ERA ratification controversy is plagued by common ignorance about the phenomenon of sex discrimination, intensified by denial of the oppression of women, by belief in the myth of women's "progress," and by propaganda that urges women to believe that women have "privileges" that "women's libbers" want to take away. If the past is prologue, the ignorance and denial of women's oppression and of the economic abuse of women in particular pose a more serious threat to women than nonratification of the ERA. In such a climate, the consequences of ratifying the ERA may well be similar to the results of women's suffrage:

The [aftermath of women's suffrage] . . . showed how little there had been to fear. The newly politically liberated womanhood of America made no move to disturb the social order; they arranged themselves instead along lines already marked out by the structure and economic interests of a society dominated by men.[10]

NOTES

1. *Frontiero v. Richardson,* 411 U.S. 677 at n. 15 (1973).

2. The AFDC applicant testified that welfare officials "short changed" her $3.50; U.S. Court of Appeals Judge Henry Friendly used her case as an example of the situations in which government should not be required to waste its resources by providing hearings to welfare applicants, in "Some Kind of Hearing," *University of Pennsylvania Law Review* 123 (1975): 1267 and 1275, n. 1.

3. Like many employers, government programmers often opt to save money by reducing or eliminating expenses incurred as to programs for women or by simply excluding women from benefits. See Colquitt M. Walker, "Sex Discrimination in Government Benefit Programs," *Hastings Law Journal* 23 (1971): 277.

4. Holly Near, "Fight Back" from the album *Imagine My Surprise* by Holly Near, Redwood Records, P.O. Box 996, Ukiah, Calif. 95482.

5. Susan Brownmiller, *Against Our Will: Men, Women, and Rape* (New York: Simon & Schuster, 1976).

6. Examples abound. *The Equal Rights Amendment: A Bibliographic Study* (Westport, Conn.: Greenwood Press, 1976) lists several, including "Harmful Effects of ERA," "Ladies! Have You Heard?" and "Warning! ERA Is Dangerous to Women!" (Fort Worth, Tex.: Women Who Want to Be Women, n.d.).

7. Selma James, *Sex, Race, and Class* (London: Falling Wall Press/ Race Today Publications, 1975).

8. See, for example, *General Electric Co. v. Gilbert,* 429 U.S. 125 (1976), in which pregnancy was labeled generally "voluntary."

9. The most notorious example is *General Electric Co. v. Gilbert,* 429 U.S. 125 (1976), in which the majority through Rehnquist held that pregnancy-based discrimination is not necessarily discrimination against women. Congress explicitly overruled this decision by amending Title VII to prohibit pregnancy-based (but arguably *not* abortion-based) discrimination. Public Law 95-555 (October 31, 1978).

10. J. R. Pole, *The Pursuit of Equality in American History* (Berkeley: University of California Press, 1978), p. 309.

————15.————

Women's Right to Full Participation in Shaping Society's Course: An Evolving Constitutional Precept

————————RUTH BADER GINSBURG

A story still in the making is the effort, pressed vigorously since 1970, to promote through litigation the acceptance of a constitutional sex-equality principle. However, A devil's advocate might ask: Isn't such a principle in place? Until the latter half of the nineteenth century married women could not contract, hold property, sue in their own names, or even control their own earnings. Then the married women's property acts swept the country from the middle to the end of the nineteenth century and changed all that. Also, the Fourteenth Amendment provides: "Government shall not deny to any *person* the equal protection of the laws." Most significantly, since 1920 women have had the right to vote.

Despite those developments, the Constitution was viewed by jurists until well past this century's midpoint as a virtually empty cupboard for sex-equality claims. A 1947 opinion by Justice Jackson (*Fay v. New York*) offers a good summary of the state of constitutional doctrine until the current decade. The Supreme Court that year rejected a challenge to New York's jury-selection system exempting a woman from service simply because she was a woman. Justice Jackson explained:

The contention that women should be on the jury is not based on the Constitution, it is based on a changing view of the rights and responsibilities of women in our public life, which has progressed in all phases of life, including jury duty, but has achieved constitutional compulsion on the states in only one particular—the grant of the franchise by the nineteenth amendment.[1]

In other words, the Nineteenth (Women's Suffrage) Amendment apart, the government was free to draw what Justice Frankfurter, the next year in his opinion for the Court in *Goesaert v. Cleary*,[2] called a sharp line between the sexes. Samples of Supreme Court decisions from 1873 to 1961 underscore that line. Government could keep (or protect) women from working in a wide range of occupations, from lawyering to bartending.[3] Government could regulate where and when a woman worked, although at first it could not, and later would not, impose such restrictions on her brother.[4]

The High Court position until 1971—its consistent affirmation of governmental authority to classify by gender—was faithful to the founding fathers' understanding. Thomas Jefferson said that all men are created equal. He also said:

Were our state a pure democracy there would still be excluded from our deliberations women who, to prevent depravation of morals, and ambiguity of issues, should not mix promiscuously in gatherings of men.[5]

What of the next era of constitution making? The Reconstruction Congress gave us a majestically encompassing equal-protection guarantee in the Fourteenth Amendment. But the legislative history of the Fourteenth Amendment explains that government, beyond question, could classify on a number of bases—prime among them age and sex. The Supreme Court clarified in 1875. Of course, women are persons within the meaning of the Fourteenth Amendment, the justices said in *Minor v. Happersett*.[6] So too are children, they added (and who would suggest that children have a constitutional right to vote or to function as lawyers?).

That association of women and children indicates a tradition still evident in some jurists' thinking. Sex classifications, in contrast to black codes, were not thought to downgrade women. Chivalrous jurists regarded lines the law drew between the sexes not as "back of the bus" regulation but as according favorable treatment to the fairer or weaker sex. Laws differentiating on the basis of gender were perceived as operating preferentially or benignly to place and keep women on a pedestal.

Given the original understanding and the prevailing social climate, few women attempted constitutional litigation to overturn sex lines until the 1970s. But in that decade, sex-discrimination challengers trooped before the courts with a barrage of complaints. They charged employment discrimination; educational inequalities (particularly in vocational and athletic training); gender-based differentials in laws governing social insurance, jury and military service, and age of majority specifications; disadvantages suffered by parent or child based on out-of-wedlock birth; disadvantageous treatment of pregnant women; and barriers blocking access to contraception and abortion. The Supreme Court, from 1974 to 1977 alone, dealt with more cases touching on the rights and responsibilities of men and women than in its entire previous history.

Why did this litigation barrage occur, particularly the resort to the Constitution, given the original understanding and the bleak state of Supreme Court precedent? Prominent in the picture was a revived feminist movement inspired in part by the black Civil Rights movement of the 1960s. But the grand inspiration provided by the movement for racial equality was only one factor. A revived, latter-twentieth-century feminist movement is not peculiar to the United States. In Sweden, for example, a country notable for its homogeneous population, the movement started earlier and has advanced at least as far.

The setting also included developments in the political arena—most conspicuously two federal laws: the Equal Pay Act of 1963 and Title VII of the Civil Rights Act of 1964. But by 1963 the equal-pay principle was hardly a novelty. The International Labour Organization had adopted a convention on the subject in 1951, and an equal-pay provision was part of the Rome Treaty that launched the European Common Market in 1958. Moreover, mixed motives were involved in congressional adoption of the Equal Pay Act. Some doubting Thomases were sold by the argument that women surely would not flood the job market as a result. If an employer must pay men and women the same, so the argument went, he would prefer a man for the job.

Title VII was the centerpiece of the comprehensive 1964 civil rights legislation. It outlaws discrimination based on race, national origin, religion, and sex in hiring, firing, and all terms and conditions of employment. Originally applicable to the private sector, Title VII was expanded in 1972 to cover public employment as well. But sex discrimination was not included in the drafters' plan for Title VII. Protection of women against job discrimination was introduced later in the legislative process. The category "sex" was added by floor amendment, an amendment proposed by a representative from Virginia whose aim was to defeat the entire measure. His tactic backfired. (Perhaps he would have been more successful had his colleagues fully appreciated what Title VII means—for example, almost all jobs must be open to women; females cannot be refused employment because they are mothers; they must be accorded retirement benefits fully equal to those male co-workers receive.)

What, then, accounts for the litigation parade and the sustained drive to tie a bedrock sex-equality principle to our fundamental instrument of government?

The revived feminist movement and the advent of equal-employment-opportunity legislation signaled a transition to a new period in the history of humankind. An early indicator of it attracted scant attention. In 1947-1961, before the Civil Rights movement captured headlines, before Betty Friedan wrote *The Feminine Mystique,* unprecedented growth occurred in the employment of women aged forty-five to sixty-four outside the home. A steep increase for younger women followed later, coinciding with, and shored up by, the revived feminist movement—a burgeoning movement caused by, and in turn spotlighting, dramatic alterations in women's lives. Among the salient factors causing women to enter the paid work force were a sharp decline in necessary home-centered activity, curtailed population goals and more effective means of controlling reproduction, and vastly extended life spans. For most of women's adult lives, children requiring close care are not part of the household. The two-earner family has become more common than the family in which a man is sole breadwinner. Persistent inflation boosts the attraction of gainful employment for wife as well as husband. The Bureau of Labor Statistics projects that within a dozen years, two-thirds of all women aged twenty-five to fifty-four will be in the paid labor force.

My Columbia colleague Eli Ginzberg appraised the sum of these changes as the most outstanding phenomenon of the twentieth century. Automobiles, planes, nuclear power plants—all brought about by technology—he termed *infrastructural changes.* Important as they are, he said, they do not go to the guts of a society—how it works and plays, how people relate to one another, whether they have children, and how they bring them up.[7]

The change Eli Ginzberg called millennial sparked the American Civil Liberties Union (ACLU) board, at the start of the 1970s, to devote substantial resources to sex-equality litigation. The ACLU is only one of several participants in this venture (although it is the one with which I am associated and know best). The venture is diffuse. Although diffusion indicates widespread interest, it also occasions problems. With many groups and individuals involved, not always marching to the same tune, it is impossible to duplicate the orderly, step-by-step litigation campaign that led to *Brown v. Board of Education*[8] (the landmark 1954 school desegregation decision).

The ACLU, although only one among many, is a major (probably to date, the major) participant at the Supreme Court level in litigation seeking to foster a secure, constitutionally based sex-equality principle. From my perspective, the ACLU enjoys two special advantages. First, its affiliate network, comprised of chapters in almost every state, makes it possible to seek and bring cases in various parts of the country. Ideally, cases with the best facts are selected and brought before the most sympathetic tribunals. (Reality inevitably falls some distance short of the ideal.) Second, in the ACLU, men and women work together. That is important if you believe, as I do, that the social change provoking the litigation parade will affect, and should involve, men as much as women.

A different perspective on that issue was offered by a colleague who works in a public-interest law firm staffed by four women and one man. She said that she would like a better sex balance but would not be happy if men became a majority. Her preference is not based on a view that women are one great sisterhood. Rather, she emphasized that although her female colleagues are independent, aggressive, and competitive, they work *together* far more than men do and avoid the nonsense—the sexist comments, the put-downs. Who needs it?

Sociologist Cynthia Epstein[9] stressed men's need. Men need to learn, she pointed out, and they do, when women show up in their midst *in numbers,* not as one-at-a-time curiosities, or only in subordinate, helping roles. Men need the experience of working with women who display a wide range of personality characteristics. They need to become working friends with women.

A pair of cases launched by the American Civil Liberties Union initiated the 1970s constitutional litigation regarding gender-based discrimination. Sally Reed of Idaho was the challenger in one case. Charles Moritz of Colorado was the petitioner in the other case. The *Reed* case[10] began with the suicide of Richard Lynn Reed at age nineteen. Sally Reed, Richard's mother, applied to be appointed administrator of his estate. Cecil Reed, Richard's father, by then separated from Sally, applied two weeks later. Idaho had a statute to resolve such controversies. It read: "As between persons equally entitled to administer a decedent's estate, males must be preferred to females."

Charles Moritz was a lifelong bachelor. Although well past sixty-three, he took good care of his mother. She lived with him, and he hired a nurse to care for her during the day when he was out working. The Internal Revenue Code at that time allowed to a never-married daughter, but not to a never-married son, an income tax deduction for part of the cost of a nurse hired under those circumstances.

Idaho lawyers argued in *Reed* that men are more experienced than women in business affairs. The Department of Justice said in the *Moritz* case[11] that women, more frequently than men, took responsibility for care of infirm relatives. Even if Sally Reed were better at numbers than Cecil Reed, that was irrelevant, Idaho attorneys said. Even if Charles Moritz took care of his mother, the Department of Justice said, that was irrelevant, for the legislature must make rules fitting the generality of cases, not the exceptional instances. The ACLU's idea in supporting both cases and attempting to get them before the Supreme Court the same season was to emphasize that sex-role pigeonholing disadvantages members of both sexes—that overbroad generalizations unfairly trap or type both men and women.

The *Reed* case was decided swiftly. Chief Justice Burger spoke for a unanimous court. He declared the gender line inconsistent with the equal-protection principle. His opinion was terse and acknowledged no break with precedent. But *Reed* marked the first departure from the High Court's "anything goes" approach to line drawing by gender. The *New York Post*[12] gave the *Reed* decision a front-page banner headline: "High Court Outlaws Sex Discrimination."

The *Moritz* case was not decided so swiftly. It lingered in the court of appeals for eighteen months, until after the Supreme Court decided *Reed.* Then Charles Moritz got his tax deduction. The court said that it was wholly arbitrary to distinguish between dutiful sons and dutiful daughters. It was the first time a provision of the Internal Revenue Code was ever held unconstitutional.

The government unsuccessfully sought review in *Moritz,* but in the process made a major contribution to the future course of events. The *Moritz* decision may seem innocuous, the solicitor general told the Supreme Court (for Congress had by this time already changed the law to neutralize the deduction). But the solicitor general warned that the ruling cast a cloud on thousands of laws across the nation. The Department of Justice computer run had turned up over 800 laws at the federal level alone containing gender-based references. A list of those laws was appended to the government's petition for review.

The list proved extraordinarily helpful. First, it provided a ready answer to those who claimed that with Title VII and the Equal Pay Act on the books, no more law-sanctioned sex discrimination existed. Second, it provided a stimulus for a next set of constitutional challenges.

Already under way by this time was the *Frontiero* case.[13] The Southern Poverty Law Center and the ACLU jointly presented the case for the Frontiero plaintiffs in the Supreme Court. Plaintiffs were Sharron Frontiero, an air force lieutenant, and Joseph, her student husband. Congress provided that married male officers in the armed forces were automatically entitled to a housing allowance added to their paycheck and health care for their wives. Married female officers, however, received those benefits for their spouses only if they supplied half of their husband's support. (That meant all of their own plus over half of their husband's support—in other words, more than three-fourths of the family's support.) Plaintiff Sharron Frontiero brought in more than half but something less than three-fourths of the family's income—hence no family benefits for the Frontieros.

The case had a number of attractive features. In essence, Sharron Frontiero had been denied equal pay. If the Equal Pay Act had covered the military, which it did not, the case would have been open and shut. The Department of Defense was already on record before Congress in support of a sex-neutralizing amendment, and the Department testified that the cost would be minimal. But the precedent potential was high, for *Frontiero* involved the most pervasive sex line in the law—treating as synonyms male and breadwinner, female and dependent.

Frontiero yielded an eight-to-one judgment. Four of the justices said that the Court should look as closely (or suspiciously) at government resort to a gender criterion (in lieu of functional description) as it looks at official line drawing based on race or national origin. But four other justices said that *Reed* was enough to support a decision for Sharron and

Joseph Frontiero. They thought that further doctrinal development was unwise, at least until the fate of the proposed Equal Rights Amendment was decided. The ACLU had advocated a "close look" approach in *Frontiero,* just as it had in *Reed.* Four votes, of course, is one vote short of a Supreme Court majority, and I believed, after *Frontiero,* that an effective five-year plan could come close to finishing the job. That estimate proved excessively optimistic.

Social security legislation provided an almost perfect illustration of the lawmakers' habit of classifying overbroadly by sex. The legislation appeared on the list the solicitor general supplied in *Moritz* and was the focus of the next challenges. The first challenge was the child-in-care provision, applicable when a wage earner died with a young child. If the wage earner were a man, monthly benefits were provided for widow and child. If the wage earner were a woman, no benefits were provided for the widower. Second, the old age and survivors insurance provisions involved a one-way dependency test virtually identical to the one in *Frontiero.* The elderly wife or widow could receive benefits under her husband's account automatically. The elderly husband or widower was entitled to such benefits only if his wage-earning wife brought in three-quarters of the family's income.

The child-in-care case was brought to court early in 1973. It was stimulated by a letter Stephen Wiesenfeld wrote to his local newspaper on November 27, 1972. The letter was headed "Social Security Inequality." It read:

Your article about widowed men last week prompted me to point out a serious inequality in the Social Security regulations.

It has been my misfortune to discover that a man cannot collect Social Security benefits as a woman can.

My wife and I assumed reverse roles. She taught for seven years. She paid maximum dollars into Social Security. Meanwhile, I, for the most part, played homemaker. Last June she passed away while giving birth to our only child. My son can collect benefits but I, because I am not a woman homemaker, cannot receive benefits.

Had I been paying into Social Security, and had I died, she would have been able to receive benefits, but male homemakers cannot. I wonder if Gloria Steinem knows about this?[14]

A friend of Gloria Steinem did know about the inequality. She was an officer in the Women's Equity Action League and lived in the town next to Wiesenfeld's. After reading his letter in the local paper, she called him and suggested that he contact the American Civil Liberties Union.

As for old age and survivors' insurance, retired New Jersey police officer Edgar Coffin had read of Wiesenfeld's case when it was filed. Coffin's wife had been a math teacher in a New Jersey public school. Her earnings were approximately equal to his. Her pension was slightly higher than his. Her employer was covered by social security, his was not. She had supplied the larger part of the family's total income, but he could receive no benefits under her account.

After Stephen Wiesenfeld's case was presented and awaiting decision in the federal district court in New Jersey, New Jersey police officer Edgar Coffin's case was filed—out of caution, but not anticipating a venue objection the government pressed—in the District of Columbia. The ACLU saw *Frontiero, Wiesenfeld,* and *Coffin* as a logical progression in the Supreme Court. Instead, Florida widower Mel Kahn's case appeared on the Supreme Court docket. Florida gave widows, but not widowers, a real property tax exemption worth fifteen dollars annually. Kahn thought the law was unfair. (It is to some observers a remarkable feature of our system that a fifteen dollar case can travel three levels in a state and end up in the Supreme Court.)

Widower Kahn's case signaled danger—danger that the Court would revert to old ways and see the tax exemption as pure favor to women. (Unlike the *Moritz* situation, the tax benefit in *Kahn* was based on status alone; it was not tied to the performance of a function—in *Moritz,* caring for a parent.) In *Wiesenfeld* and *Coffin,* the argument could be made, far more persuasively than in *Kahn,* that women were harmed by the classification, that Paula Wiesenfeld and Edna Coffin were shortchanged because the Social Security Act treated their employment as less valuable to and supportive of the family than the employment of the family's man.

To make a bad situation worse, *Kahn* was scheduled for argument in the Supreme Court on the same day as the *DeFunis* case. *DeFunis* was a challenge to the University of Washington Law School's minority admission program. The University of Washington's attorney had this concern. He feared that the Court would say the Constitution is color blind and allows no corridor for color-conscious law school admission. Widower

Kahn's attorney (I was representing the widower) had a different concern. She feared the Court would allow too broad a corridor for sex classifications rationalized as benign. This fear proved well founded.

On April 23, 1974, Justice Douglas said in *DeFunis*[15] that the Constitution does not tolerate any race-based preference. (The rest of the justices expressed no opinion, leaving the question open until some four years later when the *Bakke* case[16] was decided. The Court said that *DeFunis* was moot, for Marco DeFunis would graduate from law school in a few weeks' time.) The day after Justice Douglas offered his color-blind view in *DeFunis,* he wrote for the Court in *Kahn.*[17] Speaking for a six-member majority, Justice Douglas ruled that widows may be preferred without offense to the equal-protection principle. He viewed the fifteen dollar tax saving as legitimately compensating women for disadvantages they encountered in economic endeavor.

Not highlighted in the *Kahn* opinion, the Florida real property tax exemption was nineteenth-century legislation. It was enacted when a married woman ranked more as her husband's ward than as his peer (she had no right to contract, hold property, vote). Florida gave three groups this little tax break: the blind, the totally disabled, and widows. That juxtaposition suggested a view of women as persons of limited capacity, a view I would not characterize as "benign." Panglossian commentators, however, applauded the *Kahn* decision. They said that woman has the best of all possible worlds. *Reed* and *Frontiero* permit her to attack laws that discriminate against her; *Kahn* allows her to preserve laws that favor her.

But virtually every gender-classifying law can be characterized as favor or as discrimination, depending on one's perspective. For example, when young widower Stephen Wiesenfeld's case reached the Supreme Court, the government argued that the law favors widows over widowers; therefore *Kahn* is decisive. I argued that the law denigrates the efforts of wage-earning women; therefore *Frontiero* is decisive.

Similar arguments were made in the Louisiana jury cases heard the same term as *Wiesenfeld,* cases attacking a volunteers-only system for women. If women wanted to serve on juries, they had only to march to the clerk's office and sign up. If they did not sign up, they were not on the list. The result—less than 5 percent of those on the jury list were women.

The Louisiana attorney general said the law was obviously benign.

The state gave the woman the right to serve but did not impose it on her as a responsibility. I argued that the law was obviously invidious. A person with a right but no corresponding responsibility is less than a full citizen, for citizenship entails responsibilities as well as rights.

The Louisiana jury issue[18] was an eight-to-one success; *Wiesenfeld*[19] was an eight-to-zero victory. These decisions put the Court back on track. Things were looking up for *Coffin,* the old age and survivors' insurance challenge.

After the *Kahn* decision, but before the unanimous *Wiesenfeld* victory, the ACLU was insecure with police officer Coffin's challenge as the sole test case. Several other similar suits were instituted to increase the possibility of a winner and also to insure against mootness, since all of our plaintiffs were men of a certain age. After *Wiesenfeld,* all of those cases were winners. But one moved too fast. *Coffin,* with its excellent facts, had a year's lead time over the others. Leon Goldfarb's case,[20] the last filed, was the first decided by a federal district court, three weeks before the favorable decision obtained in *Coffin.*[21] The Supreme Court schedules cases on a first-out-of-the-lower-court/first-into-the-Supreme-Court basis. Therefore, Leon Goldfarb's case, not Edgar Coffin's, was set down for High Court argument.

On the facts, Goldfarb's case was the least sympathetic of the several similar suits instituted to challenge the same gender line. Goldfarb had earned substantially more than his wife and had received a federal civil service pension. Consequently, the government could argue more persuasively in his case, than in a case where wife and husband were equal earners, that survivors' benefits for widowers would be an unmerited windfall.

Goldfarb was paired for argument in the Supreme Court with the Oklahoma 3.2 beer case, *Craig v. Boren.*[22] Oklahoma's near-beer controversy was a curious case for Supreme Court attention. It was pressed not by any public-interest group but by Carolyn Whitener, owner of an establishment called the Honk and Holler; costs of the suit were paid by a fraternity at the University of Oklahoma. The complaint was that Oklahoma let girls buy the brew (and work in a 3.2 beer emporium) at age eighteen, but boys (because they will be boys) were made to wait until age twenty-one. The thirsty boys were big winners in the Supreme Court. The victory was seven to two. (The chief justice and Justice Rehnquist were the only naysayers.)

The Court used the near-beer case to acknowledge an important doctrinal advance. It held that a higher review standard applies to gender classifications. The standard it articulated is not as high as that applicable in race and national-origin discrimination cases but is considerably higher than the standard in the mine-run equal-protection case.

Ironically, the Court announced the heightened review standard in a men's (more accurately, boys') rights case. But the majority appeared to accept the argument critical to a genuine sex-equality principle; most of the justices indicated awareness that classification by gender generally cuts with two edges. Such classification sometimes snares a male victim, but it is rarely, if ever, pure favor to women.

Leon Goldfarb's case, on the other hand, although successful, was a cliffhanger. In principle, the case was *Wiesenfeld* all over again, but this time without the baby. True, the fact pattern fell short of the ideal. But that was not enough to explain why the eight-to-zero *Wiesenfeld* count dwindled to five to four in *Goldfarb*. [23] A possible decision-influencing factor was the price tag in *Goldfarb*—the highest in any successful gender discrimination case until 1977. (Five hundred million dollars annually was the government's estimate, an inflated estimate, I believe, although not wildly off the mark.)

But most important, the *Goldfarb* briefs and argument had to take into account and distinguish a case in the wings—a case brought by *pro se* litigant William Webster. The Court was to consider his case shortly after Goldfarb's. From 1956 to 1972, the Social Security Act gave female wage earners a slightly more favorable retirement benefit calculation than male wage earners. Congress evened things out in 1972. Men were given the same more favorable calculation formula. But William Webster was born three years too early—the congressional sex neutralization was not retroactive.

The ACLU suggested in its *Goldfarb* presentation a synthesis the Court developed in *Webster*. [24] First, post hoc rationalization was unacceptable for the laws that ranked women as men's subordinates. But when a law, in design and operation, attempts to ameliorate past disadvantage during an interim catchup period, and is narrowly tailored to that end, sex classification, as a transitional measure, is permissible.

Webster fit the bill. Congress had in fact focused on two things in 1956—depressed wages for women (unequal pay in those days was openly acknowledged) and early retirement that employers routinely forced on women but not on men. When the Equal Pay Act and Title VII directly prohibited those practices (in 1972 both acts were extended to cover most sectors of the economy), the same need for the sex classification no longer existed, and Congress dropped it. That distinction was developed not only to shore up widower Goldfarb's case, but with the idea that it might provide useful support for the University of California's position in *Bakke*.

Justice Brennan, writing in dissent for four members of the Court in *Bakke*, cited *Webster* several times as a path marker. Justice Powell, author of the *Bakke* prevailing opinion, while agreeing with the four who rejected a color-blind interpretation of the equal-protection guarantee, regarded sex-discrimination precedent as inapposite. His first point is clear: it is easier to tell who is male and who is female than to decide who belongs in the category of disadvantaged racial or ethnic minority. But his second point, one he labeled more important, is problematic: the perception of racial classifications as inherently odious, he wrote, stems from a lengthy and tragic history that gender-based classifications do not share. The Court, Justice Powell maintained, has never viewed gender classification—for the purpose of equal-protection analysis—as inherently suspect or as comparable to racial or ethnic classification.

Justice Powell's comment on gender-based classification is a cryptic part of an otherwise sizable essay. It contrasts with a statement made by Justice Blackmun two years earlier, in a 1976 opinion for the Court in *Mathews v. Lucas*.[25] Sex, like race, Justice Blackmun wrote, is an obvious badge. He further observed that historical legal and political discrimination based on sex, like discrimination based on race, has been severe and pervasive. The contrast suggests that in 1978, the Court remained insecure, still wavering, not entirely clear on what to do in sex discrimination cases absent the signal and the guidance the Equal Rights Amendment would supply.

A further indication of the Court's uncertainty was revealed by its nondecision in *Vorchheimer v. School District of Philadelphia*.[26] The *Vorchheimer* case disarmed the justices. However, the case that might have been the High Court's precedent setter was filed by the Louisiana ACLU in 1972. Jefferson Parish, Louisiana, segregated its high schools by sex the same day the schools were integrated by race. Separate and unequal opportunities were shown, and race discrimination in the background was apparent. But the trial court sat on the case for years and refused to decide it.

Meanwhile, Susan Vorchheimer's case came before the Supreme

Court. Philadelphia had two sex-segregated high schools in an otherwise predominantly coeducational system. The two single-sex schools were for academically superior students. Susan Vorchheimer preferred Central (the boys' school). She was told to content herself with Girls' High. *Vorchheimer* came to the High Court with a slim record, with virtually no showing of tangible inequalities. Also, Pennsylvania had a state Equal Rights Amendment. It was perhaps disturbing to federal judges that the case had been fought out in federal court under the equal-protection clause rather than in the state courts under Pennsylvania's own law. The result—a four-to-four even division. That meant no Supreme Court opinion and, instead, an automatic affirmance of the decision below (two to one for the school district).

To sum up the story as it had unfolded up to 1978, lower courts and lawyers felt a certain discomfort with five-to-four decisions, as in *Goldfarb*, or four-to-four splits, as in *Vorchheimer*. As one federal district court judge said: "In dealing with Supreme Court 1970s sex-discrimination precedent, lower courts judges feel like players at a shell game who are not absolutely sure there is a pea."

But constitutional doctrine concerning sex equality was in a primitive state until 1971. Until the 1960s, judges could be confident there was no pea. My estimate early in the decade that the story with respect to constitutional doctrine would be almost finished by 1978 was overly optimistic. But doctrinal development in the seven years from 1971 to 1978 clearly passed the point of return to the original understanding. The empty-cupboard days of constitutional interpretation are over. Precedent is evolving in support of women and men who seek full partnership in shaping their own lives and society's course. But that precedent, in large measure because it lacks solid foundation in our fundamental instrument of government, is variously interpreted. Ratification of the Equal Rights Amendment (ERA) would clear the air.

The ERA would supply a signal to our legislatures to eliminate a host of unnecessary gender lines in the law—a stimulus to commence in earnest, systematically and pervasively, the law reform so long deferred. Without the cleanup work, laws as silly as Oklahoma's near-beer regulation, or as dated as Alabama's statute permitting fathers—but not mothers—to recover for the wrongful death of a child, must be attacked one by one, in hand-to-hand combat in court, pressing into service eighteenth- and nineteenth-century provisions surely not envisioned by their framers to encompass a ban on sex discrimination. In case of continued legislative default or foot dragging, the ERA would give our courts a handle for sex-equality rulings far more secure than the Fifth or Fourteenth amendments. The sole office of the ERA is to guarantee to each woman and each man fully equal justice under the law.

An explicit sex-equality principle as part of our fundamental law, although in my judgment of vital importance, will still leave large work ahead to carry the nation forward from equality accepted in principle to equality put into practice in the political community, the workplace, and the home. Those committed to a society in which opportunity is genuinely equal will have to continue efforts to reach that goal on many fronts and for a long time.

For example, opening all vocational courses to girls, in itself, does not assure that girls will pursue technical subjects to the same extent as boys. Providing leave to either parent to attend to an infant or a sick child, in itself, does not mean that fathers will take time off to the same extent as mothers. Recognizing that it would be desirable to increase women's participation in politics, on the judiciary, in industrial management and unions, does not mean that when actual decisions are made, female heads will be as visible to headhunters as male heads.

But I am confident that pressures to achieve equal stature and dignity for women and men will not relent. The drive for equal opportunity has the support of self-interested groups whose consciousness and expectations have been raised, and it has the brainpower of the steadily increasing numbers of women ready and eager to gain positions outside the pink-collar ghetto.

Partnerships and alliances with other groups striving for genuinely equal status and opportunity will facilitate and reinforce the gains. Just as women have benefited from the effort to eradicate race discrimination, so members of minority groups should benefit from feminists' pursuit of equal rights and opportunity for all of humanity.

In the 1973 *Frontiero* decision, four of the Supreme Court justices, borrowing lines penned some months earlier by the California supreme court, said:

Traditionally . . . discrimination [on the basis of sex] was rationalized by an attitude of "romantic paternalism" which, in practical effect, put women not on a pedestal, but in a cage.[27]

Decades before the awakening among our High Court jurists, the same point was made by George Bernard Shaw in an essay he called "The Womanly Woman." His words serve as an appropriate conclusion to these remarks:

If we have come to think that the nursery and the kitchen are the natural sphere of a woman, we have done so exactly as English children come to think that a cage is the natural sphere of a parrot: because they have never seen one anywhere else. No doubt there are Philistine parrots who agree with their owners that it is better to be in a cage than out, so long as there is plenty of hempseed and Indian corn there. There may even be idealist parrots who persuade themselves that the mission of a parrot is to minister to the happiness of a family by whistling and saying Pretty Polly, and that it is in the sacrifice of its liberty to this altruistic pursuit that a true parrot finds the supreme satisfaction of its soul. I will not go so far as to affirm that there are theological parrots who are convinced that imprisonment is the will of God because it is unpleasant; but I am confident that there are rationalist parrots who can demonstrate that it would be a cruel kindness to let a parrot out to fall a prey to cats, or at least to forget its accomplishments and coarsen its naturally delicate fibres in an unprotected struggle for existence. Still, the only parrot a free-souled person can sympathize with is the one that insists on being let out as the first condition of making itself agreeable. A selfish bird, you may say: one that puts its own gratification before that of the family which is so fond of it. . . . All the same, you respect that parrot in spite of your conclusive reasoning; and if it persists, you will have either to let it out or kill it.[28]

POSTSCRIPT

In the year following presentation of these remarks, the Supreme Court grappled with several cases involving sex-based differentials. Three cases are of particular significance. In *Orr v. Orr,*[29] the Court held unconstitutional an Alabama law that authorized awards of alimony to wives but never to husbands. The Court explained that the legislation was freighted with the "baggage of sexual stereotypes," presumptions that men support but do not receive support from women and that women are always dependent on men. As a result of *Orr,* need for assistance and ability to pay—not sex—determine an individual's entitlement to and obligation for support following a divorce.

In *Califano v. Westcott,*[30] the Court held incompatible with the equal-protection principle the payment of welfare benefits to families with unemployed fathers but not to families with unemployed mothers. The consequence—payments are now authorized for families with an unemployed parent, whether the breadwinner temporarily out of work is female or male. The Court emphasized in *Westcott,* as it did earlier in *Orr,* that the statutory scheme had to be adjusted to cast off the "baggage of sexual stereotypes."

Along with the significant victories in *Orr* and *Westcott,* one significant loss occurred. In *Personnel Administration of Massachusetts v. Feeney,*[31] the Court upheld an absolute lifetime preference that Massachusetts accorded to veterans for Civil Service jobs. The extreme preference concededly had a devastating impact on employment opportunities for women. To become a veteran, one must be allowed to serve her country in the military. But the military has maintained highly restrictive quotas and more exacting enlistment standards for females. When litigation in *Feeney* began, over 98 percent of Massachusetts veterans were male. The practical effect of the exorbitant preference—women with perfect grades on the Civil Service examination are turned down in favor of men with barely passing scores.

Orr and *Westcott* suggest that the Court will closely review any law that explicitly invokes a gender-based classification. *Feeney* indicates that when a classification is neutral in form and is drawn for a laudable purpose, for example, aiding veterans, the Court will allow the measure to stand without modification although its adverse impact on one sex is severe and inevitable.

NOTES

1. 332 U.S. 261, 290 (1947).

2. 335 U.S. 464, 467 (1948).

3. *Bradwell v. Illinois,* 83 U.S. (16 Wall.) 130 (1873); *Goesaert v. Cleary, supra,* note 2.

4. *Muller v. Oregon,* 208 U.S. 412 (1908).

5. As quoted in Martin Gruberg, *Women in American Politics* (Oshkosh, Wis.: Academia Press, 1968), p. 4.

6. 88 U.S. (21 Wall.) 162 (1875).

7. Quoted in J. A. Briggs, "How You Going to Get 'Em Back in the

Kitchen? (You Aren't)," *Forbes* 120, no. 10 (November 15, 1977): 177-78.

8. 347 U.S. 483 (1954).

9. Professor, Queens College, and director, Program on Sex Roles and Social Change, Center for the Social Sciences, Columbia University; author of several studies on women in the professions.

10. *Reed v. Reed,* 404 U.S. 71 (1971).

11. *Moritz v. Commissioner of Internal Revenue,* 469 F.2d (10th Cir. 1972), cert. denied, 412 U.S. 906 (1973).

12. November 22, 1971.

13. *Frontiero v. Richardson,* 411 U.S. 677 (1973).

14. Ibid.

15. *DeFunis v. Odegaard,* 416 U.S. 312 (1974).

16. *Regents of the University of California v. Bakke,* 438 U.S. 265 (1978).

17. *Kahn v. Shevin,* 416 U.S. 351 (1974).

18. *Taylor v. Louisiana,* 419 U.S. 522 (1975); *Edwards v. Healy,* 421 U.S. 772 (1975).

19. *Weinberger v. Wiesenfeld,* 420 U.S. 636 (1975).

20. *Goldfarb v. Califano,* 396 F. Supp. 308 (E.D. N.Y. 1975).

21. *Coffin v. Califano,* 440 F. Supp. 953 (D.D.C. 1975).

22. 429 U.S. 190 (1976).

23. *Califano v. Goldfarb,* 430 U.S. 199 (1977).

24. *Califano v. Webster,* 430 U.S. 313 (1977).

25. 427 U.S. 495 (1976).

26. 430 U.S. 703 (1977), affirming 532 F.2d 880 (3d Cir. 1976).

27. *Frontiero v. Richardson, supra* note 13.

28. George Bernard Shaw, "The Womanly Woman," in *The Quintessence of Ibsenism,* 3rd ed. (1922; reprint ed., New York: Hill and Wang, 1957), pp. 47, 55-56.

29. 440 U.S. 268 (1979).

30. 99 S. Ct. 2655 (1979).

31. 99 S. Ct. 2282 (1979).

16.

Status Report on the Women's Movement as Indexed by a "Festival of Women" in West Virginia, Fall 1978,

ANN PATERSON, KAREN FUCHS, CAROL GIESEN, and BETSY HOBBS

A major event like the Festival of Women,[1] which attracted about 1,000 individuals to various parts of the program, raises some larger questions about the value-purpose-payoff of such an event in 1978. The festival took place on a university campus in a small town and in a state that would be considered traditional and rural. Those attending the festival were overwhelmingly women, but not primarily university faculty or students. Our feedback data suggest that the largest subgroup at most of the sessions was composed of townspeople or women who came from out of town. We are therefore confident that the festival audience represented a broad cross section of concerned West Virginia women. The audience also represented a wide age range—from teenagers to septuagenarians, although observation suggested that the festival attracted primarily women over thirty.

Because of the nature of the audience, the questions we asked can suggest the health and pulse rate of the women's movement in 1978 among women who are obviously concerned and involved, yet who are

not the vanguard or resisters to change in the status of women. These
questions were of three kinds.

First, what were the criteria that women used in assessing the festival,
that is, what made a session successful or unsuccessful? These criteria
will suggest the operating evaluative framework women use in judging
themselves and others. Will different subgroups of women make similar
assessments—does objective position in the social structure determine
which criteria are used in assessing festival sessions, or is there consensus
among subgroups of women? Were the three programmatic emphases of
the three days of the festival equally effective in the eyes of the general
audience and among audience subgroups? What might any differential
effectiveness tell us about the women who attended and the issues they
view as important?

Second, how did feedback from those who worked on the festival
differ from audience feedback in general? Were the assessments of the
festival made by nationally famous main speakers consistent with those
of the local festival participants (discussants, chairwomen, committee
workers)? More importantly, what in turn was the impact of the festival
on those who were participants? Were networks of communication and
association created or reinforced by festival participation? If so, were the
created networks of association and/or communication made across the
traditional boundaries of objective social position and between local and
national participants, or were new networks largely intragroup?

Third, in the larger context of the women's movement in the late
1970s, what do the data on the festival suggest about the current status
of the women's movement among the large group of women who are concerned about women's issues, but who are not at the core of the movement either organizationally or politically? Always a potential public
to be mobilized on any specific women's issue, this group can tell us
much about the concerns likely to endure into the 1980s as well as about
the pulse of the movement itself in the larger society.

ASSESSMENTS BY THE FESTIVAL AUDIENCES

The three days of the festival included a wide variety of activities:
eighteen speaker-discussion sessions, two round tables, two consciousness-raising sessions, fifteen films, one play, and two keynote addresses.

Additionally, the festival had informal lunches, dinners, social hours, and receptions. Evaluation data were obtained from the audiences on all of the structured events except for the play. The festival was held on three days; each a week apart, all in September 1978. Each day of the festival had a different focus: "Women's Roles in Society—Issues and Achievements" was the theme of the first day; "Women's Lives and the Impacts of Public Policy" was the theme of the second day; and "Women Facing the Future" was the theme of the third day. The first and last days, both weekdays, were similar in overall format, with speaker-discussion sessions, a round table, films, and a keynote speaker at night. The second day of the festival was held on a Saturday, with the play on the Friday evening before. No round table or keynote speaker was scheduled on Saturday, but two consciousness-raising sessions (on money), films, and speaker-discussion sessions were held during the day.

Evaluation data came from members of the various audiences who filled out forms at the conclusion of the sessions. The forms were handed to each individual entering the room, and a request was made by the chairwoman of each session to complete the forms. Forms were dropped in ballot-type boxes as members of the audience exited.

Providing feedback is a voluntary activity, and not everyone enjoys filling out forms. Aside from the films (on which we had particularly low rates of response due to dark rooms, multiple films per session, and so on), the response rate varied from 15 to 78 percent of the estimated audience, with 44 percent the mean and 50 to 60 percent the modal category. (If the audience size was overestimated, the actual return percentages were underestimated.) Overall, we thought the response rate was good and higher than expected, given our knowledge of other such events where feedback was requested.

The evaluation forms asked for certain standardized information from all of the audiences: (1) overall assessment of the session; (2) assessment of the speaker (if any) and other identifiable participants, such as discussants or chairwomen; (3) learning value of the session; (4) adequacy of coverage of the topic; and (5) whether the session had been personally or professionally relevant to the respondent. The only personal identification data requested were sex[2] and whether the individual was a West Virginia University (WVU) student, WVU faculty or staff person, local townsperson (not WVU), or someone from out of town. Additional information was obtained on special forms prepared for the films and keynote addresses. The keynote speaker forms, for example, asked respondents to check all other sessions attended earlier in the day. (Such data became the basis for estimating the actual attendance at the festival by different types of individuals.)

Overview of the Audience Feedback

By almost any criterion, the festival was judged a success by those providing feedback. A minimum of 60 percent of all of the audiences rated the *overall sessions* as "excellent" or "good," and half of all of the sessions were rated "excellent" by 40 percent or more of the audiences. Only three sessions had overall "fair" or "poor" ratings by as much as 30 percent of the audiences; three other sessions, by contrast, had not a single "fair" or "poor" rating.

The evaluations of the *speakers* were even more positive. All but three of the twenty speakers were given "excellent" ratings by at least 40 percent of the audiences, and in most cases, the speaker ratings were more laudatory than the overall session ratings. Four speakers were less successful, with over 20 percent of the reporting audience giving "fair" or "poor" ratings, but in three of these four cases, even larger percentages of the audience rated the speaker as "excellent," suggesting alternative criteria of assessment being used by different audience members. Overall, however, the speakers were the hit of the festival.

Learning "quite a bit" (rather than "a great deal," "a little," or "hardly anything") was the dominant response to the question of how much had been learned from the session. Only six sessions had as much as 30 percent of the audiences learning "a great deal," and at the other extreme, all sessions had at least 30 percent of the audiences feeling they had learned "little or nothing." *Coverage* of the session topic fared better, with at least 30 percent of twelve audiences giving an "excellent" rating to the topic coverage. At least 30 percent of five other audiences, however, gave only "fair" or "poor" ratings to the coverage.

The fifth general assessment variable was *relevance*—either personal or professional. At least 66 percent of all of the audiences indicated that the session was "relevant" to them either personally or professionally, and 90 percent of the audiences found the subject matter relevant in half of the sessions. Five of the seven sessions that had as much as 15 percent of the audience finding "no special relevance" were on the first day, which had been focused on women's accomplishments. These sessions featured women in the literary arts, the performing arts, the visual arts, legal-medical-dental careers, and "nontraditional" careers. Given the subject matter, the lack of personal or professional relevance was expected. More of the sessions were "personally" relevant than "professionally" relevant to the attendees. In all but four sessions, at least 50 percent of the audience listed the session as "personally" relevant; only one session was "professionally" relevant for 50 percent or more of the audience.

In summary then the various audiences attending the twenty-two structured sessions reported the session as having excellent speakers, good learning value, good coverage, and high levels of relevance. The overall assessments added up to "good" or "excellent" ratings for most sessions. Our concern, however, was less with these absolute ratings than with the criteria being used to assess the overall ratings of a session. What were the ingredients of an overall "excellent" rating? What were the ingredients of "fair" or "poor" ratings?

Variables Indexing Session Satisfaction

Using the percentage of the audience that gave either "excellent" or "fair-poor" ratings to the various sessions as scores, a simple regression was run using four predictor variables to predict both "excellent" overall ratings and "fair-poor" overall ratings.[3] The results of the regression analyses suggest that "excellent" sessions are predicted primarily from having excellent main speakers and for being personally relevant. If professional relevance is substituted for personal relevance, the speaker rating becomes even more important, but professional relevance makes no significant additional contribution to the overall prediction of satisfaction. At the negative end of the satisfaction continuum, poor speakers and poor coverage are the variables that contribute significantly to the overall negative ratings.

We were able to account for more of the variance in the *fair-poor* ratings (85 percent) with our four prediction variables than in the *excellent* ratings using the same four variables.[4] Variance accounted for increased when we used personal (70 percent) rather than professional (60 percent) relevance.

Correlations among the variables indicate[5] that speaker, learning, coverage, and overall satisfaction variables are all highly intercorrelated (this is slightly more true in the case of negative assessments than it is for positive assessments). Personal relevance, however, is a clearly independent variable that is correlated significantly only with overall high satisfaction, but not with high levels of learning, excellent speakers, or good coverage. Personal relevance is related not to lower levels but to higher levels of satisfaction. Professional relevance, on the other hand,[6] is not significantly correlated with any of the other variables. Professional and personal relevance are likewise uncorrelated.[7]

Variations among Subgroups of the Audience

Because our forms asked for designation of respondents as student, faculty-staff, local townsperson, or out of towner, we were able to examine differences among these groups of attendees in some of the better attended sessions. For each of eight speaker-discussion sessions with large numbers of feedback forms, we obtained an average rating of overall learning and satisfaction for each subgroup. Averaging all of these scores, we noted a remarkable degree of similarity in satisfaction and learning ratings among the four subgroups:[8] the ratings are almost identical across the four subgroups.

We also examined the extent to which these same eight sessions were of personal and professional relevance (or both) to members of the four subgroups.[9] Students are the only subgroup where a majority did not find the sessions personally relevant,[10] although a majority did find them professionally relevant.[11] The relatively low student turnout at the festival may be related to the lack of perceived personal relevance of the session topics. Although the festival deliberately sought to attract a cross section of adult women, none of the programs was specially focused on young adult women: marriage and family were stressed, not mating and dating; problems on the job were discussed, but not professional training; and so on. Faculty-staff and students found the sessions most relevant professionally; faculty-staff and out of towners (many were from other colleges) most likely found the sessions personally relevant. Overall, faculty-staff benefited most from dual relevance, perhaps not unexpectedly, as they were the largest group of planners and participants in the festival.

Variations by Day of Festival

Although overall, the four audience subgroups could not be distinguished in terms of learning or overall satisfaction, differences could be found in these ratings for the three days of the festival.[12] Clearly, the *third day* of the festival was the best in terms of both learning and satisfaction. The highest speaker ratings also came on the last day. The program on the third day focused on a set of realistic goals for the future that already seemed to be taking hold–goals that would have the effect of making the position of women brighter in the future. The topics included a variety of law-related issues, including the Equal Rights Amendment (ERA), legislation supporting nonsexist education, and affirmative action and equal-opportunity statutes. Additionally, sessions on women's studies and new family relationships also underscored what is actually being done or could be done to insure that better future. The conference ended on a note of pragmatic optimism.

The *first day* was intermediate in terms of learning, satisfaction, and speaker ratings. The program focused on the actual achievements of women–in the visual arts, the literary arts, the performing arts, the professions, and traditional and nontraditional careers. It was not surprising that learning was high on these days; most of the participants simply did not know about these women's accomplishments, since most of the speakers were not household names. The relatively high satisfaction ratings no doubt reflected both pride and pleasure upon learning of the many achievements of these women. Personal and professional relevance were least evident on this day.

The *second day* of the festival was the least satisfying of the three days for the audience, although all three days received strong positive ratings on an absolute scale. The second day was not less satisfying because the sessions were less relevant–the second-day sessions were the second most relevant set of sessions, both professionally and personally, and were clearly closer to the third than to the first day in terms of relevance.[13] We suspect that the lesser satisfaction and learning on the second day were largely a function of the topics–topics that in general, audience members knew quite a bit about. Health, mental health, money, aging, problems on the job, problems of organizing women, and continuing education are all subjects that individuals must deal with daily and at a personal level. No doubt many solutions or approaches to these concerns had been tried, perhaps unsuccessfully. Because coming to terms with such problems is imperative, more may have been at stake, and thus more dissatisfaction may have resulted when the sessions were unsuccessful.

The second day also was the only one characterized by much controversy. This was apparent in the "additional comments" written on the evaluation forms. Almost no comments were written on the first day about the substance of the talks except in one session, where a discussant was challenged for taking an excessively big-business point of view. Likewise, on the third day, almost no substantive supplementary comments were made, except on the session about new family relationships, which was the most personal of the topics of the day and one that would have fit comfortably into the second day's focus.

In contrast, the second day stood out dramatically in terms of audience feedback. Five of the eight sessions each produced a solid page of voluntary comments. These five sessions focused on health, aging, job-related problems, mental health, and organizing women. Only the continuing education session among the regular speaker-discussion sessions evoked few comments, and this was probably because it turned out to be largely an information-type session.

The substance of the comments on the five controversial sessions suggests several topics, perspectives, and/or issues that caused problems for these audiences. The following points were reiterated: (1) when speakers failed to deal with "tough" issues (such as abortion) and stuck with "safe" subjects, the feedback was negative; (2) when traditional, establishment perspectives were reiterated and feminist viewpoints ignored, the suggestions given during the session were viewed as not useful; (3) when the speakers resorted to academic jargon and complex statistics, the audience pointed out the lack of effective communication on the subject; (4) when too little time was available for discussion that was considered essential to the issues, the festival schedule was attacked; (5) when the topic was considered important but the session wandered off the topic or speakers dealt ineffectively with the topic, the audience felt cheated; and (6) when "militant" tactics were used in a session, many in the audience objected.[14]

By noting what was a problem to the audience, we can begin to understand what the festival audience members thought about women's lives and public impact. It appears that they rejected old solutions and establishment strategies as inappropriate for the present. They accepted the feminist thinking that had by now become a part of their own viewpoint over the last several years. They frowned upon aggressive tactics[15], bookishness, academic jargon, and meaningless statistics. They required relevance, but also a broad view of the subject, not just attention to singular issues. Finally, they saluted competent and effective speakers who dealt with hard realities and got to the core of the stated issue; the audience expected no less.

Implications from the Overall Evaluations

We have been interested in the criteria women used to evaluate the festival as a basis for understanding what is currently important to the cross section of women who were in our audience. First, we have clear evidence that these women admired and applauded knowledgeable and effective speakers. Heralding individual achievement has often been denigrated (or ignored) by the grass-roots segment of the women's movement because of the greater emphasis placed on the collective experience of women acting together and finding common bonds. We find here, however, no distrust of individual accomplishment or resentment of personal fame. Although most of the speakers were not household names, all were acknowledged as leaders in their field, and many women no doubt came because of that fact. The traditional American value of individual achievement is apparently surviving intact. Demonstrated personal competence is one major criterion used by the festival audience in assessing public forums.

Second, we find strong evidence that the women in our audiences were demanding that the programs and speakers be relevant. Those sessions and whole days focused on topics with which the audience could identify personally provided the greatest overall satisfaction. Although all of the sessions were designed to be relevant (and very few of our feedback forms suggested that women found the sessions irrelevant), we found that personal relevance made an independent contribution to our prediction equation for successful programs, one almost as strong as that for the main speakers. Professional relevance, on the other hand, made no independent contribution. Neither professional nor personal relevance was significantly correlated with excellent speaker ratings, learning, or good coverage. We have therefore strong evidence for a second independent and major criterion used by the audience: relevance—women value learning about things that make a difference to themselves, especially in their personal lives. Sessions were relevant if they contributed to personal insight or clarification of one's own situation. Relevance, a major concern of all factions of the 1960s and 1970s women's movement, is a clear component of late 1970s thinking of women in general.

We have additional evidence of the importance of individual achievement and relevance from the evaluation data on the two keynote speakers and from the films shown during the festival. The two *keynote speakers,* Sharon Rockefeller and Ruth Bader Ginsburg, each spoke to an audience of over 300 persons; their speeches were on the first and last days of the festival. The titles of the two addresses were, respectively, "Women in 1978: Are We the Real Silent Majority?" and "Women's Right to Full Partnership in Shaping Society's Course: An Evolving Constitutional Precept." Not surprisingly, the overall ratings for the keynote addresses were high, with 88 percent and 86 percent of the respondents giving the speakers "excellent" or "good" ratings.

On the evaluation form, we asked respondents to check the strengths of the presentations.[16] Ninety-seven of 109 respondents cited the knowledgeability of Ginsburg, and almost as many mentioned the importance of the topic as a strength of her session. Gaining new information or insight was the other factor that was checked by over 60 percent of the audience who attended this intellectual presentation on Supreme Court decisions and critical test cases on sexism. Emotional impact, speaker personality, and entertainment value were unimportant; the audience was highly satisfied with a relevant topic handled competently by a highly knowledgeable speaker.

As the wife of West Virginia's governor, Sharon Rockefeller was better known than Ginsburg, and the audience response reflected a greater interest in the speaker as an individual. Rockefeller's message was less focused on providing information than on applauding the efforts of women in effecting change. Importance of the topic and personality of the speaker were almost equally often checked, with knowledgeability and speaking style mentioned by over 60 percent of the responding audience. Fame was mentioned by half of the respondents, but emotional impact, gaining new information, and entertainment value were less commonly cited. Like the other keynote address, this one received high ratings because of the competence of the speaker (which in this case included a very effective speaking style, as well as general knowledgeability) and the importance of the topic. Relevance and competence had won again.

We also examined the criteria checked by members of the *four subgroups* who returned our keynote speaker forms—students, faculty-staff, local townspeople, and out-of-town members of the audience. For the Ginsburg speech, importance of the topic and knowledgeability of the speaker were the strengths checked most often, and in each subgroup, both were checked on at least 60 percent of the forms. The out of towners also checked "new information-insights" and "thought provoking" above the 60 percent level, but both of these were likewise cognitive evaluations and appeared to be essentially the same criterion stated in slightly different words.

For the Rockefeller keynote address, importance of the topic or personality of the speaker were put either first or second on the list by all four subgroups, and three of the four groups checked knowledgeability at the 60 percent level or higher. Several other criteria were checked by 60 percent or more of a subgroup. The students checked only the three already mentioned, faculty-staff respondents also checked effective speaking style and fame of speaker, and out of towners added fame of speaker and effective speaking style, although they alone did not cite knowledgeability of speaker at the 60 percent level. Despite the slight variation, the overwhelming agreement in the basic assessments of these speakers suggests that members of the audience shared a common perceptual-ideological orientation to the keynote addresses.

Also at the festival, twelve films ran concurrently with all of the other day sessions. Our feedback on the films was limited, but we did request that the audience indicate the strong points of the films by checking their strengths.[17] In a television- and movie-oriented culture, it was surprising to find entertainment value at the bottom of the list of strengths. Direct personal relevance was also not critical, probably because many of the films dealt with extreme behavior, such as rape, actual cases of job discrimination, and so on. The important criteria for assessing film success were "thought provoking" and "importance of the issue." Along with emotional impact, these were the only criteria that were checked on over 50 percent of the forms. However, only "thought provoking" was acknowledged as an important strength by two-thirds of the audience, making a cognitive assessment of intellectual relevance the real key to success for the festival films.

Of the criteria used by women to evaluate the festival, a third criterion

emerges from the assessment of the poorer festival sessions, that of adequacy of coverage of the material. (The first two criteria were competence and relevance.) Inadequate coverage of the topic was a significant independent contributor to fair-poor ratings. But what did "inadequate coverage" mean? The comments voluntarily written in by audience
members suggest that poor coverage sometimes meant a shortsighted view
of the subject. But poor coverage also had an ideological dimension.
Speakers or sessions that were establishment oriented or that turned into
advocacy sessions for a singular point of view were given low ratings. Ignoring feminist issues was particularly offensive to audience members and
brought comments such as "She seemed naive and brainwashed." When
speakers failed to deal with real problems and issues, many in the audience were insulted. On the other hand, by the late 1970s, militant
feminism had run its course, and any perspective that offered only extreme or singular solutions was found wanting. As a third criterion,
the festival audience wanted a *creative* and *comprehensive* approach to
the problems of women, an approach compatible with the new realities
of women's position in society and with the multidimensional and complex lives that women now lead.

Finally, we have strong evidence that the women who came to the
festival were more united across objective social categories than even
they were aware of. Faculty, professional staff, secretaries, agency personnel, housewives, and students all had remarkably similar assessments
of the festival sessions. Although we have no basis for knowing if such
similarities are more the case now than in the past, an educated guess is
that they are. Few women could have escaped the influence of the
women's movement over the last decade, and probably many have personally benefited from it. Rising expectations have an infectious quality
and likely become the informal standard against which specific behaviors
are judged. We suspect that the unity of perspective among the festival
attendees is *not* the result of common memberships and concerted collective action, but rather stems from countless individual assessments of the
quality of present life that women judged against a common picture of
the hopes and dreams projected by the women's movement. Inadvertent-
ly, women in many different circumstances arrived *individually* at similar
conclusions about what it takes to attain that future good life—competence, relevance, and creative-comprehensive perspectives on the problems that arise. One of the most important functions of the festival may

have been providing an occasion for identifying these common perspectives and actually affirming them together. Our feedback suggests that women were both pleased and surprised at discovering how many other women shared their world view.

ASSESSMENTS BY AND IMPACT ON FESTIVAL PARTICIPANTS

The second major question in our festival evaluation asked about the effects that participating in the festival would have on both the local and national participants. The "local" participants included the eighty-nine local women who worked on the various festival committees or who participated in the sessions as chairwomen, discussants, or facilitators. The "national" participants were the eighteen speakers in the speaker-discussion sessions and the two keynote speakers.

We have two kinds of data available on each group: (1) opinion data on satisfaction with the festival and so on and (2) network data on the extent to which the festival created or extended networks of communication and contact between participants.

All of the data from the national speakers come from a mail questionnaire sent out one week after the end of the festival. Fourteen of the twenty speakers replied and gave generally positive feedback on the festival. Half of the speakers thought the festival was as effective as other similar events they had participated in; the other half found it more effective. All had been satisfied with the arrangements for accommodation, transportation, and so on. Some weaknesses were noted—"should have had a more specific goal (setting up a day care center, planning a women's studies program, and so on)"; "the need for Third World women speakers . . . was considerable"; "the paucity of student participation was very strange"—but also some areas of strength—"your special strength was in the presence of people who represent a cross-discipline approach"; "enjoyed learning from women from distant places *and* from West Virginia women—good combination"; "the topics and formats were outstanding."

As part of the mail questionnaire, we asked our twenty speakers to check whether they had known any of the other speakers before the festival or whether they had met them at the festival. We also asked speakers to indicate any local participants in the festival whom they had made a point of remembering (we asked the speakers to *write in* the names of such local people; they really had to be remembered). None of the speakers on the first day, indicated prior acquaintance with any of the other speakers, and none indicated meeting more than four other speakers during the day (although six had participated in a round table together in the afternoon). As the speakers had only to check the names of those other main speakers they had met (recognition of names, not recall), we concluded that the first day had been unsuccessful in creating networks of new association between the speakers themselves. All four speakers who returned the questionnaire did, however, write in the names of local festival people they had met and wanted to remember.

The second day of the festival did not include a round table involving all of the speakers, and not surprisingly, few contacts were made among speakers. One speaker did not recall meeting any of the other speakers, but another one identified five she had met; the mean was two other speakers recalled. Again, all of the main speakers identified local participant contacts that had been established.

The third day of the festival involved another round table, but this time a presession was built into the schedule to organize the six speakers before the round table took place. The speakers were more likely to remember the other speakers on the third day. This was partly because, on this day, unlike on the previous days, some of the speakers had known each other before the festival, but probably also because of the greater level of interaction that had taken place among the speakers. Again, local contacts were recalled by all respondents.

Our overall conclusion on the national participants was that the festival had served to create a new contacts between the speakers themselves and probably created an equal number of contacts between local participants (mostly WVU faculty) and the national speakers. Overall, however, the impact of the festival *on* the national participants was at best modest.

Our data were more substantial on the festival's impact on *local* participants. Again, we had multiple types of data, but the most important was the pre-post "network survey." In July, before the September festival, we mailed each of the 89 known local participants a "network survey" that asked the respondents to identify each of 116 people on a list as "not known," "know who she is," "known slightly," or "known fairly well." The list included all of the speakers, session participants, and committee workers then on the program (there were some subsequent changes). Sixty-six questionnaires were returned and three were un-deliverable, for an initial response rate of 77 percent. A postsurvey was sent in October, about a week after the last day of the festival. This sur-vey was identical to the one sent in July but had an additional page of questions seeking reaction to the festival. Forty-two of those who re-turned the presurvey completed the postsurvey as well. The two network surveys allowed us to determine if people knew more people in October than they had known before the festival, or if they got to know more people better. We were also able to determine whether the new people met between July and October were faculty, professional staff, local townspeople, and so on.

The extra page on the October survey allowed us to obtain separate assessments of the festival by the workers (in contrast with the general audience). Additionally, one year later, in June 1979, we did a telephone survey asking local participants to reflect on the value of the festival from the perspective of a year later. We reached 43 local participants in this telephone survey.

The Network Survey Results

Comparing the July and October surveys, we looked initially to see if the local festival participants recognized the names of more of the national speakers in October or July. On the average, the twenty speakers were known by 9.3 more individuals in October than in July, an increase that is statistically significant.[18] It was still the case, however, that except for the keynote speakers, none of the other speakers' names was recog-nized in October by over 50 percent of the respondents; the average speaker was remembered by only 35 percent of the 42.0 respondents who returned both surveys.

We also analyzed the average number of people on the survey list known "slightly" or "well" in July versus October.[19] The increase in average number of people known "slightly" or "well" is statistically significant.[20]

In a similar manner, we looked *separately* at only those people known "slightly" or "well" in these two periods.[21] The increases in these totals are also statistically significant,[22] leading us to conclude that the festival was successful not only in creating networks of acquaintance but also in fostering increased intimacy among participants.

We had enough women in three of our network subgroups to do comparisons of the extent and type of network formation.[23] For these three subgroups—faculty, professional staff, and local townspeople—it is clear that the biggest increases between July and October came in the "know who she is" category. All three respondent groups significantly increased in the number of names that were now recognized, and in each respondent group, the greatest increases were in the number of out of towners who were now recognized. The professional staff, for example, now recognized on the average an additional 2.9 names of out of towners (the main speakers).

Three categories had actual decreases between October and July, possibly because people tended to get to know others better, thus reducing the number of superficial acquaintances over the period. The data do not allow us to see whether the *same* people changed categories over the four-month period; we have only summary data on the number of people in each category.

Thus the following generalizations about the three respondent groups emerge. *Faculty* alone did not get to know more people well, they became acquainted with many out of towners, and they learned the names of some professional staff and out-of-towners. The *professional staff* members got to know better both other professional staff and members of the faculty, they made almost no new contacts with any group, and they greatly increased their recognition rate of names of out of towners, local townspeople, and other professional staff. The *local townspeople* got better acquainted, especially with faculty; they met some of the out-of-towners; and they greatly increased their recognition of the names of out of towners and other local townspeople.

If we simply count significant increases in types of festival participants known, it is apparent that out of towners became more known than other subgroups. As most of these women were the main speakers, this is not surprising. The names of famous women are likely easier to retain. Faculty were the local group most likely to become better known, with professional staff and local townspeople more likely to have been met or to have their names recognized. Although faculty became better known to others, it is interesting that they in turn came to know fewer new names or people than was true of the other two respondent groups.

Whether this reflects different standards for assessing how well one knows someone—perhaps faculty were less likely to say that they know someone "fairly well"—is unclear. It is also possible that in their more pivotal roles in the festival, they became better known *to* others but had less opportunity to learn *about* others.

The Telephone Survey Results

The telephone survey was done in June 1979, almost a year after the first network survey was mailed. The telephone sample was the same as for the network surveys except that members of the Evaluation Committee (ourselves) and members of the Planning Committee (nine people) were not called. The members of the Planning Committee had been responsible for the conceptualization of the festival and therefore had a major investment in it; the topics and format of the festival reflected that committee's assessment of what would interest and was needed by local women, and end-of-festival reports written by members of that committee indicated their satisfaction with the festival experience. We thought this group could tell us little more. For the telephone survey, we wanted to reach those who had a more marginal investment in the festival and who therefore would better represent a broader segment of the community of concerned women. These are "concerned" women because all of them had agreed to some level of participation in the festival as committee workers.

Of the seventy-six individuals we tried to contact by telephone, forty-three were actually reached (60 percent). On a subgroup basis, we reached twenty-two of thirty-five potential faculty, seven of fifteen professional staff members, five of six clerical staff members, and nine of twenty local townspeople. The forty-three individuals contacted were asked to reflect on the impact of the festival from the perspective of almost a year later. More specifically, they were asked to indicate how many sessions they attended, which sessions they had found in retrospect to have had the most long-term impact, and what the overall value of festival participation had been for them personally.

Probably because this sample excluded members of two very active committees, the average number of sessions attended by the remaining participants was only 3.4, compared with the results of our second network survey reported earlier, where the median number of sessions attended was 4.5. Within the telephone sample, the average number of sessions or events attended was higher for the professional staff (4.8 sessions) and the local townspeople (3.0 sessions), with the faculty reporting only 1.8 sessions. Four of the six clerical staff contacted had attended at least 1.0 session, but their attendance record was the poorest of the subgroups. (This last group also had the greatest difficulty getting time off to attend sessions, unlike the other groups, where greater flexibility in work schedules is the rule.) All but 13 percent of the respondents indicated that they definitely would have attended at least a few more sessions had their other commitments allowed. That 13 percent either had attended everything they found interesting or else were not attracted to the festival program. Overall, however, festival participants had been positive about the program.

Each telephone respondent was asked to indicate the one session that had had the greatest impact on her and to analyze why. The session selected came in all cases from either the first day (55 percent) or from the last day (45 percent); no one cited a second-day session as the best, perhaps because no keynote address was presented on this day, and keynote addresses were most often mentioned on the other days. Professional staff especially were likely to select one of the first day's sessions, where the emphasis was on the achievements of women. A review of the reasons given for liking high-impact sessions revealed two themes. First, some sessions were remembered because a specific speaker was remembered—personalities were important. Second, festival sessions had been remembered because they provided an occasion for confirming or reassessing personal views on a subject. What we did *not* find was evidence that the high-impact sessions had been important because they provided *initial* awareness of a problem, that is, no evidence could be found that the festival provided basic consciousness raising, although some individuals did indicate that they were *re*thinking their views on a subject.

When we asked for the primary reason for a session being remembered, the bases of attractiveness of the sessions were of three types: (1) *speaker*-focused comments, such as "the speaker was articulate, knowledgeable, concrete," "the speaker was an independent woman"; (2) *audience*-focused comments, such as "good audience interaction"; and (3) *content*-focused comments, such as "extremely interesting," "context of talk."

The majority of all of the comments were speaker focused, but the faculty gave 30 percent audience-focused comments, and the professional and clerical staff were more likely to make content-focused comments. Different subgroups apparently use different criteria to judge success. Faculty, for whom less new material was learned, were more likely to judge success by effective dialogue or communication about the topic; the professional and clerical staff were more likely to have gained more actual new information. It is interesting that all of the comments by local townspeople were speaker focused; personalities were the central attraction with this group.

If a session was remembered because of a good speaker, we asked what made a good speaker. Fame was not a major reason, as often the speaker's name was not recalled, only the subject of the talk. Again, three types of reasons emerged: (1) the speaker had an exceptional *speaking ability,* for example, "spoke honestly, natural, open, casual," "was articulate"; (2) the speaker had an attractive *personality,* for example, "aggressive," "personal sincerity"; and (3) the speaker was *competent,* for example, "well informed," "achieved in her field," "spoke from experience." Again, differences by subgroup emerged; faculty and local townspeople mentioned each of the three criteria in about equal proportion, but both professional and clerical staff tended to cite either speaking skills or personality.

Earlier in this chapter, we noted that immediate feedback data on the festival stressed the importance of the speakers in predicting successfully rated sessions; the present data confirm the importance of the speakers and suggest that speakers are largely responsible for long-term impact. Although many speaker qualities are important, personality and competence are best remembered. These same qualities were mentioned again when we asked our telephone respondents to indicate qualities of speakers they would like to emulate.

The second general reason for session impact was the tendency of the session to reinforce the respondents' own viewpoint. Two-thirds to three-quarters of each respondent subgroup indicated that their own views had been supported or that they had rethought their views on a given issue.

Most women reported that participation in the festival (as a discussant, committee worker, and so on) had been a positive experience. They also indicated feeling good about being part of a group of women sharing

a common experience with comments such as, "I felt increased support
for my own point of view," "I heard another group of women saying
things I've thought," and "I liked learning of others with similar problems." Beyond mentioning shared viewpoints, we also found a "feeling
of identity" and "increased awareness of others," "an excitement about
seeing that many people together," and enjoyment at "being one of a
group with diverse backgrounds but with a sense of unity." It was probably feelings of this sort that resulted in an overall feeling of optimism
about the future status of women.

One exception to the overall feeling of group unity was that 80 percent
of the professional staff respondents reported a neutral or negative image
of the festival as a source of solidarity for themselves, although the same
women reported feeling encouraged about the future status of women.
It is not clear why professional staff women more than others would
report being "only remotely involved" or serving as a "bridge between
the audience and the participants." It is possible that professional staff
women perceived their assisting with the festival as a professional, job-
related activity. Many of these women regularly are involved in putting
on conferences and doing public relations work, and for them, the festival
may have been "more of the same."

In summary, the telephone survey documented the nature of the long-
term impact of the Festival of Women on local participants. Although
memories of specific events and names of people had faded over the year
of elapsed time, important residual effects were evident. Most remembered were the speakers—their speaking styles, personalities, and competence—although names and the specific content of their talks might
have been forgotten. Respondents also remembered when sessions had
reinforced or challenged their views on a subject, which we take to mean
that the festival had been remembered for its intellectual challenge and
its learning value. Finally, respondents had a residual memory that it
had felt good to be part of a group of women sharing similar problems
and often similar views on those problems.

The nature of the comments suggested that the festival had been well
received by the participants and that if asked in the future about successful events focused on women, the festival will serve as an exemplar. The
specific formula for a successful festival-type event appears to be providing both cognitive and affective impact by providing a context for
women to learn together from competent and attractive other women.

IMPLICATIONS FOR THE WOMEN'S MOVEMENT

The fate of social movements has long been of interest to sociologists who have studied the life cycles of movements, the ability of movements to transform their goals, and the internal changes in the leadership style and organizational structure that tend to accompany waxing and waning movement strength. Our interest here is not in the internal structures of the women's movement,—for example, the nature of core groups such as the National Organization for Women (NOW) or the National Women's Political Caucus—but in that large potential public of women that rides the ebb and flow of changing public sentiment. This group ultimately will, by its interest, determine which new issues, problems, and programs will receive large-scale focus and support and thus will determine the direction the women's movement will take and if in fact it will survive at all.

Generalizing from studies of other social movements,[24] we can suggest that the women's movement[25] structurally has built into it both the potential for its survival and the sources of its own dissolution. On the survival side, one structural feature is its inclusive membership, which means that a full range of viewpoints will likely flourish within the movement. This helps the movement to be sensitive to changing public sentiment and to reflect that general sentiment even if more radical (or conservative) viewpoints also are expressed.

Given a comprehensive membership and a wide range of issues and viewpoints expressed, movements are at the same time vulnerable to co-optation by other groups that have become identified with one or more specific issues and/or programs of the movement. Women's caucuses in industry, government, professional associations, and academia, for example, have largely taken over the fight for equal pay, leaving this somewhat of a nonissue within the women's movement itself. If too many issues are co-opted, the movement dies from lack of any clearly defined goals or causes. Boundaries that are too weak are a structural liability.

Again on the survival side, movements that rely on solidary incentives (prestige, respect, friendship) have had higher survival rates than those that have had to rely on purposive or monetary incentives. In the women's movement, solidary incentives commonly go under the rubric of "sisterhood," and new converts to feminism seldom fail to mention the wonderful discovery of other females as friends and the delights of sororal companionship. On the vulnerable side, however, those who are enjoying each other often get caught up in the sheer pleasure of the relationship and are prone to lose their focus on specific goals. Under these conditions, a movement may be transformed into a social club with primarily expressive goals, and more purposive activities largely cease.

Another survival strength of the women's movement is that it is avowedly out to change individuals as well as society. Although individual change is potentially less threatening to establishment interests than tactics aimed exclusively at changing institutions, the real point is that movements focused on individuals are not dependent on the specific accomplishments of the movement to insure movement survival. Institutionwide failures are readily indexed, and commitment is likely to wane in the absence of successes, but at the individual level, some successes are almost inevitable, and the individual failures are more readily explained away as quirks of individuals.

Finally, social movements that have "exclusive" memberships should more readily mobilize to take on new goals if survival is threatened; more "inclusive" membership movements are vulnerable to fading away— or being transformed into intrinisically satisfying groups. The very breadth of interest and nonspecificity of programs and goals in the broad-based movement make it less likely that threats to survival will be recognized or that subgroups can be effectively mobilized to transform the movement.

Using this framework, we can make an assessment of the viability of the women's movement in 1979, as seen from the perspective of the concerned women in the larger public. We are concerned about the following questions: (1) Is the women's movement's membership still "inclusive" and the issues broad; (2) are viable issues still being addressed, or have they been co-opted; (3) are solidary incentives still being provided by the movement, or have purposive ones taken over; (4) is individual change still the primary focus of the women's movement, or is institutional transformation of increasing importance; and (5) is goal transformation occurring in the women's movement?

To answer the first question, the range of people attending the festival suggests that the movement is still attracting a broad audience with diverse interests. The festival included faculty, professional and clerical staff, social service agency personnel, housewives, and students. The range of topics that attracted audiences underscores the inclusiveness of the concerns that continue to interest women. Nevertheless, certain differences in content and audience focus did emerge. Our data indicate that greatest interest (attendance and positive feedback) was either in personally relevant issues—health, homes, jobs—or in sessions focused on political and legal processes—the effective change mechanisms in our society.

Audience enthusiasm for the festival itself suggests initially an affirmative answer to the second question: viable questions are still being addressed by the movement. The women who came wanted information on or insight into ways to deal with specific personal problems, or they sought political techniques for effecting change in organizations, communities, and so on. The festival itself had no specific political or social outcomes built into it, and the failure to predefine such outcomes apparently did not deter attendance or create negative assessments of the festival. Women came to learn, not primarily to accomplish something specific.

Despite lack of specific goals, a consensus seemed to be developing across sessions of the festival about the importance of the ERA. The existence of this yet-unattained goal may in fact be serving the strategic function of providing a symbol of outward consensus among women. Throughout the festival, many speakers independently stressed the importance of the passage of the ERA. Failure to pass the ERA may be a major reason for continuation of the women's movement in the immediate future.

Although ERA passage provides a viable issue for the women's movement, interest shown in programs on political and legal strategy suggests the potential for co-optability of yet another current concern of the women's movement. Women working in diverse fields came to the festival and gained ideas and techniques for political and legal action that they could take back to use in their own areas of expertise. If successfully used, over time, the movement will become deprived of one of its present distinctive services—providing political and legal know-how. A more comprehensive answer to the second question then is mixed—the ERA currently provides the movement with a viable issue, but to the extent that women seek out the movement to learn how to get things done politically or legally, eventual co-optation (in providing these skills) by other units of our society is encouraged.[26]

The third question is related to the second. We have noted the purposive incentive provided by the ERA campaign; a related question is

whether solidary incentives are also provided. The concern with passage
of the ERA itself provides both a purposive and a solidary incentive, because this effort is at the same time both a specific goal to be obtained
and a reminder of common subordinate status. Subordinate status usually
provides an inherent basis for solidarity as long as superordinates remain
visible and conspicuously advantaged. But beyond this basis for psychological cohesiveness, the festival suggested the importance of continuing discovery by individuals of other like-minded women. Data from the
telephone survey suggested that many women attended the festival out
of an *intellectual obligation* to support women's activities rather than as
a result of being swept into such activities by existing affective ties to
other women. Existing social solidarities, in other words, did not *promote*
attendance for many (although certainly this was a factor in attendance
by some), but solidarities were often *created* by attendance at the festival.
Our network data suggest that women made new acquaintances and
deepened old ones as a result of festival participation; our telephone
interviews suggested pleasure in such ties and delight in finding that other
women shared their own views, were asking similar questions, and were
seeking similar knowledge. Even if the motivation for attendance for
many was initially purposive (an obligation to support other women), the
outcome of attendance was often the creation of a solidarity incentive
to continue such support. We can seriously ask how support could be
alternatively generated in the absence of events such as our festival. For
a movement whose issues are potentially co-optable, few occasions are
likely to create solidarity incentives in the larger public of women.[27]
The third question gets a positive answer for the movement, but a concern about the sources of solidarity incentives in the future must be raised.

The festival data provide evidence that consciousness raising about
women's status is an accomplished fact, not a current concern—sessions
that failed to deal with the issues that have been repeatedly raised by
feminists received negative assessments. But a lack of present concern
about consciousness raising does not mean a lack of focus on the
individual. The preferred topics of the festival suggest strong emphasis
on individual solutions to personal problems and strong support for the
advancement and achievement of individual women. All of these results
are indicators of a continued emphasis on the individual rather than
the sisterhood.[28]

Shared concern showed up most clearly in terms of widespread interest in learning about how to effect change. The diverse, specific interests of the audience members suggest, however, that these changes are likely to be implemented within particular organizations or units (such as health agencies or individual families) rather than on a unified national basis through events like a march on Washington.[29] Such collective responses have in the past been supported more by core groups of the women's movement than by the larger public on which we are focused, and we assume that this will continue to be the case. The institutional transformation hopes of the women's movement appear more likely to be fragmented than unified, with major successes in the movement continuing to be indexed at the level of the individual. Positive changes that do occur (in bettering the status of women) in the future therefore will be less likely identified with the movement and more likely perceived as the result of special-interest or organizational efforts. The absence of specific losses (the ERA has not yet been completely lost) strengthens the survival odds of the movement, as does the emphasis on changing individuals, but the apparent fragmentation weakens the chances for viable issues to be taken seriously on a national, collective basis.

The most difficult question is the fifth one, because our data are not from the core groups of the women's movement but from the larger public. We can, however, rephrase the question to make it relevant to our data: to what extent are the interests of the concerned, educated women who attended the festival reflected in the current programs of core groups of the women's movement as these programs have become publicly visible? (We are not concerned about the nonpublic interests of such groups.) To avoid the chicken-and-egg argument potentially involved—has general public interest forced change in the national leadership, or has national leadership redirected the thinking of the public—we can simply ask about the congruence of interests of local and national groups.

Two specific examples are suggestive. First, the extensive comments written about the second day of the festival document the importance to local women of avoiding extremist, militant solutions and methods—balanced perspectives are sought and clearly preferred by most. At the national level, the election of Eleanor Smeal to the presidency of the National Organization for Women likewise suggests a move toward moderation within that organization. Family and home life under Smeal appear to have a legitimacy that the more strident tones of Karen DeCrow, her precedessor, did not foster.

Second, the festival audience expressed great interest in social change, as shown by feedback ratings and overall high attendance on the last day of the festival. Sessions focused on women and the law, the ERA, affirmative action-equal opportunity, new family relationships, sexism in the schools, and Supreme Court decisions—all areas of public policy where the majority of women reported the session "personally relevant." We conclude that women sought out the festival to learn both about the nature of social changes that are in progress and about the change processes themselves. As this chapter was being written, the National Women's Political Caucus had identified its major programmatic theme as providing women with political insight and skills for use in the 1980 election. Political education had apparently been identified as a major need (or interest) of women, and at least one major national organization had moved to fill that void.

Both of the above examples indicate the congruence between the interests of our local audiences and the leadership of at least two core groups of the women's movement. They suggest no lack of responsiveness to the interests of the public but rather a sensitivity to such interests. As suggested above, an emphasis on change processes may facilitate long-range co-optability of the movement, but now this emphasis insures the viability of the movement.

NOTES

1. The 1978 September Festival of Women, which was held on the campus of West Virginia University, was made possible through grants from the Humanities Foundation of West Virginia and the WVU Foundation. As one of the conditions for receiving such grants, an evaluation of the festival was required. An extensive evaluation report (102 pages) was completed in December 1978 by the Evaluation Committee for the festival. This article uses data from that report but has been entirely rewritten to fit this book. The four members of the Evaluation Committee all have had training in evaluation; at the time of the festival, two were on the faculty of West Virginia University in sociology and education,

and two were doctoral candidates in psychology. The committee operated with complete autonomy and was responsible for the conceptualization of the evaluation strategy, the design of all evaluation forms, and the analysis of all of the data. The conslusions reached in this chapter are the responsibility of the committee and do not necessarily reflect the views of the Planning Committee of the festival or other festival participants. Appreciation is expressed to Margie Marguez, who did much of the original data tabulation, and to Kenette Carlson, Debbie Bizick, and Sherry Wilson for manuscript typing.

2. So few men were present at most of the sessions that separate analysis by sex was not done. Responses by males are not included in the reported results unless noted.

3. The resulting beta weights for the four variables are given in the table below. Part A uses *personal* relevance as one of four variables to predict overall "excellent" ratings; Part B uses *professional* relevance in the same prediction equation. In the prediction of "fair-poor" overall satisfaction (Part C), the percentages of the audience citing "no special relevance" were used in the equation. Because beta weights are on the same scale, they may be directly compared; that is, in Part A, "excellent" main speaker ratings are weighted more than high learning or excellent coverage ratings. At the other end of the scale, "fair-poor" speaker ratings and "fair-poor" coverage ratings are about equally weighted in terms of predicting "fair-poor" overall ratings.

BETA WEIGHTS FOR FOUR VARIABLES USED TO PREDICT OVERALL "EXCELLENT" AND "FAIR-POOR" RATINGS WITH THE FESTIVAL SESSIONS, WITH MULTIPLE CORRELATION COEFFICIENTS

PART A

Predictor Variables (%)	Beta Weights for Predicting Overall "Excellent" Ratings	
"Excellent" main speaker	0.46^a	
"Great deal" learning	0.18	$R^2 = 0.70$
"Excellent" coverage	0.16	
"Personal" relevance	0.33^a	$R = 0.84$

PART B

Predictor Variables (%)	Beta Weights for Predicting Overall "Excellent" Ratings	
"Excellent" main speaker	0.57[a]	$R^2 = 0.60$
"Great deal" learning	0.15	
"Excellent" coverage	0.13	$R = 0.77$
"Professional" relevance	-0.05	

PART C

Predictor Variables (%)	Beta Weights for Predicting Overall "Fair-Poor" Ratings	
"Fair-poor" main speaker	0.58[a]	$R^2 = 0.85$
"Little or no" learning	-0.10	
"Fair-poor" coverage	0.54[a]	$R = 0.92$
"No special" relevance	0.01	

[a]Beta weight significant at 0.05 level.

---

4. Note the multiple R's at the right of the beta weights (see footnote 3).

5. The intercorrelation matrices are given in the table below.

INTERCORRELATION AMONG OVERALL SATISFACTION, SPEAKER RATINGS, LEARNING RATINGS, COVERAGE RATINGS, AND PERSONAL-PROFESSIONAL RELEVANCE FOR *HIGH* OVERALL SATISFACTION RATINGS AND *LOW* OVERALL SATISFACTION RATINGS

	(1)	(2)	(3)	(4)	(5)
(1) Overall satisfaction	—	0.84	0.79	0.82	0.10
(2) Main speaker	0.75	—	0.76	0.63	-0.08
(3) Learning	0.62	0.66	—	0.84	0.02

(4) Adequacy of coverage	0.64	0.72	0.71	—	0.25
(5) Personal relevance	0.43	0.17	0.07	0.06	—
Professional relevance	0.07	0.20	-0.06	0.11	—

Note: High satisfaction ratings below the diagonal; low satisfaction ratings above the diagonal.

Values for relevance (item 5) vary according to whether personal or professional relevance is considered; the correlation between personal and professional relevance is -0.03.

In all of the above correlations, N = 22, except in the case of the main speaker variable, where N = 18, as four sessions did not have main speakers but could be assessed on the other variables. For N = 22, a correlation of 0.423 or above is significantly different from zero; for N = 18, the critical value is 0.468 ($p = 0.05$).

6. See second row of values for item 5 in the preceding table.
7. $r = 0.03$.
8. Both variables have a possible score range from 1 to 4. Table is based on eight sessions only (all sessions had at least thirty-nine forms returned).

LEARNING AND SATISFACTION RATINGS AMONG FOUR SUBGROUPS

	MEAN LEARNING	MEAN SATISFACTION
Students	2.80	3.12
Faculty-staff	2.80	3.22
Local townspeople	2.81	3.29
Out of towners	2.87	3.20

9. The average percentages of the four subgroups who found the sessions personally and/or professionally relevant are given in the following table. Table is based on eight sessions only. These eight sessions

represented the most popular sessions of the festival. The only one on the first day, the round table, focused on reconciling home and career. The second day's sessions focused on job-related problems, aging, mental health, and organizing women; the last day's sessions among the eight were on the ERA, new family relationships, and a look at the future (fifty years ahead).

PERSONAL AND PROFESSIONAL RELEVANCE OF FESTIVAL SESSIONS TO FOUR SUBGROUPS (IN PERCENTAGES)

	PERSONAL ONLY	PROFESSIONAL ONLY	BOTH PERSONAL AND PROFESSIONAL	"TOTAL" PERSONAL	"TOTAL" PROFESSIONAL
Students	22	36	24	46	60
Faculty-staff	21	24	44	65	68
Local townspeople	36	26	22	58	48
Out-of-towners	31	21	37	68	58

10. Combining the "personal only" and "both" categories to get "total" personal relevance.

11. Combining the "professional only" and "both" categories to get "total" professional relevance.

12. These figures represent averages over the structured day sessions: seven on the first and third days, eight on the second day.

LEARNING AND SATISFACTION RATINGS BY DAYS OF FESTIVAL

	MEAN LEARNING	MEAN SATISFACTION
First day (issues and achievements)	2.85	3.25

Second day (women's lives and the impact of public policy)	2.68	3.14
Third day (women facing the future)	3.05	3.51

13. The table below shows the percentages of the audience finding each day's sessions personally or professionally relevant.

PERSONAL AND PROFESSIONAL RELEVANCE
OF FESTIVAL SESSIONS BY DAY OF FESTIVAL

	"TOTAL" PERSONAL RELEVANCE	"TOTAL" PROFESSIONAL RELEVANCE
First day (issues and achievements)	48	40
Second day (women's lives and the impact of public policy)	66	52
Third day (women facing the future)	74	58

14. The session on organizing women was distinguished by audience members from the National Organization for Women capturing much of the discussion period and actually passing out petitions to be signed on the spot and sent to Congress. Many in the audience thought that this was a planned part of the program (which it was not), and many comments expressed resentment of the NOW presence and tactics.

15. The NOW approach.

16. The figures reported in the table below are the actual number of people checking each response.

STRENGTHS OF THE PRESENTATIONS

	GINSBURG (N = 109)	ROCKEFELLER (N = 92)
Importance of topic	87	78

New information-insights provided	66	26
Thought provoking	55	35
Emotional impact	15	27
Interesting-entertaining	39	37
Knowledgeability of speaker	97	62
Personality of speaker	28	74
Fame of speaker	51	51
Effective speaking style	47	68

17. The following table does not control for the rating of each film by the audience, but we do know that seven of the twelve films had over 50 percent of the audience indicating that the film was "excellent." Again, the numbers refer to the actual number of responses made indicating a strength of one of the twelve films. The table below summarizes 170 evaluation forms but represents fewer individuals, as many people saw several films.

STRENGTHS OF THE FILMS

	RESPONSE
Thought provoking	115
Importance of the issue	99
Emotional impact	86
Timeliness of topic	77
Good technically	72
Universality of theme	70
Well paced	66
Personally relevant	57
Entertaining	56

18. $p < 0.001$.

19. The table below presents the averages for July and October for people checking one of two categories.

AVERAGE NUMBER OF PEOPLE CHECKED AS "KNOWN SLIGHTLY" OR "KNOWN FAIRLY WELL" IN JULY AND OCTOBER

	"KNOWN SLIGHTLY" OR "KNOWN FAIRLY WELL"
July	23.72
October	27.45

20. $p < 0.001$.

21. The table below presents the averages for each category for July and October.

AVERAGE NUMBER OF PEOPLE CHECKED AS "KNOWN SLIGHTLY" OR "KNOWN FAIRLY WELL" IN JULY AND OCTOBER

	"KNOWN SLIGHTLY"	"KNOWN FAIRLY WELL"
July	10.95	12.78
October	13.28	14.18

22. $p < 0.05$.

23. The following table is complex, but it will be easier to follow if it is remembered that the *columns* represent the three subgroups of *respondents* (faculty, professional staff, and local townspeople) who answered the July and October network surveys; the *rows* represent four categories of people (including out of towners) who became known to the survey respondents: Part A indicates how many more people in each of four categories were now recognized by name; Part B indicates how many new acquaintances were made among people in each category; and Part C indicates the number of people in each category whom the survey respondents got to know better.

MEAN NUMBER AND TYPE OF CONTACTS MADE
BY THREE GROUPS OF FESTIVAL PARTICIPANTS

PART A: KNOW WHO SHE IS

		Network Respondents	
Categories of People Known by Respondents	*Faculty (N = 22)*	*Professional Staff (N = 10)*	*Local Townspeople (N = 7)*
Faculty	0.5	0.3	1.6
Professional staff	0.4^a	0.5^a	-0.1
Local townspeople	-0.1	0.8^a	1.3^b
Out-of-towners	2.1^a	2.9^b	3.9^b
Total group^c	3.1^a	4.7^a	6.3^b

PART B: KNOW HER SLIGHTLY

		Network Respondents	
Categories of People Known by Respondents	*Faculty (N = 22)*	*Professional Staff (N = 10)*	*Local Townspeople (N = 7)*
Faculty	0.5	0.4	0.4
Professional staff	0.3	-0.4	0.3
Local townspeople	0.5	0.2	0.4
Out-of-towners	1.7^a	0.2	1.6^b
Total group^c	3.0^a	0.4	2.6

PART C: KNOW HER FAIRLY WELL

		Network Respondents	
Categories of People Known by Respondents	*Faculty (N = 22)*	*Professional Staff (N = 10)*	*Local Townspeople (N = 7)*
Faculty	-0.5	1.5^a	3.0^b
Professional staff	0.2	1.0^a	0.4

Local townspeople	0.1	0.1	0.9
Out-of-towners	0.1	0.3	0.4[a]
Total group[c]	0.0	4.0[b]	4.5[b]

[a]$p < 0.05$ (one-tail t-test)
[b]$p < 0.01$ (one-tail t-test)
[c]Total group includes a few students and clerical staff who were known to the network respondents. So few in these groups returned the network surveys that further analysis was not possible.

---

24. Mayer N. Zalk and Roberta Ash, "Social Movement Organizations: Growth, Decay, and Change," in *Collective Behavior and Social Movements,* ed. Louis E. Genevie (Itasca, Ill.: F. E. Peacock Publishers, 1964), pp. 259-75. This section draws heavily on the insights of Zalk and Ash.

25. "Women's movement" is being used here in the broadest sense of the many local and national activities since 1966 that have been self-consciously focused on improvement in the status and well being of women.

26. This co-optation was, of course, the basis for creating the consensus that promoted the movement in the early 1970s, as noted by Jo Freeman, "The Origins of the Women's Liberation Movement," *American Journal of Sociology* 78 (January 1973): 792-811. Although initially the movement co-opted the other units of society to take on its cause through the use of those units' communication networks, we suggest that those other units are now in a position to co-opt a major function of the movement. Such co-optation may be seen as an index of the long-range success of the movement despite the fact that it may lessen the chances for future long-term survival of the movement. Survival, paradoxically, may index defeat.

27. As a result of our concern for this question, we have recommended the continuation of at least a "minifestival" each year.

28. For an excellent discussion of the tension within the women's movement over the individual versus the collective, see Joan Cassell, *A Group Called Women* (New York: David McKay Company, 1977), especially chapters 10 and 11.

29. More than 100,000 people marched on Washington, D.C., in July 1978, in support of ratification of the Equal Rights Amendment.

Bibliographical Essay

GENERAL AND THEORETICAL STUDIES

The reemergence of a women's movement in the late 1960s has been accompanied by a comprehensive literature, speculative and literary, scholarly and empirical, identifying and documenting the grievances of women in twentieth-century America. Some of the best and most incisive of this literature was published in volumes of essays in the early 1970s. These essays identified the issues about which the organized women's movement was to struggle and identified those areas of concern about which more detailed and scholarly studies have since emerged.

Collections such as Vivian Gornick and Barbara K. Moran, eds., *Woman in Sexist Society: Studies in Power and Powerlessness* (New York: Basic Books, 1971); Judith Hole and Ellen Levine, *Rebirth of Feminism* (New York: Quandrangle, 1971); Anne Koedt, Ellen Levine, and Anita

Rapone, eds., *Radical Feminism* (New York: Quadrangle, 1973); and
Robin Morgan, ed., *Sisterhood Is Powerful: An Anthology of Writings
from the Women's Liberation Movement* (New York: Vintage, 1970),
are still basic sources for an understanding of the issues behind the
modern women's movement. Presenting some of the same themes but in
a more moderate tone are Joan Huber, ed., *Changing Women in Changing
Society* (Chicago: University of Chicago Press, 1973), and Jo Freeman,
ed., *Women: A Feminist Perspective* (Palo Alto, Calif.: Mayfield Publishing Company, 1975).

More detailed and comprehensive studies, which not only discuss the
issues on which the women's movement has focused but also offer an
analysis of that movement as a political force responding to those issues,
include Barbara Sinclair Deckard, *The Women's Movement: Political,
Socioeconomic, and Psychological Issues* (New York: Harper and Row,
1975), presenting an overview of the movement as a whole; and Maren
Lockwood Carden, *The Feminist Movement* (New York: Russell Sage,
1974), a study of the nature of feminist groups and their membership.
Jo Freeman, *The Politics of Women's Liberation* (New York: David
McKay, 1975), traces the development of the women's movement and
its relationship to the establishment of public policy; and Constantina
Safilios-Rothchild, *Women and Social Policy* (Englewood Cliffs, N.J.:
Prentice-Hall, 1974), delineates strategies, social action, policies, and
laws necessary to eradicate effectively sexism in American society.
A recent work summarizing the impact of women's changing roles on
social and economic life around the world, including the United States,
is Kathleen Newland, *The Sisterhood of Man* (New York: W. W. Norton
and Company, 1979).

Other studies attempt to go beyond a definition of the condition of
women based on the view that women as a group experience powerless-
ness vis-à-vis men and offer a Marxist or class analysis of the condition
of women in modern society. Such studies include Juliet Mitchell,
Women's Estate (New York: Pantheon, 1971); Sheila Rowbotham,
Woman's Consciousness, Man's World (Baltimore: Penguin, 1973);
Heleieth I. B. Saffiota, *Women in Class Society* (New York: Monthly
Review Press, 1978); and Zillah R. Eisenstein, ed., *Capitalist Patriarchy
and the Case for Socialist Feminism* (New York: Monthly Review
Press, 1979).

WOMEN IN THE PROFESSIONS AND THE ARTS

Access to the male-dominated professions of medicine, dentistry, and law has been a major demand of the contemporary women's movement. The obstacles, both internal and external, that confront women entering the professions have been the subject of many recent studies, such as Elizabeth A. Ashburn, *Motivation, Personality, and Work-Related Characteristics of Women in Male-Dominated Professions,* Ruth Strang Research Award Monograph Series, no. 2 (Washington, D.C.: National Association for Women Deans, Administrators, and Counselors, 1977); Barbara J. Harris, *Beyond Her Sphere: Women and the Professions in American History* (Westport, Conn.: Greenwood Press, 1978); Ruth B. Kundsin, *Women and Success: The Anatomy of Achievement* (New York: William Morrow and Company, 1974); Jacquelyn A. Mattfeld and Carol G. Van Aken, *Women and Scientific Professions* (Cambridge, Mass.: MIT Press, 1965); Margaret A. Campbell, *"Why Would a Girl Go into Medicine?" Medical Education in the United States: A Guide for Women* (Old Westbury, N.Y.: Feminist Press, 1973); Mary Roth Walsh, *"Doctors Wanted: No Women Need Apply," Sexual Barriers in the Medical Profession, 1835-1975* (New Haven: Yale University Press, 1977); Carolyn Spieler, ed., *Women in Medicine, 1976* (New York: Josiah Macy, Jr., Foundation, 1977); and Dorothy Rosenthal Mandelbaum, *The Career Persistence of Women Physicians* (New York: Praeger Special Studies, 1979). An index of the current status of women in the health professions can be found in the Department of Health, Education, and Welfare publications: *Minorities and Women in the Health Fields: Applicants, Students, and Workers.*

In the literary arts, studies have focused on women as writers as well as on the development of a feminist criticism insisting that literature cannot be judged on internal content and style alone. Josephine Donovan, ed., *Feminist Literary Criticism: Explorations in Theory* (Lexington: University of Kentucky Press, 1975), provides an overview of the state of the art of feminist criticism. Overlapping discussions of women writers and criticism are works by Elizabeth Hardwick, *Seduction and Betrayal: Women and Literature* (New York: Random House, 1974); Mary Ellman, *Thinking about Women* (New York: Harcourt, Brace, and World, 1968);

and Patricia Meyer Spacks, *The Female Imagination* (New York: Knopf, 1975).

Two studies examining the effects of literature in creating and maintaining particular forms of social relations are Lillian S. Robinson, *Sex, Class, and Culture* (Bloomington: Indiana University Press, 1978), and Ann Bar Snitow, "Mass Market Romance: Pornography for Women Is Different," *Radical History Review* 20 (Spring/Summer 1979): 141-61.

WOMEN'S PRIVATE LIVES

"Control over our own bodies" has been a major theme of the new women's movement, manifested through demands for legal and institutional change as well as for redefinitions of health and illness. A feminist critique of prevailing ideas and practices in mental health can be found in Phyllis Chesler, *Women and Madness* (Garden City, N.Y.: Doubleday, 1972), one of the earliest works on the subject. Jean Baker Miller, ed., *Psychoanalysis and Women* (Baltimore: Penguin Books, 1973), contains sixteen essays on women written by well-known analysts describing the impact of the women's movement on psychoanalysis. Dorothy Tennov, *Psychotherapy: The Hazardous Cure* (New York: Abelard-Shuman, 1975), and Violet Franks and Vasanti Burtle, eds., *Women in Therapy: New Perspectives for a Changing Society* (New York: Brunner/Mazel, 1974), explore the contemporary status of psychotherapy and its response to the changing role of women in today's society. Anica Vesel Mander and Anne Kent Rush, *Feminism as Therapy* (New York: Random House, 1974), reject traditional approaches to the treatment of emotional illness as male-dominated and capitalistic and describe collective self-help consciousness-raising activities as an alternative form of therapy.

Many of the emotional conflicts that confront the contemporary woman originate in the relationship between men and women within marriage and the family. Some works that elaborate on the impact of traditional relationships on the social roles of the two sexes are Jessie Bernard, *The Future of Marriage* (New York: World, 1972); Eva Figes, *Patriarchal Attitudes* (New York: Stein and Day, 1970); Shulamith Firestone, *The Dialectic of Sex: The Case for Feminist Revolution* (New York: William Morrow and Company, 1970); John Scanzoni, *Sexual Bargaining: Power Politics in the American Marriage* (Englewood Cliffs, N.J.:

Prentice-Hall, 1972); and Robert Seidenburg, *Marriage between Equals: Studies from Life and Literature* (New York: Anchor Press, 1973).

Feminist critiques of the medical establishment and a redefinition of what constitutes acceptable health care for women can be found in works such as the now-classic *Our Bodies, Ourselves: A Book by and for Women* (New York: Simon and Schuster, 1976); Ellen Frankfurt, *Vaginal Politics* (New York: Quadrangle, 1972); and Sheryl Burt Ruzek, *The Women's Health Movement: Feminist Alternatives to Medical Control* (New York: Praeger Special Studies, 1978). A historical perspective of the treatment accorded women by the health care system is the focus of two books by Barbara Ehrenreich and Deirdre English, *Complaints and Disorders: The Sexual Politics of Sickness* (Old Westbury, N.Y.: Feminist Press, 1973) and *For Her Own Good: 150 Years of Experts' Advice to Women* (New York: Doubleday, 1979); such a perspective is also provided by Linda Gordon, *Woman's Body, Woman's Right: Birth Control in America* (New York: Penguin Books, 1977).

Because menopause is a health issue specific to women, the way it has been defined in medical theory and practice provides an instructive guide to the sexual politics of medicine. Some works that challenge prevailing medical theory regarding menopause are Vidal S. Clay, *Women, Menopause, and Middle Age* (Pittsburgh, Pa.: Know, 1977); Jane Page, *The Other Awkward Age* (Berkeley, Calif.: Ten Speed Press, 1977); Rosetta Reitz, *Menopause: A Positive Approach* (Radnor, Pa.: Chilton Book Company, 1977); and Paula Weideger, *Menstruation and Menopause* (New York: Knopf, 1976).

WOMEN FACING THE FUTURE

How women are viewed according to the law is a reflection of their status in the society at large. Comprehensive textbook surveys of legal discrimination and its remedies can be found in Barbara Babcock, Ann Freedman, Eleanor Holmes Norton, and Susan Ross, *Sex Discrimination and the Law: Causes and Remedies* (Boston: Little, Brown, 1975), and Kenneth M. Davidson, Ruth Bader Ginsburg, and Herma H. Kay, *Sex-Based Discrimination* (St. Paul, Minn.: West Publishing Company, 1974). Karen DeCrow, *Sexist Justice* (New York: Random House, 1974), covers similar material in a more accessible although less comprehensive manner.

Albie Sachs and Joan Hoff Wilson, *Sexism and the Law: Male Beliefs and Legal Bias* (New York: Free Press, 1978), examine the impact of sexism on the thinking and structure of the legal profession and the judiciary. Ellen Switzer, *The Law for a Woman: Real Cases and What Happened* (New York: Scribner's, 1975), explains women's legal rights in marriage, the family, work, education, housing, and credit through case histories; and Judith A. Baer, *The Chains of Protection: The Judicial Response to Women's Labor Legislation* (Westport, Conn.: Greenwood Press, 1978), examines the origins, objectives, and effects of early-nineteenth-century protective labor legislation.

A critical issue for the future of women and an objective still unachieved by the women's movement is the Equal Rights Amendment (ERA) to the United States Constitution. Several studies analyze its possible impact in reshaping American society. Mary A. Delsman, *Everything You Need to Know about ERA* (Riverside, Calif.: Meranza Press, 1975), provides an easy-to-read guide to the issues surrounding ERA. The California Commission on the Status of Women has published a collection of eighteen articles concerning the ERA's impact on concerns such as affirmative action, marital roles, employment, and the courts in *Impact ERA: Limitations and Possibilities* (Millbrae, Calif.: Les Femmes Publishing, 1976). An in-depth study of women's treatment under the law and the implications of the ERA for state laws is provided by Barbara A. Brown, Ann E. Freedman, Harriet N. Katz, and Alice M. Price, *Women's Right and the Law: The Impact of the ERA on State Laws* (New York: Praeger Special Studies, 1979). An extensive reference guide to materials on the ERA is *The Equal Rights Amendment: A Bibliographic Study* (Westport, Conn.: Greenwood Press, 1976), which contains 5,800 entries.

Since education has historically played such an important role in the transmission of cultural values, the availability of appropriate schooling as a key to individual and social improvement has received a lot of attention from the women's movement. The focus has been not only on the physical exclusion of women from professional positions but also on the consequences of curriculum content that fails to recognize and value the contributions of women to the functioning of a society. Works documenting inequities in higher education include the Carnegie Commission on Higher Education, *Opportunities for Women in Higher Education* (New York: McGraw-Hill, 1973), and Saul D. Feldman, *Escape from the*

Doll's House: Women in Graduate and Professional Education (New York: McGraw-Hill, 1974), as well as John A. Centra, *Women, Men, and the Doctorate* (Princeton, N.J.: Educational Testing Service, 1974).

Collections of essays dealing with a variety of issues affecting women in higher education, including women's studies, can be found in Florence Howe, ed., *Women and the Power to Change* (New York: McGraw-Hill, 1975); W. Todd Furniss and Patricia Albjerg Graham, eds., *Women in Higher Education* (Washington, D.C.: American Council on Education, 1974); Elizabeth Steiner Maccia, ed., *Women and Education* (Springfield, Ill.: Charles C. Thomas, 1974); and Alice S. Rossi and Ann Calderwood, eds., *Academic Women on the Move* (New York: Russell Sage, 1973).

Identifying the nature of sexism in the educational system and suggesting remedies are studies by Nancy Frazier and Myra Sadker, *Sexism in School and Society* (New York: Harper and Row, 1973); Diane Gersoni-Stavn, *Sexism and Youth* (New York: Bowker, 1974); Judith Stacey, Susan Béreaud, and Joan Daniels, eds., *And Jill Came Tumbling After: Sexism in American Education* (New York: Dell, 1974); Barbara Grizzuti Harrison, *Unlearning the Lie: Sexism in School* (New York: Liveright, 1973); and Barbara Sprung, *Non-Sexist Education for Young Children: A Practical Guide* (New York: Citation, 1975).

BIBLIOGRAPHIES

Finally, an in-depth study of any of the areas covered in this book should begin with one or more of the numerous bibliographic guides to books and articles on women. An extremely useful and descriptive guide to recent books on women, covering eighteen subjects from abortion to work, is Barbara Haber, *Women in America: A Guide to Books, 1963-1975* (Boston, Mass.: G. K. Hall and Company, 1978). Another comprehensive and partially annotated guide to more than 8,600 English-language publications concerning the status of women around the world is Albert Krichmar, *The Women's Movement in the Seventies: An International English Language Bibliography* (Metuchen, N.J.: Scarecrow Press, 1977).

An article containing indispensable information on women in a number of fields is Patricia K. Ballou, "Bibliographies for Research on

Women," *Signs* (Winter 1977): 436-50. Elizabeth H. Oakes and Kathleen Sheldon, *Guide to Social Science Resources in Women's Studies* (Santa Barbara, Calif.: American Bibliographical Center/Clio Press, 1978), provide sources on women from a variety of fields in the social sciences and evaluate the suitability of these materials for use in undergraduate courses.

Bibliographic guides to specific topics include Esther Manning Westervelt, Deborah A. Fixter, and Margaret Comstock, *Women's Higher and Continuing Education: An Annotated Bibliography with Selected References on Related Aspects of Women's Lives* (New York: College Entrance Examination Board, 1971); Henel S. Astin, Nancy Suniewick, and Susan Dweck, *Women: A Bibliography on Their Education and Careers* (Washington, D.C.: Human Service Press, 1971); and Nancy W. Huang, *Women's Continuing Education* (Ann Arbor, Mich.: Center for Continuing Education). Sandra L. Chaff, Ruth Haimbach, Carol Fenichel, and Nina B. Woodside, *Women in Medicine: A Bibliography of the Literature on Women Physicians* (Metuchen, N.J.: Scarecrow Press, 1977), provide comprehensive coverage with 4,087 annotated entries of literature in all parts of the world from the eighteenth century through December 1975.

The bibliographical work on women in literature is expanding rapidly, including Florence Boos, "1974 Bibliography of Women in British and American Literature: 1600-1900," *Women and Literature* 3 (Fall 1975): 33-64; Florence Boos, "1975 Bibliography of Literature in English by and about Women," *Women and Literature* 4 (Supplement, Fall 1976); Paula R. Backschneider and Felicity A. Nussbaum, *An Annotated Bibliography of Twentieth-Century Critical Studies of Women and Literature, 1660-1800* (New York: Garland Publishing, 1977); Narda Lacey Schwartz, *Articles on Women Writers, 1960-1975* (Santa Barbara, Calif.: American Bibliographical Center/Clio Press, 1978); and Barbara A. White, *American Women Writers: An Annotated Bibliography of Criticism* (New York: Garland Publishing, 1977).

Biographical Notes

CAROL BAEKEY is a lawyer in the District of Columbia and a member of the Women's Legal Defense Fund. She is active in the areas of women's rights, women and addiction, tenants' rights and related housing issues, grand jury abuse, and local politics.

PAULINE BART is Associate Professor of Sociology and Psychiatry at The Abraham Lincoln School of Medicine, University of Illinois. In the spring of 1980, she was Distinguished Visiting Professor of Women's Studies at San Diego State University. She has written extensively, primarily on the interface between sex roles and health issues and sex roles and violence against women.

EDITH BREEN holds a Ph.D. in psychology from The George Washington University and is a practicing feminist therapist in Fairfax, Virginia. She has conducted numerous seminars and workshops in the area of women and mental health.

MARILOU BURNETT is Associate Professor of Human Development and Counseling at Sangamon State University, Springfield, Illinois. She is associated with the Humana Network of Virginia Satir and is preparing a book entitled *Family Reconstruction: A Method of Owning Your Life.*

NANCY DATAN is Professor of Psychology at West Virginia University and best known for her contributions to life-span developmental psychology (*Normative Life Crisis,* Academic Press, 1975; *Dialetical Perspectives in Experimental Research,* Academic Press, 1977). She has lectured nationally and internationally on her research on women's roles, a cross-cultural study of 1,200 women in five Israeli subcultures (*A Time To Reap,* Johns Hopkins University Press, in preparation).

MARY DUNLAP is staff attorney for Equal Rights Advocates, Inc., based in San Francisco. She has taught on an adjunct basis in several law schools and is also a published poet.

KAREN FUCHS is Assistant Professor of Psychology at Colgate University.

CAROL GIESEN teaches at West Virginia University and is pursuing a doctorate in psychology.

ELAINE GINSBERG is Chairwoman of the Department of English at West Virginia University. She teaches and writes in the fields of early American literature, American fiction, and women's studies.

RUTH BADER GINSBURG is Professor of Law at Columbia Law School. As director of the American Civil Liberties Union's Womens Rights Project, she argued eight successful gender-based discrimination suits before the U.S. Supreme Court in the 1970s, helping to establish a constitutional basis for equality between the sexes.

BETSY HOBBS is Assistant Professor of Reading at West Virginia University and associate coordinator of the West Virginia Board of Regents Bachelor of Arts Degree Program.

CORRINNE JACKER is a playwright with a number of books, plays, and television scripts to her credit. She has won Emmy citations for "Actor's Choice" (NET, 1970); "Benjamin Franklin (CBS, 1974); the

Cine Golden Eagle Award for "Virginia Woolf: The Moment Whole" (NET, 1972); and her play "Chinese Restaurant Syndrom" was included in the Best Short Plays of 1978.

MARYAT LEE, inspired by medieval theater, is credited with originating modern American street theater when she, in 1951, developed *Dope*, a play with and about the people of East Harlem. In 1968 she formed the Soul and Latin Theater group in New York and since 1975 has directed ECOTheater based in rural West Virginia. On September 1, 1980 ECOTheater was featured on the "Today Show."

JUDITH L. LICHTMAN is an attorney and executive director of The Women's Legal Defense Fund in Washington, D.C. In monitoring the enforcement of federal laws affecting women, she works closely with many national women's organizations.

ANN PATERSON is Associate Professor of Sociology and Chairwoman of the Department of Sociology and Anthropology at West Virginia University.

ELLEN PERLMUTTER is a doctoral candidate in clinical psychology at the Northwestern University Medical School in Chicago, Illinois.

RUTH M. PHILLIPS is Associate Professor, Department of Pediatrics, West Virginia University School of Medicine, and serves as its Women's Liaison Officer to the American Association of Medical Colleges.

NANCY REYNOLDS is Professor of Dentistry and Assistant Dean for auxiliary programs for the College of Dentistry at Ohio State University. She has contributed several chapters to textbooks in the field of dentistry, edited with Susan S. Boundy *Current Concepts in Dental Hygiene* (St. Louis: Mosby, 1977) and is past president of the American Association of Dental Schools.

ADELLE F. ROBERTSON is Dean of the Division of Continuing Education at the University of Virginia. She has been active in promoting the expansion of public continuing education programs to serve the needs of women.

JUDITH STITZEL is a professor of English and Coordinator of Women's Studies at West Virginia University. She has been a participant in the

Modern Language Association/Fund for the Improvement of Post-Secondary Education project—"Teaching Women's Literature from a Regional Perspective"—and in the Modern Language Association/National Endowment For the Humanities Institute—"Women's Nontraditional Literature: Theory and Practice."

MARY ELLEN VERHEYDEN-HILLIARD is President of Verheyden and Associates, a Washington, D.C.-based consulting firm concerned primarily with efforts to reduce sex stereotyping in education. She previously managed Sex Equality in Guidance Opportunities (SEGO), a project funded by the U.S. Office of Education and has served on numerous public and private committees concerned with career opportunities for women.

Index

About the Editors

BETTY JUSTICE is an Instructor in Labor Studies at West Virginia University in Morgantown. She is the author of a forthcoming book on basic labor law.

RENATE PORE is employed by the West Virginia Department of Health and is an Adjunct Faculty Member at the College of Graduate Studies in Charleston, West Virginia. She is the author of *A Conflict of Interest: Women in German Social Democracy, 1919-1933* (Greenwood Press, 1981).